A HISTORY
OF THE
RESTORATION PLEA

by

HAROLD W. FORD

Professor of New Testament
Instructor in Church History
Lincoln Bible Institute

Minister Christian Church
Elkhart, Illinois

Being a history of the statements of the Plea
of the churches of Christ for Christian unity
upon the basis of a Restoration of the church
of the New Testament.

SEMCO COLOR PRESS
Oklahoma City, Oklahoma
1952

FOREWORD

Professor Harold W. Ford has made a great contribution to the cause of the New Testament message of unity by gathering together this *History of the Statements of the Plea of the Churches of Christ for Christian Unity Upon the Basis of a Restoration of the Church of the New Testament.*

These statements show that God's message has been understood by men of this age. Since it has been and is being understood today by many, it is possible for all men to understand.

Christian unity is based upon full and complete conversion, for unity is a result not a cause in God's plan. For this reason this book should be read and studied carefully. All who profess Christ as Lord and Saviour need to examine these statements in the light of the word of God.

We need to present a united voice to the confused and divided religious world. A close study of the statements which harmonize with the Bible will show that when men are truly converted and follow God's word they are one. They become one through conversion and continue to be one through the process of continuing in the faith given unto the saints.

Read this masterpiece and thank God for a Christian scholar who has presented the unchangeable history of the statements of men concerning the Plea. Read this book and see the error of those who have not caught the full significance of the Movement to restore the spirit, life, doctrine and practice of the church revealed in the Scriptures. Then ask yourself the question, Why do the leaders fail in their conception of the great plea of God?

Above all read this book and in the light of the Bible see the great opportunity we have to bring the message to the world which will create Christian unity in order that the world may believe that Jesus is the Christ.

EARL C. HARGROVE, *President*
LINCOLN BIBLE INSTITUTE.

January, 1952,
Lincoln, Illinois.

PREFACE TO THE BOOK

The material which constitutes this book was put together originally in the form of a thesis submitted to the School of Religion of Butler University, Indianapolis, Indiana, as partial fulfillment of the requirements for the Bachelor of Divinity degree which was granted in the Spring of 1949. Some explanation may be due as to why it is being put into book form at this late date.

At the time of its completion as a thesis some intention but very little hope that it would be published was entertained. However, upon coming to Lincoln Bible Institute as Professor of New Testament and Instructor in Church History, I have used this material many times as the basis of a course which has been called "History of the Restoration Plea." Each year the students who have enrolled in the class have called for the publication of the thesis as a book.

The group of students who took the course in the school year of 1950 and 1951 was especially zealous that this be done. A petition was circulated among the students of the Institute resulting in a sizeable number expressing their desire to have a book and pledging their backing financially. One student enlisted the support of several gracious and generous men of the congregation where he ministers, and it began to appear that what had at first been but an idle dream was fast approaching the realm of reality.

The balance of the story is known to all who will read these pages. My only regret is that I have not been able to do a better job. The importance of the theme is, in my judgment, without measure and deserves the finest treatment possible. However, I herewith submit it to the public for thoughtful reading. It appears as it was written originally with but few changes. Two of the statements which appeared in the original have been deleted, because copyright owner's permission to quote them could not be obtained. In addition a few paragraphs have been added to clarify certain issues. Its value rests, not in what I have composed, but in what has been recorded from the pens of many individuals. Careful consideration of the statements of the Plea recorded herein will repay adequately any interested inquirer.

Appreciation is herewith acknowledged: to the Standard Publishing Company for granting permission to quote material published and copyrighted by them; to the MacMillan Company for permission to quote W. M. Forrest's *Do Fundamentalists Play Fair?*, published by them in 1926; to Charles Clayton Morrison for permission to quote from his recent book, *What is Christianity?*, to Miss Elsie T. Sweeney for permission to quote from Z. T. Sweeney's set on *New Testament Christianity*, to Dr. C. C. Crawford for permission to quote from his *Sermon Outlines: The Restoration Plea*, to the Christian Board of Publication for permission to quote from B. A. Abbott's *The Disciples, An Interpretation*, to George Walker Buckner, Jr., for permission to quote from his *The Winds of God*, to C. C. Ware for permission to quote from *A History of the North Carolina Disciples of Christ*, to the Christian Century Publishing Company for permission to quote from Herbert L. Willett's *Our Plea for Union and the Present Crisis* and W. T. Moore's *The Plea of the Disciples of Christ*, to Fleming H. Revell for permission to quote from W. T. Moore's *A Comprehensive History of the Disciples of Christ* and Peter Ainslie's *The Message of the Disciples for the Union of the Church;* to Dr. O. L. Shelton and the School of Religion of Butler University for permission to publish the thesis as a book. Without the gracious consideration of the above named individuals and companies this book could not have been published.

In sincere appreciation for the confidence shown by the students in calling for the publication of this material, I herewith dedicate this work to them and to the generous men of the church of Christ in Covington, Indiana, whose interest in a practical way has made it possible. My prayer is: May God speed the cause of the Restoration movement and may He use these humble efforts in some way to accomplish His purpose among men.

H. W. F.

Lincoln, Illinois,
January, 1952.

PREFACE TO THE THESIS

In the preparation of a thesis such as this, many acknowledgments of assistance are due. It would be impossible, however, to name personally all who have encouraged when progress was slow and aided when help was needed. In particular, three persons have been of great assistance in many practical ways. It would be unjust to close this work without stating that fact for those who may care to read these pages.

Appreciation should be expressed for the assistance given by Dr. Dean E. Walker. The idea of writing upon this subject was born in the classroom while studying under Dr. Walker. The supreme significance of the Plea was brought home again and again. Clear it became that this was not only the solution but the only solution to the ills of the church.

In addition, Enos Dowling, librarian of the School of Religion rendered great service in the form of accommodation. He also aided considerably in finding material and information when it was not possible to travel to the school and do it personally. For all of this I am deeply grateful.

Finally, appreciation must also be expressed to my loving wife, Berniece, for the encouragement and assistance rendered during the time of composition of the thesis. It is doubtful that the work would ever have been completed, were it not for the contribution which she has made. Also, I must express my thanks to her for typing the final draft and for offering many suggestions which have materially improved the finished work.

To any who may read this work it should be said that the statements contained herein should be read with extreme care and with a discerning eye. They speak much that has been beyond bringing out in this dissertation.

H. W. F.

Lincoln, Illinois,
May, 1949

TABLE OF CONTENTS

CHAPTER I

RESTORATION BEGINNINGS

INTRODUCTION

The ideas of men, as well as their activities, leave records in the passage of time. In many cases, the activities of men can be far more clearly understood if the motivating ideas are taken into consideration. In this dissertation, the object of consideration is the history of an idea. It is our interest to determine and clarify this idea from the record left behind by its originators, and to restate it for the consideration of those who seek to follow in the wake of the movement brought to be by its original propagation.

The idea to which reference is made is: the restoration of the Christianity of the New Testament and the resultant rebuilding of the church of Christ as it is recorded in that volume, looking to the unity in Christ of all people in the world who wish to be known as Christians and, ultimately, to the conversion of the world. It was a firm conviction in the rightness of this idea and a burning zeal for the working of it that resulted in the initiation of one of the most significant religious movements since the beginning of time.

It is certainly not a hidden fact that, today, there are many notions about the movement and consequently various understandings of "the plea" to restore the faith and practice of the church of the New Testament. Within the movement, at the present time, there are at least four groups representing to be in line of descent from the original "plea" and to be presenting the message of the Restoration movement, the Message of New Testament Christianity, in historically correct fashion. The interest of this history is in a correct definition or statement of the Plea and an accurate evaluation of the movement today in search for the most nearly correct representation of the Plea.

History has the very distinct characteristic of being absolutely unchangeable, since it is made up of the happenings of time. Attempts to change the facts of history or to erase the things that have been recorded, would be about as futile as trying to change the course of the sun or the flow of the tides. Facts do not change. We may wish them changed, but our wishes will not change them. They must stand as they took place.

This universally confessed character of history makes possible such research as this. Our recourse is to the facts recorded. The idea of restoring the faith and practice of the church of the New Testament is recorded. The ideas of the original advocates of the Plea are in print. We need not take the word of others about it, but we may go directly to their written word. This, precisely, is the plan this investigation shall follow. Our procedure shall be to investigate the various statements of the Plea as they have been formulated and presented by those men of the movement who chose to record such statements. The statements will be compared and analyzed. In this manner, it is hoped that the place and reason for departure from the Plea may be determined and the way pointed for a reconciliation of the varied elements. It is not the purpose

1

of this thesis to enter the field of Christian doctrine and to discuss the various teachings of the New Testament, but to confine itself as strictly as possible to the statements of the Plea.

This history of the movement has been divided into five distinct periods. The determination of these periods has not been arbitrary, but has been arrived at by the recognition of certain divergent elements within the statements of the Plea or by the recognition of certain divergent practices within the movement. Each statement of the Plea is included in its proper chronological section and is accredited to its proper author.

The selection of the statements has been made through the reading of the greater proportion of the material available on the subject. Repetition of ideas has been avoided in so far as possible. No attempt, however, has been made to determine the trend of the Plea through the listing of some statements and the elimination of others. The picture of the Plea as it reveals itself in the chronological listing of the statements is a true one.

It was hoped at first that a short biographical sketch could be included, identifying each person making a statement, but it has proven impractical to do so. The reader, no doubt, will be able to identify some of the individuals from his personal knowledge of the movement, others he will perhaps be able to identify with little difficulty.

The material available upon the subject of this research is voluminous. Nearly everything that has been written about the Restoration movement contains some note about the Plea of the movement, while much has been written about the Plea itself. The latter, of course, has been largely useful in this investigation. Many tracts and pamphlets have been written on the subject also, and biographies have been an important source. However, the periodicals of the movement have been without peer in this investigation. The *Christian Baptist*, the *Millennial Harbinger*, the *Christian Messenger*, the *Christian Century*, the *Scroll*, the *Christian Record*, the *American Christian Review*, the *Octographic Review*, the *Christian Standard*, the *Christian Evangelist*, and others, as listed in the bibliography, all entered into the reading matter.

There are several terms which will be used in this thesis which might be well to define at the outset. "The Plea" refers to the distinctive message of the churches of Christ for the unity of all Christians. At first, the preachers of the movement referred to the "Cause we plead." Later, they referred to "the plea." "Restoration" is a term descriptive of the means to be used in accomplishing the desired objective, the restoration of the Christianity recorded for and presented to the world in the New Testament. It is not a movement to reform the existing denominationalism, but to go back of all tradition and opinion to the original record and build again the institution recorded therein, i. e., to restore the church of the New Testament. "Denominationalism" is a term denoting the divided state of the church. The concept of denominationalism is a concept of parallels. A denomination, then, is a party or sectarian group, an organization of local churches, existing by the side of or parallel to other parties or sectarian groups, having absolutely no connection or reference in any way to the others, yet claiming that all are bound for the same destination but by different roads, though calling itself by a distinctive name to distinguish it from all other "Christian" groups. Other terms may be defined or clarified as they arise in the discussion.

The significance of this study cannot be overestimated. Our Lord's prayer, recorded in the seventeenth chapter of John, is a very humiliating object of study when the divisions among Christians are taken into consideration. There are, no doubt, thousands of people in the world who will never hear the gospel and thousands more who will not accept it until the people of God are one in Christ. The road to unity was once very clearly pointed out to the church. Christ was the first to plead for the oneness of his people, and the apostle Paul followed closely with the same advocacy. Others through the history of the church have worked diligently for this same end. At the turn of the eighteenth to the nineteenth century, there arose a people pleading again for the oneness of the Christians of the world. Their chief concern was for an unsaved world, which they believed would never be saved until unity was accomplished. The means by which they sought to regain the oneness of Christ's people was the restoration of the Christianity of the New Testament, and the elimination of everything foreign to it. In short, it was an addition as well as a subtraction.

There was a time when the ardent preachers of the gospel and advocates of the Plea expected to see a united church in their own day. Now the forces, which claim to be pleading for the unity of Christians, are divided themselves. Is the Plea valid, or is it in itself divisive? What is the unity for which we plead? What was the desired object of those men who first conceived of the idea under investigation in this thesis? These are some of the questions that need to be answered in this day. A restatement of the Plea is gravely needed; the churches of Christ need to be recalled to original ground, if the Restoration movement is to be an effective agency in bringing about the unity of Christians and, through this unity, the conversion of the world to our Lord.

To facilitate understanding and to clarify the goal to which we hope ultimately to arrive in this investigation, it seems well to anticipate something at this point. The Plea is for unity, but not unity for unity's sake. The consideration uppermost in the thinking of the early advocates of the Plea was that the divided church would never win the world to Christ. In other words, the ultimate object of their work and the cause they sought to plead was the conversion of the world. In the consideration of this ultimate object may be seen the basis of the unity they sought to accomplish. If conversion is the object, then those things that make for conversion must be the basis of unity. Thus, the conversion of the individual, bringing that individual to unity in Christ, is the grand object of the Restoration movement. From that point, the rebuilding of the church of Christ, according to the expressed injunctions and approved precedents of the New Testament, as a simple local fellowship of those united in Christ, becomes a part of the object of the movement. The requirements for salvation become the only tests of that fellowship, and beyond that the widest freedom must be allowed.

RESTORATION BACKGROUNDS

The Restoration movement cannot be properly understood nor can the Plea be properly appreciated without some knowledge of the backgrounds of the

3

movement. The movement did not spring full-grown from the head of any single person, but arose as an evolution of thought in the minds of many in widely separated sections of the country and of the world. It was the work of many and, most certainly, not the work of one man. To call the movement by the name of one man is to demonstrate a very profound ignorance of the history of the Plea. It was the "confluence of six streams of Christian action"[1] which brought to be the total movement to restore to the world the Christianity of the New Testament.

> These are, in origin, quite distinct. Arising simultaneously, they discovered each other and clarified their objectives within a generation. The story of the beginnings is therefore necessarily scattered at first, but unifies toward the fourth decade of the nineteenth century.[2]

It is well that consideration be given each of these six major streams of action, but space will not allow a detailed discussion of them. If further information is desired, reference may be made to the books quoted here.

① The Republican Methodists. — Not Campbell, not Stone, but James O'Kelly and the Republican Methodists were the first of these lines of activity. The American Revolution had brought independence not only to the nation but to the American Methodists as well. They had been released from all foreign control. Francis Asbury, Thomas Coke, and others came to re-establish the supremacy of Wesley,[3] but, at Manakin Town, North Carolina, on December 25, 1793, Asbury's assumption of episcopal powers met considerable opposition from James O'Kelly and others who pled for a congregational form of church government, claiming that the New Testament was sufficient reference in all matters of discipline.[4] The episcopal party being the largest element in the controversy, O'Kelly and those who held like position with him were forced to withdraw.[5]

At first they were called "Republican Methodists" because of their objection to the episcopal form of church government and their advocacy for the congregational form of the New Testament. In 1794, Rice Haggard made a motion to the effect that "henceforth the followers of Christ be known as Christians simply," and A. M. Hafferty suggested that the Bible itself be taken as their only creed.[6] The assembled group passed both motions, and the first church was established in North Carolina at Chapel Hill.[7]

In addition to the above material gleaned from a portion of the written record concerning the activities of James O'Kelly, the following statements are inserted here to give testimony to the personal faith of the man:

> MY *ideas* on creation are plain and simple: I pretend to no astronomical depths on that subject. As to the rise and fall of angels, I am *guided* by scripture, and reasonable suppositions. As touching the *rise* and fall of man, I *have* followed revelation. I have considered that Adam, the personal transgressor, being *acquitted,* and that children of a *thousand* generations to be doomed to *endless* torment, for a grandfather's sin, would appear repugnant to the eternal rule of right!

---

[1]Dean E. Walker, *Adventuring for Christian Unity,* (Birmingham: The Berean Press, 1935), p. 17.
[2]*Ibid.*   [3]*Ibid.*

[4]Robert Richardson, *Memoirs of Alexander Campbell,* (Cincinnati: The Standard Publishing Company, 1897), II, 185.

[5]*Ibid.*   [6]Walker, *op. cit.*   [7]*Ibid.*

Respecting divine foreknowledge, predestination, etc., God hath decreed to punish *vice*, and reward virtue. His works of providence are mysteries, and too deep for mortals to scan: but sure I am, that *his* work is perfect, and *his* ways are judgment. If there be a secret number of souls unconditionally elected, such were never to be lost. But Christ came to *seek*, and to save the lost.

After we become actual transgressors, and by the Judge condemned, yet we discover our lives are prolonged, because the Judge will *do right*: though *just* to destroy, yet *right* to spare; and give an offer of mercy on gospel terms. But after grace is despised, mercy slighted, then it is both *just* and *right* to execute! . . . .

Respecting the *doctrine* of faith, it appears still to me to be a *simple idea*, produced in the reasonable soul; arising as the exercise of belief, from the *evidences* of holy writ. Those *evidences* convey *light*, and that *light* is grace, which produces faith: therefore, we are saved through grace: Acts XVIII, 27 . . . .[1]

Pure orthodoxy is a doctrine that always leads to God and godliness. The holy scripture is the rule to believe by; as also a rule of life; and of course a rule of judgment.[2]

With regard to the doctrine of perseverance, I still urge that it is the practical part of a believer's righteousness, and not an absolute promise, nor an irresistable work of grace.[3]

. . . . After the sinner slights the redeeming blood, eternal punishment is his reward, of just necessity; because it is right! God spares sinners long enough, and useth means sufficient to reclaim and regenerate them; but they refuse: and if they could live forever in this world, God knows they would sin forever: therefore, according to foreknowledge, the will is taken for the eternal deed; and they sink to rise no more.[4]

The above is purely a repudiation of the basic doctrines of Calvinism. He is sure that the Word is sufficient guide and grants sufficient evidence upon which faith may be based.

The movement, characterized by its inherited Methodist evangelism, grew quite rapidly.[5] Many of its advocates, however, moved westward with the tide of the population. Some of them established churches after the form agreed to; others, not so active, kept their thoughts until the awakening on the frontier, which came soon after the turn of the century. It was a humble beginning, perhaps, but its influence was to be felt by others within a decade. The potentiality of the concept which brought about their bold action could not, at the time, be measured, and, while this movement was later swallowed up by the larger stream, James O'Kelly and his co-laborers should be remembered as "pioneers of the restoration idea."[6]

② *The New England Christians.* — A few years after James O'Kelly rebelled against the episcopal aspirations of Asbury and Coke, Dr. Abner Jones of Hartland, Vermont, observing the error of sectarian names and creeds, withdrew from the Baptist church and established, in 1800, a church of but twenty-five members at Lyndon, Vermont. Soon he followed this work by establishing churches after the same simple pattern at Bradford, Vermont, and Pierpont, New Hampshire.

---

[1]James O'Kelly, *Original Truth*, (Raleigh; Printed by Joseph Cales), p. 51.
[2]*Ibid.*, p. 52.   [3]*Ibid.*   [4]*Ibid.*, p. 53.   [5]Walker, *op. cit.*
[6]Frederick D. Kershner, *The Restoration Handbook*, (Cincinnati: The Standard Publishing Company, 1918), I, 11.

"True piety alone," he maintained, should be made the ground of Christian fellowship."[1]

Not long after Dr. Jones started his reformatory activities, Elias Smith, a Baptist minister who was laboring in Portsmouth, New Hampshire, came into contact with his work. He was at once impressed and concluded to adopt the views advocated by Dr. Jones. In so doing, he carried his entire congregation with him. His action was followed by several other Regular and Freewill Baptist ministers of the region.[2]

This newly formed simple gospel effort, refusing to be bound by the traditional theologies of the day,[3] adopted the name "Christians," and upheld the Bible as their only source of authority in matters of faith and practice.[4] While they did not at once realize the full importance of the stand they had taken, they had begun the work. Assisted by the newly founded *Herald of Gospel Liberty*, and by the zealous evangelism which characterized its advocates, this movement made many converts in New England and swept on into New York, Pennsylvania, Ohio, and up into the Eastern British provinces.[5]

Like the Christians of the O'Kelly movement, yet entirely separate from and unknown to them, these people, imbibing the spirit of simple evangelical Christianity, began to move westward with the flow of the population. Their meeting upon the Western Reserve was inevitable. Undoubtedly they contributed largely to the Restoration movement in that region, and it was here that the greatest strides were made in the early days.

(3) *The Kentucky Christians.* — The third of the lines of Christian activity which eventually converged to unity in the Restoration movement by the third decade of the nineteenth century was the group who labored with Barton Warren Stone. He was a Presbyterian Minister who came to Cane Ridge, Kentucky, with the western flow of the population following the Revolutionary War. He at once became alarmed at the prevailing immoral conditions on the frontier and sought at once to do something about it.[6]

In the Spring of 1801, Stone traveled south to attend a much publicized camp meeting which was to be under the direction of James McGready, a Cumberland Presbyterian minister, in Logan County, Kentucky.[7] Upon returning to Cane Ridge, he experienced for the first time in his own labors the sort of phenomena that he had witnessed in the McGready revival. In August of 1801, Mr. Stone instituted what has come to be known as the Cane Ridge Revival. It was the most extensive thing of its sort ever conducted in the United States, and some have said that it stemmed the tide of Atheism in this country. The preaching of the gospel in this meeting was accompanied by a very strange phenomena again, as

---

[1]Richardson, *op. cit.*, p. 186.   [2]*Ibid.*

[3]Walker, *op. cit.*   [4]Richardson, *op. cit.*

[5]*Ibid.*   [6]Walker, *op. cit.*, p. 18.

[7]Richardson, *op. cit.*, p. 192.

it had been in the revival of McGready in the Cumberland territory and afterward in Stone's own work at Cane Ridge.[1]

While Mr. Stone never denied the allegations of some that the peculiarities accompanying the preaching at the Cane Ridge Revival were manifestations of the working of the Holy Spirit, he did maintain that they were not necessarily signs of conversion. The thing that struck Mr. Stone's mind's eye was the preaching done at the meeting and the change in the people who attended. The preachers abandoned their peculiarities of preaching and expression and spoke alone in Bible terms. The day of religious bickering and prejudice seemed to have ended.[2]

However, Mr. Stone had not taken his ecclesiastical superiors into consideration. He, according to their complaints, had not only been guilty of association with preachers of Methodist and Baptist denominations, he had departed from traditional Calvinism. Together with Robert Marshall, John Dunlavy, Richard McNemar, John Thompson, and David Purviance, Stone withdrew from the Synod, and formed the "Springfield Presbytery." To defend their action they published *The Apology of the Springfield Presbytery*, which severely indicts human creeds as bonds of communion and expresses a conviction that the Bible alone is sufficient in these matters.[3]

A new passion took the heart of Barton W. Stone following the revival at Cane Ridge and its subsequent reactions. He now saw the great need of Christian union, and this ideal now obsessed his mind. The partisan nature of even the Springfield Presbytery was at once seen, and this body was dissolved with the publication of *The Last Will and Testament of the Springfield Presbytery*, which came from the presses in 1804. The name Christian simply was adopted by the group, at the suggestion of Rice Haggard.[4] The name Haggard is to be remembered, for he played a similar role a few years before for the co-laborers with James O'Kelly.

The content of *The Last Will and Testament of the Springfield Presbytery* will not be noted nor discussed at this juncture, for it will be fully quoted and analyzed in the next chapter of this work. It is only mentioned here in explanation of the course taken by these men under the able leadership of Barton Stone.

This movement was to play a larger part in the history of the Restoration movement in the union to be accomplished in later years. It was brought to be by men of strong convictions and strong in their bravery to face changes in conviction adverse to the prevailing thought of the time. Above this, however, towered their stronger conviction that Christian unity was an essential to the conversion of the world.

(4) *The Blue River Christians.* — In the early 1800's, as the population of the young nation surged westward, the people soon found themselves trodding on the soil of a territory which was to become the state of Indiana. It was here under the leadership of John Wright of Blue River, Washington County, that

---

[1]*Ibid.*, pp. 192, 193.   [2]Walker, *op. cit.*
[3]*Ibid.*   [4]*Ibid.*, p. 19.

the fourth of the streams of Christian activity, which have the claim of our attention, was begun.

John Wright first set foot in Indiana in the year 1807. In 1810 he moved to Blue River, followed soon after by his father, Amos, and his brother, Peter. Being school teachers and preachers, they at once set about forming a Free Will Baptist church. In the ten years following, they formed ten such churches that together made up the Blue River Association.[1]

However, from the first, John Wright had desired to make the Bible alone the rule of faith and practice for the church. In 1819, he made a resolution which advocated the discarding of party names. Said he, "As individuals we should be called Friends, Disciples, or Christians and as a body, should be known as the church of Christ or the church of God." The next year the Blue River Association was dissolved, and it was agreed to have a simple annual meeting.[2] Adopting Wright's resolution with common consent, they began to plead for Christian unity upon this adopted basis. The Bible became their creed "without note or comment."[3]

Soon, upon this basis, an association of some fifteen German Baptist churches joined with them. This group, then, united with the New Lights as the followers of Barton W. Stone were known. Later, the Silver Creek Association of Baptist churches, which had become convinced of the New Testament position through reading the writings of Alexander Campbell, united with them.[4] By the year 1821 there was scarcely a Baptist church in the region, for all had become Christians only.[5]

In possession of the writer during the time of writing of this thesis was the record of the formation and the Articles of Faith of the Silver Creek Association of Baptists. Also, included in the record book are the minutes of the annual meetings of the association from the time of its formation in 1812 to its dissolution in 1837. The Articles of Faith upon which the Silver Creek Association was constituted, July 24th and 25th, 1812, read as follows:

1st. We believe in one only living and true God, the father, the word (or son) and the holy ghost, equal in wisdom, power and glory.

2nd. We believe the scriptures of the old and new testament to be of divine authority, and the only infallible rule of faith and practice.

3rd. We believe, in the total depravity of human nature, and that a recovery from that situation, is wholly, and entirely, of the sovereign, free, unmerited grace of God in Christ Jesus.

4th. We believe, that god purposed in himself, for his own glory, to make a display of his wisdom, power, justice, goodness and truth, in the works of creation, which he hath made in the dispensations of his providence.

5th. We believe, that god from eternity, purposed to save a people from their sins, for his holy name's sake, and that in infinite wisdom he devised the plan, and appointed every means necessary to accomplish the great end of their redemption, which he effects in his own time, by the operation or his Holy Spirit.

6th. We believe, that sinners are justified before god, alone by the imputed righteousness Jesus Christ.

---

[1]C. W. Cauble, Disciples of Christ in Indiana, (Indianapolis: Meigs Publishing Co., 1930), p. 30.
[2]Ibid.   [3]Walker, op. cit., p. 19.   [4]Ibid.   [5]Cauble, op. cit.

7th. We believe, all such as are born of the spirit of God, are kept by the power of god through faith unto eternal salvation.

8th. We believe, that good works, are the effects of the faith of God's elect, and follow, being born of the spirit of god, and in this point of view, are evidences of a gracious state.

9th. We believe, Baptism, and the Lord's Supper, are ordinances of the gospel, instituted by Jesus Christ, and none but those who profess faith in Christ, and obedience to his will, are fit subjects of either.

10th. We believe, immersion, according to the scriptures and apostolic practice, to be the only proper mode of Baptism.

11th. We believe, the sanctity of the first day of the week, or Lord's day, ought to be observed, and spent in the publick or private worship of God, and that we should abstain from our worldly concerns, except in cases of necessity and mercy.

12th. We believe, in the resurrection of the Body, both of the just and unjust, and that god will judge the world in righteousness, by that man whom he hath appointed.

13th. We believe, the righteous will forever abide in the peaceful presence of god their redeemer, and his pardoning grace and forgiving love will be the theme of their song—While the wicked shall remain in everlasting torment.

The articles of faith were presented to the association by Wm. M'Coy of the Silver Creek Church on the 24th day of July, 1812.

An important step was taken in the meeting of the association in August, 1836. According to the minutes:

The Breth. met according to the adjournment, meeting being opened and organized in the usual form. After closing several correspondences, came to the following conclusion:

Agree by unanimous consent to amend our constitution by erasing the articles of faith (finding them to be superfluous believing as we do that the Scriptures are a divine-authority and the only infallible rule of faith and obedience) and so much of the rules of decorum as may be understood or construed to give the association authoritative power.

In 1837, the second step of importance was taken, according to the minutes:

The Brethren met at Friendship meeting house according to adjournment. After being called to order in the usual form it was agreed to do away with the name of the association and to have an annual meeting on the same day of the year—commencing on the Friday before the fourth Lord's day in each and every year and to dispense with all forms and usages belonging to authoritative bodies.

Both of the above records are signed by A. Littell, scribe. Thus formed upon Calvinistic articles of faith, the association was dissolved over its insistence upon the New Testament as an infallible and sufficient rule of faith and practice. Certainly these developments, drawn from the original records of the association, reveal what was going on in the minds of these men. Step by step they were assuming the New Testament position.

For forty years Wright labored in Washington County in the work of the Lord. Also associated with him were such men as Absolom and J. T. Littell and Mordecae Cole. In this time he proved one great truth, the workability of the

9

Plea for Christian unity upon the basis of the New Testament, for, with this plea, he united over nineteen various kinds of Baptists, who previously would have nothing to do with each other, and brought about their formation into simple congregations after the New Testament pattern. The plan will bring results; it needs only to be worked. The work of John Wright is important to the history of the Restoration movement for many reasons, far from the least of which is the anticipation it represented of the events of 1832, "the consolidation of the restoration movement."[1]

6) *The Scotch Baptists.* — The Scotch Baptist movement, of seldom recognized importance to the Restoration movement, is the fifth of the streams of Christian activity to claim our attention. The movement arose during the time of Oliver Cromwell, having been established during the Scottish rebellion by English soldiers who were quartered there.[2]

Later, during the days of Queen Anne, the Evangelical Revival began to assert itself in Scotland. A similar condition or movement in the United States was known as the Great Awakening. This movement may be characterized by the attitude that pervaded it, "We need a more free attitude toward religion." Toward the end of the eighteenth century, James Alexander Haldane and Robert, his brother, took prominent places of leadership in this movement. They undertook the ministry as their life work and set about preparing for the mission field in India. Denied this privilege by the East India Company, they devoted their lives and their money to the evangelical movement.[3] They were instrumental in establishing churches and Sunday schools in Scotland, Ireland, and England.[4]

About this time, Robert Sandeman came to the conclusion that immersion was the only Baptism. His newly found truth resulted in his ejection from the Scottish "Kirk," but he founded a church of his own after the New Testament pattern and in harmony with the Scotch Baptist idea.[5] There are still others of lesser importance of this time who entered into this movement under similar circumstances, but it is deemed not necessary to mention them all.

From 1800 to 1820, large numbers of Scotsmen came to America. In keeping with their custom, they brought with them the independent concept of the church which was characteristic of the evangelical movement. By the year 1816, Scotch Baptist churches had been founded at New York, Baltimore, Philadelphia, Danbury, (Conn.), Pittsburgh, and many other places. There were two things which characterized these people: 1) Their devotion to the Bible; 2) Their earnest search for the New Testament pattern of the church.[6]

Henry Errett was the first convert of the movement which located in New York. His wife was Sophia, daughter of Robert Sandeman. They had only recently come from England, and united with the movement in New York. Jane and Anne Darsy, who had been baptized before sailing, came along soon after Henry and Sophia Errett. If the names of Darsy and Errett are taken from

---

[1]Walker, *op. cit.*

[2]Dean E. Walker, *History of the Restoration Movement*, (Indianapolis: Class Notes from Butler University on Subject, 1939).

[3]*Ibid.*   [4]*Ibid.*   [5]*Ibid.*

[6]Walker, "Adventuring for Christian Unity," *op. cit.*, p. 20.

the history of the Scotch Baptists in this country, not very much remains, so important were they to the movement.[1]

Walter Scott, namesake of the famous Sir Walter, was among the people brought to the New Testament position by this Scotch Baptist movement. His importance to the Restoration movement cannot be overestimated. His analytical thinking made a tremendous contribution, and he deserves far more credit than he is often given. The signal importance of the Scotch Baptists is in the intellectual contribution to the Restoration idea, an illustration of which may be well noted in Walter Scott. Further, they played a great part in the spread of the movement in England, Scotland, South Africa, Ireland, Australia, and New Zealand.[2]

(6) *The Campbellian Contribution.* — The sixth of the streams of Christian action under consideration was initiated by the Campbells. Thomas Campbell, a minister of the Old Light, Anti-Burgher, Seceder branch of the Scottish Presbyterian church, was forced by ill health to migrate to the United States. He set out ahead of his family to establish a home in the new world, expecting to send for them later.[3]

When he arrived in this country, he found the Synod of his denomination in session, and he was assigned to a Presbyterian church near the city of Pittsburgh, in Washington, Pennsylvania, in the Presbytery of Chartiers.[4] Only a short time after settling and getting his ministry under way in his new location, Thomas Campbell was severely censored by his Presbytery for inviting Presbyterians other than Seceders to commune with the latter.[5] This brought about his withdrawal from the Presbytery and the formation of "The Christian Association of Washington, Pennsylvania."[6] The group who were with Campbell, like their leader, did not seek to found a new church or a new denomination. They designed only to arouse the Christian world against human creeds. They were still Protestants and interested in the union of Protestants.[7]

The swiftness with which this entire transaction took place may be noted in the following comparison. Campbell landed in America in the year 1807, and by 1809 he had withdrawn from the Presbyterians, formed the Christian Association of Washington, and published the *Declaration and Address* which was sent forth with the intention of clarifying the aims of the group.[8] This document, like the *Last Will and Testament of the Springfield Presbytery* of Barton W. Stone and his followers, will be analyzed and discussed in the next chapter of this work. The *Declaration and Address* is beyond question one of the most important documents in the history of the church, and should be carefully perused by all who sincerely seek a basis for Christian unity. The basis, of course, is not the document itself, but the basis upon which all Christians can scripturally become one is set forth clearly in the document for all who care to seek it.

The views Mr. Campbell proposed in the *Declaration and Address* were quite revolutionary, even for him, and he wondered how Alexander, his son, would respond to those views, little knowing that Alexander, through his as-

---

[1]Walker, "History of the Restoration Movement," *op.cit.*
[2]*Ibid.*   [3]Richardson, *op. cit.*, I, 78, 79.   [4]*Ibid.*, p. 88.   [5]*Ibid.*, pp. 224, 225.
[6]*Ibid.*, pp. 229-241.   [7]Walker, "Adventuring for Christian Unity," *op. cit.*, p. 20.
[8]Richardson, *op. cit.*, p. 242.

sociations with the Haldanes and others at the University of Glasgow, had come to almost the identical position and was to rejoice at his father's conclusions.[1] While the text of the *Declaration and Address* was being set into form by the printer, Thomas Campbell traveled to meet his family who were coming overland to Washington. Their reunion was one of great rejoicing,[2] and while they journeyed homeward again, Thomas went into great detail concerning his treatment by the Presbytery and the conclusions to which he had come.[3]

In an attempt to prevent the formation of another denomination, Thomas Campbell sought admission to the Pittsburgh Synod of the Presbyterian church for his followers in reform. The refusal of the synod to accept them brought on the formation of the Brush Run church, in which an attempt was made to put into practice the ideals and principles advocated in the *Declaration and Address*. The Lord's supper was observed weekly, since it was considered to be an "approved precedent" of the church of the New Testament. However, a problem arose when one of their number, Joseph Bryant, refused to partake, because he had never been baptized. The fact that he had been voted a member of the church made no difference in his decision to refrain from communing. At Bryant's insistence, he was immersed by Thomas Campbell on July 4, 1811. It was also Thomas Campbell who immersed the first convert of the new congregation.[4]

The birth of Alexander Campbell's first child on March 13, 1812, brought the matter to a climax. The question was, was the child to be sprinkled according to the accepted orthodox custom? Complete and thoroughgoing search of the scriptures was made in attempt to allow the Word to answer the question for them. As well, he ordered all of the books he could locate on the subject of infant sprinkling and read them well. The conclusion was that believer's baptism, the immersion of a believer in water in the name of Jesus, was the only baptism. The question was no longer, "May we safely reject infant baptism as a human invention?" It now became, "May we omit believer's baptism, which all admit to be divinely commanded?"[5]

The conclusion to which they had come resulted in the immersion of the Campbells in Buffalo Creek on the 12th of June, 1812.[6] It was a mark of progress, not only in their personal thinking, but in the course of the Restoration movement, which now most certainly was to bring again to the world the simple plan of salvation, preached by the apostles and the New Testament church, but lost for ages in the rubble of apostasy and error. The Campbells and their co-laborers united first with the Redstone Baptist Association and then with the Mahoning Association, after Alexander's "Sermon on the Law" resulted in their withdrawal from the former.[7] In 1823 the *Christian Baptist* was started and in 1830 the *Millennial Harbinger*. 1827, however, really began the greatest strides of forward movement with the appointment of Walter Scott to the position of evangelist for the Mahoning Association. The Restoration movement was to sweep across the Western Reserve and into many states, not to be stopped, or even slowed down, for almost a century.

---

[1]*Ibid.*, p. 220.   [2]*Ibid.*, pp. 215, 216.   [3]*Ibid.*, p. 246.
[4]Walker, "Adventuring for Christian Unity," *op. cit.*, pp. 22, 23.
[5]*Ibid.*   [6]*Ibid.*   [7]*Ibid.*, pp. 26, 27.

How many others were involved in the streams already mentioned or whether there were other streams of less importance than the ones to which attention has been called providence alone can tell. It was the attitude of the time that brought these forth. They had come from different lands; they had originated without knowedge of each other. Like the tributaries of a great river, all of them joined, at least in part, in the main flow of the Restoration movement.

The balance of this thesis will concern itself with the statements of the position these people sought to hold and with an analysis of those statements in an attempt to find the Plea. Consideration will be given alone to those men and those statements coming from the movement in the United States. To have gone beyond this limit would have been a task beyond hope of completion at this time, and would have added nothing to the purpose intended.

CHAPTER II

THE PERIOD OF THE LAST WILL AND TESTAMENT AND THE DECLARATION AND ADDRESS: 1804 - 1823

The period in the history of the Restoration movement which is under consideration in this chapter is so named, because the two documents, *The Last Will and Testament of the Springfield Presbytery* and the *Declaration and Address* of the Christian Association of Washington, were produced in this period, thus inaugurating, in a public manner and by a public notice, movements to restore the faith and practice of the church of the New Testament. The importance of these two documents deserves their consideration in such a prominent position. They represent the first attempt of any note to put the principles of the movement into the form of a statement directed to the world of Christians.

It is well to remember in considering this section and these two historic documents that the men who set them down were not cognizant of the far reaching consequence of their moves. It was like a man setting out upon a strange journey on a strange road. He is conscious of the fact that he is leaving the land where he has dwelt for years. He has mapped out, in so far as he is able, the path he intends to follow. In part, at least, he is hopeful of the position or place to which he will arrive at the end of his journey, but the place to which his path will take him is not clearly understood as the first steps along the way are taken.

The rightness of the position Mr. Stone and Mr. Campbell took in these early days was not debatable with them. They were conscious of the hindrances to the progress of the church in the form of bickering, jealousy, tradition, creeds, and opinion. They were sick of the whole affair. The one thing they recognized to be right in all Christendom was the New Testament, the Bible. They were willing to lay aside all else, and come alone to this, following the road it pointed out for them, regardless of where it would take them or the consequence it would bring them. To do as they were doing they considered to be right in the sight of the Author of the Book, if not in the sight of men.

We shall not consider again here the instances that brought about the publication of these documents, since we have already cared for this matter in another section of this thesis. The reader is referred again to the section in which these backgrounds are discussed for information desired on that point. We turn now to the discussion of the text of the documents.

The Last Will and Testament is not a large document, but it should be read in consideration of the size of the idea it presents and not merely in consideration of the number of words it contains. Note should be taken of the words chosen and the satirical nature of the work. It will be found recorded as follows:

> The PRESBYTERY OF SPRINGFIELD, sitting at Caneridge, in the county of Bourbon, being through a gracious Providence, in more than ordinary bodily health, growing in strength and size daily; and in perfect

soundness and composure of mind; but knowing that it is appointed for all delegated bodies once to die; and considering that the life of every such body is very uncertain, do make, and ordain this our last Will and Testament, in manner and form following, viz:

Imprimis. We *will*, that this body die, be dissolved, and sink into union with the Body of Christ at large; for there is but one body, and one Spirit, even as we are called in one hope of our calling.

Item. We *will*, that our name of distinction, with its *Reverend* title be forgotten, that there be but one Lord over God's heritage, and his name one.

Item. We *will*, that our power of making laws for the government of the church, and executing them by delegated authority, forever cease; that the people may have free course to the Bible, and adopt the *law of the Spirit of life in Christ Jesus.*

Item. We *will*, that candidates for the Gospel ministry henceforth study the Holy Scriptures with fervent prayer, and obtain license from God to preach the simple Gospel, which the *Holy Ghost sent down from heaven,* without any mixture of philosophy, vain deceit, traditions of men, or the rudiments of the world. And let none henceforth *take this honor to himself, but he that is called of God, as was Aaron.*

Item. We *will*, that the church of Christ resume her native right of internal government—try her candidates for the ministry, as to their soundness in the faith, acquaintance with experimental religion, gravity and aptness to teach; and admit no other proof of their authority but Christ speaking in them. We will, that the church of Christ look up to the Lord of the harvest to send forth laborers into his harvest; and that she resume her native right of trying those *who say they are apostles, and are not.*

Item. We *will* that each particular church, as a body, actuated by the same spirit, choose her own preacher, and support him by a free will offering, without a written *call* or *subscription*—admit members—remove offences; and never henceforth *delegate* her right of government to any man or set of men whatever.

Item. We *will*, that the people henceforth take the Bible as the only sure guide to heaven; and as many as are offended with other books, which stand in competition with it, may cast them into the fire if they choose; for it is better to enter into life having one book, than having many to be cast into hell.

Item. We *will*, that preachers and people, cultivate a spirit of mutual forbearance; pray more and dispute less; and while they behold the signs of the times, look up, and confidently expect that redemption draweth nigh.

Item. We *will*, that our weak brethren, who may have been wishing to make the Presbytery of Springfield their king, and wot not what is now become of it, betake themselves to the Rock of Ages, and follow Jesus for the future.

Item. We *will*, that the Synod of Kentucky examine every member, who may be suspected of having departed from the Confession of Faith, and suspend every such suspected heretic immediately; in order that the oppressed may go free, and taste the sweets of gospel liberty.

Item. We *will*, that Ja————, the authority of two letters lately published in Lexington, be encouraged in his zeal to destroy partyism. We will, moreover, that our past conduct be examined into by all who may have correct information; but let foreigners beware of speaking evil of things which they know not.

Item. Finally we *will*, that all our sister bodies read their Bibles carefully, that they may see their fate there determined, and prepare for death before it is too late.

Springfield Presbytery,)
) L. S.
June 28th, 1804.   )

Robert Marshall,   )
John Dunlavy,   )
Richard M'Nemar,) Witnesses.[1]
B. W. Stone,   )
John Thompson,   )
David Purviance,   )

The first point set forth by these men is a strong statement to the effect that the Springfield Presbytery is not dying a natural death, but was being willed out of existence by its creators. It has "more than ordinary bodily health," and has "perfect soundness and composure of mind." This, no doubt, answered those critics who remained behind, in the Presbytery from which Stone and his followers had withdrawn, claiming that the Springfield Presbytery was not to be worried about since it would not last long anyway. This document is certainly a stricture against the assumed authority of men over Christ's church; it is an appeal for a free gospel ministry; it is an appeal to the church to resume her native right of local autonomy; it is an appeal to the people to take the Bible alone "as the only sure guide to heaven;" it is an encouragement for those in opposition to partyism to continue in their opposition; and it is an appeal to the people in the "sister bodies" to read their Bibles and come to the truth.

Two points seem to stand out in this statement in very clear outline: 1) These men were entering a protestation against the oppressions of the ecclesiastics and proclaiming their favor of local church autonomy. 2) They were conscious that the Bible was the only sure guide in existence, pertaining to matters of eternal life. The conclusion that must be drawn from this is that they were advocating the elimination of all that is human in the church and the acceptance of all that is divine. It is to be especially noted that they were interested in a sure guide to heaven, in other words, it was the salvation of the world that took first place or at least a prominent place in their considerations at this time.

THE DECLARATION AND ADDRESS

Thomas Campbell's document, the *Declaration and Address*, is much larger and far more fluent and oratorical than the *Last Will and Testament*. Mr. Campbell was careful to go into extreme detail in pointing out the position to which he had come and the reasons involved in the decision he had made. It is an appeal to the people to think, and its appeal is to the intelligence. In this quality it is, perhaps, more appealing than the *Last Will and Testament*. The length of the work, however, seems to be against it in its appeal to the popular mind. The short, concise, and satirical statements of Stone would probably be more effective in this field, but Campbell's work has a greater cultural appeal and those really interested would not be concerned about its length.

---

[1] John Rogers, *The Biography of Elder Barton Warren Stone*, (Cincinnati: J. A. and U. P. James; 1847), pp. 51-53.

Some of the most outstanding statements from the *Declaration and Address* are all that we have room for in this dissertation, but it is believed that a careful reading of these statements will give a good general understanding of the total impact of the article. Says Mr. Campbell:

> . . . . We are persuaded that it is high time for us not only to think, but also to act, for ourselves; to see with our own eyes, and to take all measures directly and immediately from the Divine Standard; to this alone we feel ourselves divinely bound to be conformed; as by this alone we must be judged . . . .[1]

> . . . . We are also of opinion that as the divine word is equally binding upon all so all lie under an equal obligation to be bound by it, and it alone; and not by any human interpretation of it: and that therefore no man has a right to judge his brother, except in so far as he manifestly violates the express letter of the law.[2]

This is distinctly an appeal to the authoritative nature of the Bible. We should take all "measures directly and immediately" from it, for by it we shall be judged. Furthermore, all are under equal obligation to be bound by its express letter and by no other.

Mr. Campbell continues:

> . . . . Being well aware from sad experience, of the heinous nature, and pernicious tendency of religious controversy among Christians; tired and sick of the bitter jarrings and janglings of a party spirit, we would desire to be at rest; and, were it possible, we would also desire to adopt and recommend such measures as would give rest to our brethren throughout all the churches;—as would restore unity, peace, and purity to the whole church of God . . . .[3]

> . . . . Our desire, therefore, for ourselves and our brethren would be, that rejecting human opinions and the inventions of men, as of any authority or as having any place in the church of God, we might forever cease from further contentions about such things; returning to, and holding fast by the original standard; taking the divine word alone for our rule; the Holy Spirit for our teacher and guide, to lead us into all truth; and Christ alone as exhibited in the word, for our salvation that, by so doing, we may be at peace among ourselves, follow peace with all men, and holiness, without which no men shall see the Lord.[4]

The first statement is an expression of disgust. Mr. Campbell is tired and sick of all the "jarring and jangling" of party spirit and disunity in the church of God. He desires to restore "unity, peace and purity" to the church, all three, not merely unity. His plan is well expressed: the rejection of human opinions and inventions of men and a holding fast to the "original standard." It is much the same appeal, in other words, that was made by Stone.

The formation of an association is next proposed by Mr. Campbell, for the purpose of promoting "simple evangelical Christianity" free from human opinion and tradition. Each member of the association is to pledge a sum to be used to support a pure gospel ministry, to reduce to practice the "doctrine, worship, discipline, and government" of God's word, and to provide scriptures for the

---

[1]Thomas Campbell, *Declaration and Address*, (Pittsburgh: Washington, Pennsylvania, Christian Missionary Society, 1909), p. 3.   [2]*Ibid.*   [3]*Ibid.*   [4]*Ibid.*, pp. 3, 4.

poor. Further, they intended to promote the formation of similar societies. Mr. Campbell is clear to state the association is not a church, but only advocates for church reformation. It is concluded that the association and its members shall support only such preachers as proclaim and practice "the original form of Christianity" without opinion or anything for which there is not a "thus saith the Lord either in express terms or approved precedent." A standing committee is provided for to see to the promotion of the interests of the society. It was arranged for the society to meet twice each year: on the first Thursday of May and of November, at least. The proceedings of the meetings are set forth, each one to be opened with a sermon. An expression of reliance upon Christ is also included here.[1]

Something of the effect of partyism and sectarianism is next set forth by Mr. Campbell:

> What awful and distressing effects have those sad divisions produced! What adversions, what reproaches, what back-bitings, what evil surmisings, what angry contentions, what enmities, what excommunications, and even persecutions!!! And indeed, this must in some measure, continue to be the case so long as those schisms exist, for, said the Apostle, where envying and strife is, *there* is confusion and every evil work. What dreary effects of these accursed divisions are to be seen, even in this highly favored country, where the sword of the civil magistrate has not yet learned to serve at the altar. Have we not seen congregations broken to pieces, neighborhoods of professing Christians first thrown into confusion by party contentions, and, in the end, entirely deprived of gospel ordinances; while in the meantime, large settlements, and tracts of country, remain to this day entirely destitute of a gospel ministry; many of them in little better than a state of heathenism: the churches being either so weakened with divisions, that they cannot send them ministers; or, the people so divided among themselves, that they will not receive them. Many at the same time who live at the door of a preached gospel, dare not in conscience go to hear it and, of course, enjoy little more advantage in that respect, than if living in the midst of heathens . . . .[2]

It is an expression of concern not alone for the divisions that exist, but for the persons who are, because of those divisions, deprived of a gospel ministry and the persons who are deprived of the gospel altogether.

The plan to be used in ending this terrible condition is also suggested by Mr. Campbell:

> Dearly beloved brethren, why should *we* deem it a thing incredible that the church of Christ, in this highly favored country, should resume that original unity, peace and purity, which belong to its constitution, and constitutes its glory? Or, is there any thing that can be justly deemed necessary for this desirable purpose, but to conform to the model, and adopt the practice of the primitive church, expressly exhibited in the New Testament. Whatever alterations this might produce in any or all of the churches, should we think, neither be deemed inadmissable nor ineligible. Surely such alteration would be every way for the better, and not for the worse; unless we should suppose the divinely inspired rule to be faulty, or defective. Were we, then, in our church constitution and managements, to

---

[1]*Ibid.*, pp. 4, 5.   [2]*Ibid.*, pp. 6. 7.

19

exhibit a complete conformity to the Apostolic church, would we not be in that respect, as perfect as Christ intended we should be? And should not this suffice us?[1]

This solution he proposes is clearly stated: "To conform to the model, and adopt the practice of the primitive church, expressly exhibited in the New Testament;" doing this would make us "as perfect as Christ intended we should be."

The *Declaration and Address* continues with an assertion that there are many agreements among the denominational bodies and that the greater number of disagreements are in matters human and not divine. In Thomas Campbell's own words:

> It is, to us, a pleasing consideration that all the churches of Christ, which mutually acknowledge each other as such, are not only agreed in the great doctrines of faith and holiness; but are also materially agreed, as to the positive ordinances of gospel institution; so that our differences, at most, are the things in which the kingdom of God does not consist, that is, about matters of private opinion, or human invention. What a pity, that the kingdom of God should be divided about such things!! Who then, would not be the first amongst us to give up with human inventions in the worship of God; and to cease from imposing his private opinions upon his brethren; that our breaches might *thus* be healed? Who would not willingly conform to the original pattern laid down in the New Testament, for *this* happy purpose? Our dear brethren, of all denominations, will please to consider, that we have our educational prejudices, and particular customs to struggle with as well as they. But this we do sincerely declare, that there is nothing we have hitherto received as matter of faith or practice, which is not expressly taught and enjoined in the word of God, either in express terms, or approved precedent, that we would not heartily relinquish, that so we might return to the original constitutional unity of the Christian church; and in this happy unity, enjoy full communion with all our brethren, in peace and charity. The like dutiful condescension we candidly expect of all that are seriously impressed with a sense of the duty they owe to God, to each other, and to their perishing fellow-brethren of mankind. To this we call, we invite, our brethren, of all denominations, by all the sacred motives which we have avouched as the impulsive reasons of our thus addressing them.[2]

We must drop opinions and the inventions of men and conform to the original standard, and Mr. Campbell leads the way in stating that he would not hesitate to drop anything of a human sort in order to gain the unity of his "brethren of all denominations." However, he states definitely that he expects the same thing of others, so that all might "return to the original constitutional unity of the Christian church." It is in this happy unity, the original constitutional unity of the Christian church, that Mr. Campbell hopes to meet his brethren. Most certainly it is not a mere union that he is pleading for in these passages.

Mr. Campbell demonstrated his willingness to drop all opinions and inventions of men, when, later, he dropped the opinion of sprinkling and was himself immersed in Buffalo Creek. This illustrates, it seems, a fundamental concept of the restoration idea. It is a subtraction, but it is also an addition. The rubble of tradition and opinion must be taken away, but the positive ordinances of Christ must be added to the practice of the churches, if part is to be had in the "original constitutional unity of the Christian Church."

[1]*Ibid.*, p. 10   [2]*Ibid.*, pp. 10, 11.

Lest there be quibbling over the point of essentials and non-essentials, Mr. Campbell writes:

> You are all, dear brethren, equally included as the object of our love and esteem. With you all we desire to unite in the bonds of an entire Christian unity—Christ alone being the head, the centre, his word the rule—an explicit belief of, and manifest conformity to it, in all things—the terms. More than this, you will not require of us; and less we cannot require of you; nor, indeed, can we reasonably suppose, any would desire it; for what good purpose would it serve? We dare neither assume, nor purpose, the trite indefinite distinction between essentials, and non-essentials, in matters of revealed truth and duty; fully persuaded, that, whatever may be their comparative importance, simply considered, the high obligation of the Divine Authority revealing, or enjoining them, renders the belief or performance of them, absolutely essential to us, in so far as we know them . . . . [1]

Here again is an appeal to the authoritative nature of the word of God. The statements therein set forth are to be considered as essential, says Mr. Campbell, whether we think them important or not, merely because God chose to give them to us. It is the exact gospel of the New Testament for which he pleads and to which he calls his denominational friends, just as recorded and for what it is worth, regardless of our personal judgment.

Mr. Campbell next brings up a very important item. What if no such divine basis of unity exists? What is our hope then? Says he:

> . . . . Indeed if no such divine and adequate basis of union, can be fairly exhibited, as will meet the approbation of every upright and intelligent Christian: nor such mode of procedure adopted in favor of the weak, as will not oppress their consciences, then the accomplishment of this grand object upon principle, must be forever impossible. — There would, upon this supposition, remain no other way of accomplishing it, but merely by voluntary compromise, and good natured accommodation. That such a thing however will be accomplished, one way or other, will not be questioned by any that allow themselves to believe, that the commands and prayers of our Lord Jesus Christ will not utterly prove ineffectual. Whatever way, then, it is to be effected; whether upon the solid basis of divinely revealed truth; or the good natured principle of Christian forbearance and gracious condescension; is it not equally practicable, equally eligible to us, as ever it can be to any; unless we should suppose ourselves to be destitute of that Christian temper and discernment, which is essentially necessary to qualify us to do the will of our gracious Redeemer, whose expressed command to his people is that there be no division among them; but that they all walk by the same rule, speak the same thing, and be perfectly joined together in the same mind and in the same judgment? We believe then it is as practicable, as it is eligible. Let us attempt it. "Up and be doing, and the Lord will be with you."[2]

Certainly this is not a plea for unity upon the basis of "voluntary compromise, and good natured accommodation!" Such is the attempt of some in our day, as Mr. Campbell here prophesied the case would be, if an attempt was not made upon the "solid basis of divinely revealed truth." The latter basis will work, he says, so let us be about this business, and see to its working in our own day. The appeal here, surely, is for an attempt to obtain the unity of Christians upon a

---

[1] *Ibid.*, p. 11.   [2] *Ibid.*, p. 12.

solid basis, a divine basis, before any attempt to obtain a simple union upon a basis of human compromise.

The thirteen propositions of Thomas Campbell's *Declaration and Address* have been long quoted as the crux of the thought of the document. In many ways this is true, however, they should not be emphasized to the exclusion of the balance of the material. The thirteen propositions follow, at least in part, for inclusion of all statements in them would make too lengthy a quotation and would add nothing of value. The essential idea of each proposition is included. Mr. Campbell introduces them:

Let none imagine that the subjoined propositions are at all intended as an overture towards a new creed, or standard, for the church, or, as in any wise designed to be made a term of communion;—nothing can be farther from our intention. They are merely designed for opening up the way, that we may come fairly and firmly to original grounds upon clear and certain premises: and take up things just as the Apostles left them—That thus disentangled from the accruing embarrassments of intervening ages, we may stand with evidence upon the same ground on which the church stood in the beginning—Having said so much to solicit attention and prevent mistake, we submit as follows:

Prop. 1 THAT the church of Christ upon earth is essentially, intentionally, and constitutionally one; consisting of all those in every place that profess their faith in Christ and obedience to him in all things according to the scriptures, and that manifest the same by their tempers and conduct, and of none else as none else can be truly and properly called Christians.

2. That although the church of Christ upon earth must necessarily exist in particular and distinct societies, locally separate one from another; yet there ought to be no schisms, no uncharitable divisions among them . . . .

3. That in order to this, nothing ought to be inculcated upon Christians as articles of faith; nor required of them as terms of communion; but what is expressly taught and enjoined upon them, in the word of God. Nor ought anything be admitted, as of divine obligation, in their church constitution and managements, but what is expressly enjoined by the authority of our Lord Jesus Christ and his Apostles upon the New Testament church; either in expressed terms, or by approved precedent.

4. . . . . The New Testament is as perfect a constitution for the worship, discipline and government of the New Testament church, and as perfect a rule for the particular duties of its members; as the Old Testament was for the worship, discipline and government of the Old Testament church, and the particular duties of its members.

5. That with respect to the commands and ordinances of our Lord Jesus Christ, where the scriptures are silent, as to the express time or manner of performance, if any such there be; no human authority has power to interfere, in order to supply the supposed deficiency, by making laws for the church; . . . .

6. That although inferences and deductions from scripture premises, when fairly inferred, may be truly called the doctrine of God's holy word; yet are they not formally binding upon the consciences of Christians farther than they perceive the connection, and evidently see that they are so; . . . .

7. That although doctrinal exhibitions of the great system of divine truths, and defensive testimonies in opposition to prevailing errors, be highly expedient; and the more full and explicit they be, for those purposes, the

22

better; yet as these must be in a great measure the effect of human reasoning, and of course must contain many inferential truths, they ought not to be made terms of Christian communion: . . . .

8. . . . . Their having a due measure of scriptural self-knowledge respecting their lost and perishing condition by nature and practice; and of the way of salvation thro' Jesus Christ, accompanied with a profession of their faith in, and obedience to him, in all things according to his word, is all that is absolutely necessary to qualify them for admission to his church.

9. That all that are enabled, thro' grace, to make such a profession, and to manifest the reality of it in their tempers and conduct, should consider each other as the precious saints of God, should love each other as brethren, ...

10. That division among Christians is a horrid evil, fraught with many evils. It is anti-christian, as it destroys the visible unity of the body of Christ: as if he were divided against himself, excluding and excommunicating a part of himself . . . .

11. That, (in some instances,) a partial neglect of the expressly revealed will of God; and, (in others,) an assumed authority for making the approbation of human opinions, and human inventions, a term of communion by introducing them into the constitution, faith, or worship, of the church: are, and have been, the immediate, obvious and universally acknowledged causes, of all the corruptions and divisions that have ever taken place in the church of God.

12. That all that is necessary to the highest state of perfection and purity of the church upon earth is, first, that none be received as members, but such as having that due measure of scriptural self-knowledge described above, do profess their faith in Christ and obedience to him in all things according to the scriptures; nor, secondly, that any be retained in her communion longer than they continue to manifest the reality of their profession by their tempers and conduct. Thirdly, that her ministers, duly and scripturally qualified, inculcate none other things than those very articles of faith and holiness expressly revealed and enjoined in the word of God. Lastly, that in all their administration they keep close by the observance of all divine ordinances, after the example of the primitive church, exhibited in the New Testament; without any additions whatsoever of human opinions or inventions of men.

13. Lastly, That if any circumstantial indispensably necessary to the observance of divine ordinances be not found upon the page of express revelation, such, and such only, as are absolutely necessary for this purpose, should be adopted, under the title of human expedients, without any pretence to a more sacred origin—so that any subsequent alteration or difference in the observance of these things might produce no contention nor division in the church.[1]

These thirteen articles have been summarized many times before, but it seems well to reduce them to shorter form at this time. In the first place, Mr. Campbell has indicated that the church is essentially, in the very nature of its work necessarily; intentionally, by its founder intended to be; and constitutionally, its constituents being brothers in Christ; one, while necessarily separated by space and time. He contends for the authority of the scriptures, but proclaims that only what is expressly taught and enjoined in the New Testament is binding upon Christians. Expedients of human opinion, inferences and deductions from scripture premises, and human interpretations of scriptural truths

[1]*Ibid.*, pp. 15-18.

are not to be binding upon Christians. Divisions in the church result from: 1) neglect of the word of God, 2) making human authority binding in the church. The cure for the division of the church is to bring to be again the highest perfection and purity of the church. This may be had by: 1) accepting only those who possess faith in and are obedient to Christ in all things according to his word, 2) keeping in membership only those who manifest the genuineness of their profession of faith in their conduct and life, 3) making only the articles of faith expressly taught and enjoined upon the New Testament church binding upon Christians, 4) emulating the New Testament church without addition or subtraction.

The twelfth article is worthy of special note and emphasis. While the other articles dwell upon the problem of division and the introduction of human opinion and expedients, the article mentioned deals with the solution Mr. Campbell is suggesting. This proposition brings to the fore all that Mr. Campbell considers necessary to the "highest state of perfection and purity of the church." In short, here is the very crux of the *Declaration and Address*.

Mr. Campbell's purpose in suggesting these thirteen propositions, he states for himself:

> . . . . To prepare the way for a permanent scriptural unity amongst Christians, by calling up to their consideration fundamental truths, directing their attention to first principles, clearing the way before them by removing the stumbling blocks—the rubbish of ages which has been thrown upon it, and fencing it on each side, that in advancing toward the desired object, they may not miss the way through mistake, or inadvertency, by turning aside to the right hand or to the left—is, at least, the sincere intention of the above propositions.[1]

That he believed the *Declaration and Address* would find response in the mind of every Christian is revealed in the following:

> Ye lovers of Jesus, and beloved of him, however scattered in this cloudy and dark day, ye love the truth as it is in Jesus, (if our hearts deceive us not) so do we. Ye desire union in Christ, with all them that love him; so do we. Ye lament and bewail our sad divisions; so do we. Ye reject the doctrines and commandments of men that ye may keep the law of Christ; so do we. Ye believe the alone sufficiency of his word; so do we. Ye believe that the word itself ought to be our rule and not any human explication of it, so do we. Ye believe that no man has a right to judge, to exclude, or reject his professing christian brother; except in so far as he stands condemned, or rejected, by the express letter of the law: so do we. Ye believe that the great fundamental law of unity and love ought not to be violated to make way for exalting human opinions to an equality with express revelation, by making them articles of faith and terms of communion— so do we. Ye sincere and impartial followers of Jesus, friends of truth and peace, we dare not, we cannot, think otherwise of you;—it would be doing violence to your character; it would be inconsistent with your prayers and profession, so to do. We shall therefore have *your* hearty concurrence.[2]

Mere reading of this appeal of Mr. Campbell will bring to realization that it is the individual follower of Jesus to whom he is speaking. This is a fundamental concept. The unit in the unity we seek is the individual in the denominations

---

[1]*Ibid.*, pp. 18, 19.   [2]*Ibid.*, p. 21.

and out, most certainly not the denomination itself. Note his words are addressed to "ye lovers of Jesus," and "ye sincere and impartial followers of Jesus."

Whether they had taken the proper ground was not a question in the mind of Mr. Campbell. He was certain that, if they had not taken a valid stand, they would never find one.

> . . . . All we shall venture to say as to this, is that we trust we have taken the proper ground, at least, if we have not, we despair of finding it elsewhere. For if holding fast in the profession and practice whatever is expressly revealed and enjoined in the divine standard does not under the promised influence of the divine spirit, prove an adequate basis for promoting and maintaining unity, peace and purity, we utterly despair of attaining those invaluable privileges, by adopting the standard of any party . . . .[1]

It is in a restoration of the "profession and practice" of the church of the New Testament that Mr. Campbell sees a basis for unity. He would not attempt unity without restoration, as some would define his intentions, while at the same time saying that it is by returning to the purity of the apostolic church that he hopes to accomplish the unity desired. Further closing appeals follow this statement, and the document bears the signatures of "Thos. Campbell and Thos. Acheson."

To the *Declaration and Address* is attached a rather lengthy appendix in which the position is reviewed and further assertions are made "to prevent mistakes." Mr. Campbell continues his discussion of the issues:

> All we shall say to this at present, is, that if the divine word be not the standard of a party—Then we are not a party, for we have adopted no other. If to maintain its alone sufficiency be not a party principle: then we are not a party—If to justify this principle by our practice, in making a rule of it, and of *it alone,* and not of our own opinions, nor of those of others be not a party principle—then are we not a party—If to propose and practice neither more nor less than it expressly reveals and enjoins be not a partial business, then are we not a party. These are the very sentiments we have approved and recommended, as a society formed for the express purpose of promoting christian unity, in opposition to a party spirit . . . .[2]
>
> . . . . As for ourselves, we have taken all due care, in the meantime to take no step, that might throw a stumbling block in the way; that might prove now, or at any future period, a barrier to prevent the accomplishment of that most desirable object; either by joining to support a party; or by patronizing anything as articles of faith or duty, not expressly revealed and enjoined in the divine standard; as we are sure, whatever alterations may take place, that will stand. And that considerable alterations must and will take place in the standards of all the churches, before that glorious object can be accomplished, no man, that duly considers the matter, can possibly doubt.[3]

Again he asserts that it is a unity in the principles and practice of the church of the New Testament he seeks and pleads for. This he says is not and cannot be a party spirit. That such a position will bring about changes and alterations in the present practices of the churches he has no doubt, but, whatever alterations may be necessary to come to the divine standard, *"that* will stand."

Mr. Campbell next asserts that the root cause of all the bitter divisions of the church is the introduction of private opinion into the work and worship of the church as articles of faith.

---

[1]*Ibid.,* p. 22.   [2]*Ibid.,* p. 25   [3]*Ibid.,* p. 26.

. . . . To cease from all such things, by simply returning to the original standard of christianity—the profession and practice of the primitive church, as expressly exhibited upon the sacred page of the New Testament scripture, is the only possible way, that we can perceive, to get rid of those evils. And we humbly think that a uniform agreement in *that* for the preservation of charity would be infinitely preferable to our contention and divisions: nay, that such a uniformity is the very thing that the Lord requires, if the New Testament be a perfect model—a sufficient formula for the worship, discipline and government of the Christian church. Let *us* do, as we are there expressly told *they* did, say as *they* said: that is, profess and practise as therein expressly enjoined by precept and precedent, in every possible instance, after their approved example; and in so doing we shall realize, and exhibit, all that unity and uniformity, that the primitive church possessed, or that the law of Christ requires. But if after all, our brethren can point out a better way to regain and preserve that Christian unity and charity expressly enjoined upon the church of God, we shall thank them for the discovery and cheerfully embrace it.[1]

The fact that he so forcefully advocates unity upon the express injunctions and approved precedents of the New Testament scripture is indicative of the fact that he expects no other to be found, even though he promises cheerful acceptance of any other basis should it be found. He was convinced of the rightness and of the authority of the New Testament.

Some, then as now, would say that all parties already accept the New Testament as their only rule of reference. To them and in refutation of this argument, he says:

Should it still be urged, that this would open a wide door to latitudinarianism, seeing all that profess christianity, profess to receive the holy scriptures; and yet differ so widely in their religious sentiments. We say, let them profess what they will, their difference in religious profession and practice originates in their departure from what is expressly revealed and enjoined; and not in their strict and faithful conformity to it—which is the thing we humbly advise for putting an end to those differences. But you may say, do they not already agree in the letter, though differing so far in sentiment? However this may be, have they all agreed to make the letter their rule; or rather to make it the subject matter of their profession and practice? Surely no; or else they would all profess and practice the same thing . . . . [2]

. . . . Union in truth, amongst all the manifest subjects of grace and truth, is what we advocate. We carry our views on union no farther than *this*, nor do we presume to recommend it upon any other principle than truth alone. Now surely truth is something certain and definite; if not, who will take upon him to define and determine it? This we suppose God has sufficiently done already in his Holy Word. That men therefore truly receive and make proper use of the Divine word for walking together in truth and peace, in holiness and charity, is, no doubt, the ardent desire of all the genuine subjects of our holy religion. This we see, however, they have not done, to the awful detriment, and manifest subversion of, what we might almost call, the primary intention of Christianity. We dare not therefore follow their example, nor adopt their ruinous expedients. But does it therefore follow, that christians may not, or cannot, take proper steps to ascertain that desirable and preceptive unity, which the Divine word requires, and enjoins? Surely no—at least we have supposed no such thing;—but on the contrary, have overtured to our brethren, what

[1]*Ibid.*, p. 35.   [2]*Ibid.*, p. 36.

appears to us undeniably just, and scripturally evident; and which we humbly think, if adopted and acted upon, would have the desired effect— adopted and acted upon, not indeed as a standard for the doctrine, worship, discipline, and government of the church; for it pretends not to determine these matters; but rather supposes the existence of a fixed and certain standard of divine original; in which every thing that the wisdom of God saw meet to reveal and determine, for *these*, and all other purposes, is expressly defined and determined; betwixt the Christian and which, no medium of human determination ought to be interposed . . . .[1]

It is Mr. Campbell's conviction that the interposition of human opinion is the cause of division, and that men are not following the divine standard, however much they may claim to be so doing. In that case, he says, they would all "profess and practice the same thing." It is union in truth that is the object of his plea. He would not follow nor adopt "their ruinous expedients." Even the *Declaration and Address* is not to be thought of "as a standard for the doctrine, worship, discipline, and government of the church." Instead it presupposes the existence of these items in the divine "original." So reasons Mr. Campbell in the above two paragraphs.

The New Testament, the original standard, is the rule to which the *Declaration and Address* points the Christians among men. Giving further particulars about how this truth is arrived at and the reasons for giving the new pre-eminence over the old, Mr. Campbell relates:

> . . . . As to the rule itself, we have ventured to allege that the New Testament is the proper and immediate rule, directory, and formula, for the New Testament church, and for the particular duties of Christians; as the Old Testament was for the Old Testament church, and for the particular duties of the subject under that dispensation; at the same time by no means excluding the old as fundamental to, illustrative of, and inseparably connected with the new; and as being every way of equal authority, as well as of an entire sameness with it, in every point of moral natural duty; though not immediately our rule, without the intervention and coincidence of the new; in which our Lord has taught his people, by the ministry of his holy Apostles, all things whatsoever they should observe and do, till the end of the world. Thus we come to the one rule, taking the Old Testament as explained and perfected by the new, and the new as illustrated and enforced by the old; assuming the latter as the proper and immediate directory for the Christian church, as also for the positive and particular duties of Christians, as to all things whatsoever they should observe and do.[2]

> . . . . For this purpose we have overtured a certain and determinate application of the rule, to which we presume there can be no reasonable objection, and which, if adopted and acted upon, must, we think, infallibly produce the desired effect, unless we should suppose that to say and do, what is expressly said and done before our eyes upon the sacred page, would offend the believer; or that a strict uniformity, and entire scriptural sameness in profession and practices, would produce divisions and offenses amongst those, who are already united in one spirit, one Lord, one faith, one baptism, one hope of their calling, and in one God and Father of all, who is above all, and through all, and in them all; as is confessedly the case with all of the character throughout all the churches . . . .[3]

The last section of the last above quoted paragraph is, without question, satire approaching that of the Springfield Presbytery's *Last Will and Testament*. It is

---

[1]*Ibid.*, pp. 45, 46.   [2]*Ibid.*, p. 49.   [3]*Ibid.*, p. 50.

perfectly obvious that Mr. Campbell does not believe that Christians are already united, otherwise he would not be making such a lengthy appeal. It is further obvious that he does not believe that an appeal for unity upon the basis of the divine and original standard will produce division, or he certainly would not be making such an appeal. It is a rare example of the use of a glaring untruth to establish the certainty of truth. The rule is valid, and the suggested application of it is valid; it needs only to be accepted and acted upon to bring the desired happy result.

The closing lines of the *Declaration and Address* reveal the heart's desire of Mr. Campbell, the consideration uppermost in his thinking as he directs this magnificent appeal to the non-Christian world.

> . . . . Alas! poor people! how do our divisions and corruptions stand in your way? What a pity that you find us not upon original ground, such as the Apostles left the primitive churches? Had we but exhibited to you their unity and charity; their humble, honest, and affectionate deportment towards each other and towards all men: you would not have had those evil and shameful things to object to our holy religion, and to prejudice your minds against it. But your conversion, it seems, awaits our reformation—awaits our return to primitive unity and love. To this may the God of mercy speedily restore us, both for your sakes and our own; that *his way* may be known upon earth, and his saving health among all nations. Let the people praise thee, O God; let all the people praise thee. Amen and amen.[1]

The conversion of the world is the chief concern of the author of this historic document. His is certainly not an appeal for unity, simply for the sake of unity, nor for a restoration of the church of the New Testament simply to be able to point others to it and proudly exclaim, "Look upon our work! See the rightness of our position! Isn't it beautiful and glorious?" His purpose was more deeply rooted than that, his plan more sublime than that. The church, weakened by partyism and sectarianism, could not and would never save the world. It needed the strength of unity to bring about this divinely appointed accomplishment, unity in evangelism.

Since the purpose here stated, the ultimate over all purpose of the *Declaration and Address* and the restoration movement, is the conversion of the world, it may be fairly reasoned from here that the things to be restored have to do with conversion or with the unity of the individual with his Christ. The relationship of Christian to Christian will not be a point of concern when this unity exists in reality.

If one were to summarize the impact of the entire *Declaration and Address* and put it into simple form, without the inclusion of theological terminology and intricate phraseology, he might set it forth as follows: 1) The *Declaration and Address* asserts the rightness of the New Testament due to the authority of its author, 2) it exposes the inadequacy and divisive nature of all human expedients and opinions when thrust forward as authoritatively binding upon Christians, 3) it emphasizes that the conversion of the world awaits the unity of believers, 4) it suggests a solution to the problem in calling all Christians to the express injunctions and approved precedents of the original divine standard. The purposes of the movement in this period were held in common by all associated with it; though more definite expressions of that purpose and more frequent proclamations of them are to be found in the next period.

---

[1]*Ibid.,* p. 54.

CHAPTER III

THE PERIOD OF THE RESTORATION OF THE ANCIENT ORDER OF THINGS: 1823 - 1837

While the *Declaration and Address*, together with the *Last Will and Testament of the Springfield Presbytery*, ushered in a new period in the history of the restoration idea, the year 1823 began a still more clearly defined period. At this time, the leadership in the propagation of the newly discovered idea changed from father to son, and, while Thomas Campbell remained actively engaged in the program of restoring the New Testament church, his son Alexander became the leading figure in the presentation of the principles of the "current reformation."

One of the reasons for this change in leadership may be noted in the debates in which Alexander engaged with the leading exponents of the traditional thought of the day. In 1820 Mr. Campbell met John Walker, a Presbyterian, at Mt. Pleasant, Ohio, on the subject of infant baptism. He was at first hesitant about engaging in such a controversy, but the results of the debate were so beneficial to the reform that he decided such would probably be one of the most effective means of promoting the new movement.[1]

In 1823 Mr. Campbell undertook another debate, this time with another Presbyterian, William McCalla, at Washington, Kentucky. Mr. Campbell argued against infant baptism on two grounds: 1) the difference in the covenants, the new being the rule of reference in the church of Christ, thus ruling out infant baptism as coming in the room of circumcision, 2) the design of baptism, as making it ineffective except to those capable of confession and repentance. The debate gained many friends for Mr. Campbell among the Baptists of Kentucky and among the co-laborers with Barton Warren Stone.

The success of the debates mentioned and the widening reputation and influence of Alexander Campbell prompted him, in 1823, to begin the publication of a religious periodical, which he called the *Christian Baptist*. It was a small paper, according to our standards of measuring things today, but it was to be large in its influence. In the year 1830 the *Christian Baptist* was ceased, but a larger and, to become far more influential, paper was started. This paper Mr. Campbell called the *Millennial Harbinger*. Through these papers, first the *Christian Baptist* and then the *Millennial Harbinger*, Mr. Campbell placed before the public the cause he had given his life to plead.

THE CHRISTIAN BAPTIST

One can get a fair notion of a project about to be begun by asking the author of that project what his intentions are and what his goal might be. This, it seems, is true of the *Christian Baptist*. In the dedication of this publication, Mr. Campbell says:

To all those, without distinction, who acknowledge the scriptures of the

---

[1]Walker, "Adventuring for Christian Unity," *op. cit.*, p. 27.

Old and New Testaments to be a true revelation from God, and the New Testament as containing the religion of Jesus Christ: who, willing to have all religious tenets and practices tried by the Divine Word: and, who, feeling themselves, in duty bound, to search the scriptures for themselves, in all matters of religion, are disposed to reject all doctrine and commandments of men, and to obey the truth, holding fast the faith once delivered to the saints. This work is most respectfully and affectionately dedicated by the Editor.[1]

Mr. Campbell clearly states the starting point of his program. The New Testament is the source of authority. This premise must be agreed to before any discussion upon the subjects involved is permissable. The reasonableness of this major premise of Christianity is at once apparent. If the Bible is not the sole source of reference, if it is not agreed to as such by the disputants in any question of a Christian nature, then no common ground exists and one man's opinion would be as good as another. However, granted that the New Testament is authoritative a common ground of argument exists and a chance for a conclusion upon that basis is possible.

Something further expressive of the hope Mr. Campbell had for the accomplishment of his new journal is revealed in the prospectus which was printed in the first issue:

THE "CHRISTIAN BAPTIST" shall espouse the cause of no religious sect, excepting that Ancient Sect, called "CHRISTIANS FIRST AT ANTIOCH." Its sole object shall be the eviction of truth, and the exposure of error in doctrine and practice. The editor acknowledging no standard of religious faith or works, other than the Old and New Testaments, and the latter as the only standard of the religion of Jesus Christ will, intentionally at least, oppose nothing which it contains, and recommend nothing which it does not enjoin. Having no worldly interest at stake from the adoption or reprobation of any article of faith or religious practice—having no gift nor religious office of any worldly emolument to blind his eyes or to pervert his judgment—he hopes to manifest that he is an impartial advocate of truth.[2]

Who can deny that the position Mr. Campbell hopes to assume is honorable in the sight of all men? Accepting the word of God in general and the New Testament in particular, as the rule for Christians, he will espouse the cause of no sect but the sect therein presented. Of this truth he is to be an impartial advocate, since he has no advantage at stake in the advocation of any other point of view. How well Mr. Campbell accomplished his stated purpose can be well attested to by those who have made a careful perusal of his editorial works over the period of years in which he was engaged in that work.

Without question, the most significant series of essays printed in the *Christian Baptist* during the seven years of its publication was the series entitled "A Restoration of the Ancient Order of Things." We cannot hope to review the entire series here, but some of the most important statements must be considered in order to present the thought of Alexander upon the principles of the movement at this time. The series began in the year 1824, and in the first essay Mr. Campbell says:

All reformations in religious opinions and speculations have been fated

---

[1] *Christian Baptist*, Vol. I, No. I, p. 3. [2] *Christian Baptist*, Vol. I, No. I, p. 5.

like the fashions in apparel. They have lived, and died, and revived, and died again. As apparel has been the badge of rank, so have opinions been the badge of parties, and the cause of their rise and continuance. The green and orange ribbon, as well as the blue stocking, have been as useful and as honorable to those that have worn them, as those opinions were to their possessors, which have been the shibboleths of religious parties.

Human systems, whether of philosophy or of religion, are proper subjects of reformation; but Christianity can not be reformed. Every attempt to reform Christianity is like an attempt to create a new sun, or to change the revolutions of the heavenly bodies—unprofitable and vain. In a word, we have had reformations enough. The very name has become as offensive as the term "revolution" in France.

A RESTORATION *of the ancient order of things* is all that is necessary to the happiness and usefulness of Christians. No attempt "to reform the doctrine, discipline, and government of the church," (a phrase too long in use,) can promise a better result than those that have been attempted and languished unto death. We are glad to see, in the above extract, that the thing proposed, is to bring Christianity and the church of the present day up to the standard of the New Testament. This is in substance, though in other terms, what we contend for. To bring the societies of Christians *up* to the New Testament, is just to bring the disciples, individually and collectively, to walk in the faith, and in the commandments of the Lord and Saviour as presented in that blessed volume; and this is to *restore the ancient order of things.*[1]

The logic here presented is clear. Human systems, being, by virtue of their humanity, imperfect, are subjects for reformation, but Christianity, being, by virtue of the fact that it is a revelation from God, perfect, cannot be reformed. To change perfection, one must, in the very nature of the case move towards imperfection. To restore the church to that perfect system, is the ambition Mr. Campbell here reveals to us.

The totality involved in the "restoration of the ancient order of things" is the next item Mr. Campbell mentions:

But a *restoration of the ancient order of things* it appears is all that is contemplated by the wise disciples of the Lord; as it is agreed that this is all that is wanting to the perfection, happiness, and glory of the Christian community. To contribute to this is our most ardent desire—our daily and diligent inquiry and pursuit—Now, in attempting to accomplish this, it must be observed, that it belongs to every individual and to every congregation of individuals, to discard from their faith and practice every thing that is not found written in the New Testament of the Lord and Saviour; and to believe and practice whatever is there enjoined. This done, and every thing is done, which ought to be done.[2]

It has been previously observed that the restoration idea proposed, not only a subtraction from practice of all not set forth in the word, but also an addition to practice of all things not in practice but yet expressly taught in the word. Mr. Campbell asserts this same point of view again in the above statement.

He continues:

But to come to the things to be discarded, we observe that, in the ancient order of things, there were no creeds or complications of doctrine

---

[1] *Christian Baptist*, Vol. II, No. VII, pp. 155, 156.
[2] *Christian Baptist*, Vol. II, No. VIII, pp. 176, 177.

in abstract terms, nor in any terms, other than the terms adopted by the Holy Spirit in the New Testament. Therefore, all such are to be discarded. It is enough to prove that they ought to be discarded, from the fact that none of those now in use, nor ever at any time in use, existed in the Apostolic Age. But as many considerations are urged why they should be used, we shall briefly advert to these, and attempt to show that they are perfectly irrational and consequently foolish and vain.[1]

. . . . It is argued that human confessions of faith are necessary to *the unity* of the church. If they are *necessary* to the unity of the church, then the church cannot be united and one without them. But the church of Christ was united and one in all Judea, in the first age without them. Therefore, they are not *necessary* to the unity of the church. But again, if they are *necessary* to the unity of the church, then the New Testament is defective; for if the New Testament was sufficient to the unity of the church, then human creeds would not be necessary. If any man, therefore, contend that human creeds are *necessary* to the unity of the church, he, at the same time, and by *all the same arguments*, contends that the scriptures of the Holy Spirit are insufficient—that is, imperfect or defective. Every human creed is predicated upon this inadequacy, that is, the imperfection of the Holy Scriptures.

But the records of all religious sects, and the experience of all men of observation, concur in attesting the fact, that human creeds have contributed always, since their first introduction, to divide and disunite the professors of the Christian religion.

Every attempt to found the unity of the church upon the adoption of any creed of human device is not only incompatible with the nature and circumstances of mankind, but is an effort to frustrate or to defeat the prayer of the Lord Messiah, and to subvert his throne and government . . . .[2]

. . . . To attempt to unite the professing disciples by any other means than the word of the Apostles, by the Westminster, or any other creed, is, then, an attempt to over rule the will of heaven, to subvert the throne of the great King, to frustrate the prayers of the Son of the Blessed. As the heavens are higher than the earth so are God's thoughts and ways higher than ours. He knows, for he has willed, and planned, and determined, that neither the Popish, the Protestant, the Presbyterian, the Methodistic, nor the Baptist creed shall be honored more than the Apostles' testimony, shall be honored as much as the Apostles' testimony, shall be honored at all . . . .[3]

The editor of the *Christian Baptist* had set out to "show that they (the creeds or human expressions of divine truths so called) are perfectly irrational, and consequently foolish and vain." Who would deny that the aim he set for himself was accomplished in the three short paragraphs above quoted? The arguments presented are about as fine an illustration of *reductio ad absurdum* as one will find in the writings of men.

That Jesus intended his followers to look to the Apostles' testimony as a basis for unity Mr. Campbell points out in the following statement:

"HOLY FATHER—now I do not pray for these only, but for those who shall believe on me THROUGH THEIR WORD, *that they all may be* ONE.—That THE WORLD MAY BELIEVE *that thou hast sent me.*" The Testimony of the Apostles, the Saviour makes the grand means of the enlargement and consolidation of his empire. He prays that they who

---

[1]*Ibid.*   [2]*Ibid.*, pp. 178, 179.   [3]*Ibid.*, p. 182.

believe on him through their testimony may be united. And their union he desires, that the world may believe that he was sent of God, and acted under the authority and according to the will of the God and Father of all. The word of the Apostles, the unity of those who believe it, and the conviction of the world are here inseparably associated. All terminate in the conviction of the world.[1]

Thus, the Apostles' testimony becomes the principle of unity in the church of Christ. The preaching of it will drive away those who will not or cannot believe it, and it will draw those to Christ who will and can believe it. Those so drawn will be one in Him and one with each other, making Christian unity an accomplished fact. It is to be further noted in regard to the above statement that the conviction or conversion of the world is both the end of the Apostles' testimony and the unity of the church, again supporting an already stated contention that, the conversion of the world being the purpose of the unity of the church, the restoration of those things which are essential to conversion, unity in evangelism, is one of the foremost aims of the movement to restore the church of the New Testament.

From the above premises, Mr. Campbell continues his argumentation:

But the constitution of the Kingdom of the Saviour is the New Testament, and this alone is adapted to the existence of his Kingdom in the world. *To restore the ancient order of things* this must be recognized as the only constitution of this Kingdom. And in receiving citizens they must be received into the Kingdom, just as they were received by the Apostles into it, when they were in the employment of setting it up. And here let us ask how did they receive them?—Did they propose any article of religious opinions; did they impose any inferential principles; or require the acknowledgment of any dogmas whatever? Not one. *The acknowledgment of the King's supremacy, in one proposition, expressive of a fact, and not an opinion, and a promise of allegiance expressed in the act of naturalization, were every item requisite to all the privileges of citizenship . . . .*[2]

Mr. Campbell is here arguing for a restoration of the New Testament terms of fellowship in the church or of citizenship in Christ's Kingdom. These are to become more clearly stated as time passes in the history of the restoration idea.

One point will be noticed in all of Mr. Campbell's statements contending for the restoration of the New Testament church, the necessity for the restoration of a "pure speech." This necessity he points out in the next statement chosen from his series of essays on "A Restoration of the Ancient Order of Things." He asserts:

. . . . Now as all correct ideas of God and things invisible are supernatural ideas, no other terms can so suitably express them, as the terms adopted by the Holy Spirit, in adapting those supernatural truths to our apprehension. He that taught man to speak would, doubtless, adopt the most suitable terms in his language to reveal himself to his understanding. To disparage those terms, by adopting others in preference, is presumptuous, and insolent on the part of man. Besides when men adopt terms to express supernatural truths it is not the truths themselves, but their ideas of them they communicate. They select such terms as suit their apprehensions of revealed truth, and hence the terms expressive only of their conceptions of divine things, and must just be as imperfect as their con-

---

[1] *Christian Baptist*, Vol. II, No. IX, pp. 198, 199.   [2] *Ibid.*, p. 201.

ceptions are. It is impossible for any man, unless by accident, to express accurately that which he apprehends imperfectly. From this source spring most of our *doctrinal* controversies—Men's opinions, expressed in their own terms, are often called bible truths. In order then to a full restoration of the ancient order of things there must be a "pure speech" restored. And I think the Lord once said, in order to a restoration, that he would restore unto the people "a pure speech." We know that the ancient order of things, amongst the Jews could not be restored after their captivity in Babylon, until the law of the Lord containing the primitive institutions of the Jews' religion was read and understood by the people, and the dialect of Babylon was abandoned, as far as it corrupted the primitive simplicity of that religion. Hence the scribes read them the law from morning to evening, gave them the sense and made them understand the reading. This became necessary because of the corrupt dialect they had learned in Babylon, on account of which their revelation was unintelligible to them, until the language of Canaan was purged from the phraseology of Ashdod. It will, we apprehend, be found precisely similar in the antitype, or in the return of the people of God from the captivity of Babylon the great, the mother of abominations.[1]

The purpose intended in this statement and the excellence of the illustration in clarifying the issue cannot be mistaken. The things revealed in the word have not been a source of contention in the church, but what man has said in opinion or speculation about them has been the source of contention. The restoration of a "pure speech" is needed in the church of Christ.

Another point of importance brought up in this series of essays is the authority of the teaching and example of the Apostles. Says Mr. Campbell:

THE Apostles were commanded by the Lord to teach the disciples to observe all things he commanded them. Now we believe them to have been faithful to their master; and, consequently, gave them to know his will— Whatever the disciples practiced in their meetings, with the approbation of the Apostles is equivalent to an Apostolic command to us to do the same— To suppose the contrary is to make the half of the New Testament of none effect. For it does not altogether consist of commands, but of approved precedents—Apostolic example is justly esteemed of equal authority with an Apostolic precept.[2]

The truth of this statement is certain. It would be unreasonable to suppose that the Apostles would leave a categorized statement of the things necessary to the constitution of the church of Christ, but it is reasonable to suppose that what the early church practiced with the consent of the Apostles was a part of their teaching "whatsoever I commanded you." It is the church of the New Testament, its precept and example, to which we would return and which we would restore.

At this point in the series, Mr. Campbell turns to the "Ancient order," and begins a discussion of the doctrine and practice of the New Testament church. Since this history must confine itself to a discussion of the history of the statements of the Plea, we must allow this to suffice for our interest at this juncture. It is believed that Mr. Campbell's conception of the intent of the movement at this time in its history can be fairly and clearly derived from the statements

[1] *Christian Baptist*, Vol. II, No. XI, p. 256.   [2] *Christian Baptist*, Vol. III, No. II, p. 30.

we have here quoted. For additional information, the reader is referred to the balance of the essays on "A Restoration of the Ancient Order of Things."

Further information on Mr. Campbell's attitude toward the movement and his conception of the restoration idea may be noted in other statements made in the *Christian Baptist.* Of these the following is important:

1. The pretensions of the Bible to a divine authority or origin, are to be examined by our reason alone. Its evidences are addressed to our reason, and by our reasoning powers the question is to be answered, *"Is the Bible of divine or human origin?"* So soon as reason has decided this question, then

2. The truths of the Bible are to be received as first principles, not to be tried by our reason, one by one, but to be received as new principles, from which we are to reason as from intuitive principles in any human science.

3. The *terms* found in the Bible are to be interpreted and understood in the common acceptation, as reason or use suggests their meaning; but the *things* taught are to be received, not because we have *proved* them by our reason to be truths, but because God has *taught* them to us.[1]

This series of statements, Mr. Campbell suggests as the "order of doctrinal investigation," and was made in the year 1827, the year in which Walter Scott was chosen evangelist for the Mahoning Association. The meaning of the statements and their order are self evident.

In the year 1829 several questions, sent in by readers or proposed by Mr. Campbell himself, are printed and answered in the pages of the *Christian Baptist.* These, too, are important in their revealing Mr. Campbell's conception of the position he had assumed.

HAVE you any objection to the Constitution of a church, published in your last number?

Answer—I have. I object to both *matter* and *form*. This Constitution or covenant, besides other minor matters, is objectionable because it admits an *unimmersed* person to all the ordinances of the christian community or congregation, as an *occasional* member; and yet refuses to receive such as regular and constant members. I know of no scriptural authority for such a discrimination. It is arbitrary and unreasonable. If I can admit an unimmersed person once a month for a year to all social ordinances, I can for life on good behavior. When I say, *I can do so,* I mean that all precepts, precedents, and scriptural reasons, authorize such a course.

But I object to making it a rule, *in any case,* to receive unimmersed persons to church ordinances:—

1st. Because it is no where commanded.

2nd. Because it is no where precedented in the New Testament.

3rd. Because it necessarily corrupts the simplicity and uniformity of the whole genius of the New Institution.

4th. Because it not only deranges the order of the kingdom, but makes *void* one of the most important institutions ever given to man. It necessarily makes immersion of non effect. For, with what consistency or propriety can a congregation hold up to the world either the *authority* or *utility* of an institution which they are in the habit of making as little of, as any human opinion.

---

[1] *Christian Baptist,* Vol. V, No. III, p. 65.

5th. Because, in making a canon to dispense with a divine institution of momentous import, they who do so assume the very same *dispensing power* which issued in that tremendous apostacy which we and all Christians are praying and laboring to destroy. If a Christian community puts into its magna charta, covenant, or constitution, an assumption to dispense with an institution of the Great King, who can tell where this power of granting license to itself may terminate? For these five reasons I must object to the aforesaid constitution, however much I respect the benevolence and intelligence of those who framed it.[1]

A more clearly defined answer to the question of present day "open membership" would be difficult to construct.

Other problems, however, raised by this answer to the original query, are brought to attention by the querist:

Query 12—What, then, will we do with all our paido-baptist follow disciples?

Answer—Teach them the way of the Lord more perfectly; and tell them if they greatly desire our society, it can be had just on being born of water and Spirit, as the Lord told Nicodemus. Our society cannot be worth much, if it is not worth one immersion.

Query 13—But do you not make schisms by so doing?

Answer—No. He makes no schism who does no more than the Lord commands, and all know that Christian immersion is a divine institution. It is he who makes a *new institution*, such as the sprinkling of an infant, and contends for it, that makes the schism. It was not he that obeyed the first commandment, but he that made the golden calf, who made confusion in Israel.[2]

It was probably certain that this question would come up then, and it is no doubt to be expected that the question will arise today. However, Mr. Campbell has given an excellent answer. The man who holds to the original design of baptism and appeals to others to accept the ordinance as it was practiced by the New Testament church is not the one who makes the schism. It is he who substitutes something else or leaves it off altogether who is guilty. There will be more to say upon this subject later in this research.

Thomas Campbell, last heard from as author of the *Declaration and Address*, is found to contribute quite often to the pages of the *Christian Baptist*. One of his contributions, appearing in the *Baptist* in the year, 1829, the last year of its publication, is in the form of a series of "unity questions." They are important for reference as to Thomas Campbell's point of view at this time. Says he:

THE following QUERIES, for the purpose of promoting a genuine, scriptural reformation amongst the sincere professors of christianity, are respectfully submitted to their consideration:—

1. Is not the Christian Community in a sectarian condition, existing in separate communities, alienated from each other?

2. Is not such a condition the native and necessary result of corruption; that is, of the introduction of human opinions into the constitution, faith, or worship of christian societies?

---

[1]*Christian Baptist*, Vol. VI, No. VIII, pp. 183, 184.   [2]*Ibid.*, p. 185.

36

3. Is not such a state of corruption and division anti-natural, anti-rational, anti-christian?

4. Is it not the common duty and interest of all concerned, especially of the teachers, to put an end to this destructive anti-scriptural condition?

5. Can this be accomplished by continuing to proceed as hitherto; that is, by maintaining and defending each his favorite system of opinion and practice?

6. If not, how is it to be attempted and accomplished, but by returning to the original standard and platform of christianity, expressly exhibited on the sacred page of New Testament Scripture?

7. Would not a strict and faithful adherence to this, by preaching and teaching precisely what the Apostles preached and taught, for the faith and obedience of the primitive disciples, be absolutely, and to all intents and purposes, sufficient for producing all the benign and blissful intentions of the christian institution?

8. Do not all these intentions terminate in producing the faith and obedience, that justifies and sanctifies the believing and obedient subject?

9. Is not everything necessary for the justification and santification of the believing and obedient, expressly taught and enjoined by the Apostles in the execution of their commission for the conversion and salvation of the nations; and fully recorded in the New Testament?

10. If so, what more is necessary, but that we expressly teach, believe, and obey what we find expressly recorded for these purposes? And would not our so doing happily terminate our unhappy scandalous, and destructive divisions?

N. B. The two following queries are subjoined for the sake of a clear definition of the leading and comprehensive terms, viz. *faith* and *obedience*—which comprehends the whole of the christian religion:—

11. Are not law and obedience, testimony and faith, relative terms, so that neither of the latter can exist without the former; that is, where there is no law, there can be no obedience; where there is no testimony, there can be no faith?

12. Again, is not testimony necessarily confined to facts, and law to authority, so that without the latter the former cannot be? That is, where there are no facts, there can be no testimony—no authority—no law. Wherefore, in every case, faith must necessarily consist in the belief of facts; and obedience in a practical compliance with the expressed will or dictate of authority. N. B. By facts is here meant some things said or done.

CONCLUSION: Upon the whole, these things being so, it necessarily follows, that christianity, being entirely a divine institution, there can be nothing human in it; consequently it has nothing to do with the doctrines and commandments of men: but simply and solely with the belief and obedience of the expressly recorded testimony and will of God, contained in the Holy Scriptures—and subjoined by the authority of the Christian community.[1]

As may be seen, this series of questions proposes to answer the many problems involved in the restoration of the New Testament church by asking other questions, questions to which the answers are perfectly obvious or suggested within themselves. The answer granted in each case, the development toward a conclusion harmonious to the restoration idea is certain.

---

[1] *Christian Baptist*, Vol. VII, No. I, pp. 11, 12.

So much for the statements of the Plea as found in the *Christian Baptist*. That the publication was successful in getting before the public the reformation in which the Campbells and others were engaged is not at all questioned by those acquainted with the history of the movement. Some persons claim that Mr. Campbell was too dogmatic in many instances in his advocacy for the truth in the *Baptist*, but it must be remembered that the age in which he lived was so steeped in traditional theology and so bound to human creedal expressions that a hard blow was necessary even to stir the people to think about them. It would be well for those questioning the wisdom of Mr. Campbell's editorial policy to read sufficiently to acquaint themselves with it before drawing any conclusions.

THE MILLENNIAL HARBINGER

The statements of the Plea to be considered under this section are not entirely from the *Millennial Harbinger*. This division is so named only because the *Harbinger* begins it. There were many statements during this period which are found outside the pages of that publication, as will be noted in the reading of the section.

The 1829 Volume of the *Christian Baptist* ended its publication. To take its place and to continue to plead the cause of the "current reformation," Mr. Campbell began, in the year 1830, in January, the publication of the *Millennial Harbinger*. His purpose was to enlarge the circulation of his publication and to enlarge its influence by enlarging the paper itself. Later in the year the Mahoning Association, at the suggestion of Walter Scott, dissolved itself into a mere annual meeting of Christians.[1] The name given to the new publication has been a source of wonder and concern to many, but it was chosen for two reasons. In the first place it was far removed from any connection with any sectarian movement of the day and, thus, could not be construed to have any such connection. In the second place it illustrates Mr. Campbell's firm conviction that the Millennium awaited the union of Christians. "Union was not an end, but a means to the culmination of the present age and the total victory of the Kingdom of God over the kingdoms of the earth."[2]

This idea is well presented in the prospectus of the *Millennial Harbinger* and included in the first issue:

THIS work shall be devoted to the destruction of sectarianism, infidelity, and anti-Christian doctrine and practice. It shall have for its object the development and introduction of that political and religious order of society called THE MILLENNIUM, which will be the consummation of that ultimate amelioration of society proposed in the Christian Scriptures. Subservient to this comprehensive object, the following subjects shall be attended to:—

1. The incompatibility of any sectarian establishment, now known on earth, with the genius of the glorious age to come.

2. The inadequacy of all the present systems of education, literary and moral, to develop the powers of the human mind, and to prepare man for rational and social happiness.

3. The disentanglement of the Holy Scriptures from the perplexities

[1]Walker, "Adventuring for Christian Unity," *op. cit.*, p. 31.   [2]*Ibid.*

of the commentators and system-makers of the dark ages. This will call for the analysis of several books in the New Testament, and many disquisitions upon the appropriated sense of the leading terms and phrases in the Holy Scriptures and in religious systems.

4. The *injustice* which yet remains in many of the political regulations under the best political governments, when contrasted with the *justice* which christianity proposes, and which the millennial order of society promises.

5. Disquisitions upon the treatment of African slaves, as preparatory to their emancipation, and exaltation from their present degraded condition.

6. General religious news, or regular details of the movements of the religious combinations, acting under the influence of the proselyting spirit of the age.

7. Occasional notices of religious publications, including reviews of new works, bearing upon any of the topics within our precincts.

8. Answers to interesting queries of general utility, and notices of all things of universal interest to all engaged in the proclamation of the *Ancient Gospel* and a *Restoration of the Ancient Order of things.*[1]

The work was to be devoted to the "destruction of sectarianism, infidelity, and anti-christian doctrine and practice." Some claim that the message of the *Harbinger* was toned down from that of the *Baptist*, but the prospectus does not so read. It was not so much a change in emphasis as it was an enlargement of emphasis. The Plea, now as then, will never succeed, aside from the elimination of all partyism and sectarian spirit. In the very nature of the case this is so.

In his prefatory remarks, Mr. Campbell continues to explain his intended purposes in the *Harbinger*:

All I wish to remark on this occasion, is, that the first step towards the introduction of this glorious age, is to dissipate the darkness which covers the people and hides their eyes from the Sun, the quickening, renewing, animating Sun of Mercy. We expect no new Sun, no new religion, only that it shall be disinterred from the rubbish of the dark ages, and made to assume its former simplicity, sublimity, and majesty. The demons of party must be dispossessed, and the false spirits cast out. The human mind must be emancipated from the bondage of error, and the information not only augmented, but extended to all the community.

Light is certainly increasing—charity enlarging the circle of its activities—the mountains of discord diminishing, and the deep vallies which separated christians, are filling up. But much is to be done before all flesh shall enjoy the salvation of God. If all who love the Lord and the salvation of men, would unite their energies and bury the tomahawk of party conflicts, no seer could predict how rapid would be the march and how extensive the triumphs of the gospel.

But the mighty agent, or rather the successful means, of this most desirable revolution, will be the Ancient Gospel. There are many gospels now preached. The gospels of every sect are something different from each other, and something different from the apostolic. There can be, in truth, but *one* gospel; but there may be many new-modified and perverted gospels. Some make their own god and worship him; and all who create a new god invent a gospel to suit his character. Surely no man of good com-

---

[1]*Millennial Harbinger*, Vol. I, No. 1, p. 1.

mon sense can imagine that the god of the Calvinists and the god of the Arminians are the same god. He that fancies that the god of the Trinitarians and the god of the Unitarians are one and the same divinity, can easily believe in transubstantiation.[1]

The object of Mr. Campbell's labors, as he states it here, is to end the darkness by bringing in the light of the gospel. Attention is called again here to a very principal point in his arguments, the conversion of the world awaits the unity of Christians. It is the restoration of the "Ancient Gospel" that is needed, for this will bring about the unity of Christians and is essential to the conversion of the world. Certainly no one can conceive of any means by which the world can be converted to Christ other than to hear, to believe, and to obey the precepts of the original gospel.

Remarking upon those things which make up the "ancient gospel," Mr. Campbell says, in 1830:

> Some of the preachers of the gospel preach more than the ancient gospel. They launch out into matters pertaining to the designs of ancient prophecy, which they do not so well understand. They also go into details of christian teaching or doctrine, and the internal affairs of Christ's kingdom. All these may be useful, and on some occasions necessary, but belong not to the proclamation of the gospel, and ought not to be confounded with it.

> In presenting the gospel (for there is but one gospel which we for the present distress call the ancient) there are only a few topics which rightfully belong to it. These are faith, repentance or reformation, immersion for the remission of sins, the Holy Spirit, and eternal life. These topics appear in one shape in the Extra No. 1; but they are diffusely exhibited there. They are capable of being exhibited in many ways, and presented like a picture in many positions to the eye of the mind. But still these are great topics, and from these every argument to turn men to God may be deduced. Turning men to God is the great object and end of proclaiming the gospel.[2]

It has been already stated that since the conversion of the world was the ultimate aim of the movement, the restoration of the things that make for conversion was the immediate aim of the idea to restore the church of the New Testament. Mr. Campbell, in the above statement, especially when taken in the light of the previous statement, distinctly supports this contention.

In order to present something of the thinking of Barton Warren Stone at this juncture in the movement, the following quotations from his publication, the *Christian Messenger*, are called to attention. They appear in the form of query and answer in the year 1830.

> Q. By the same (reference made to a previous question and answer). Is any one lawfully a subject of the kingdom of Christ, before he is immersed into his name?

> A. I think that in a former number it was proved, that to be baptized or immersed into a person, or into the name of a person, or into a body of persons, signifies union, or incorporation with that person or body of persons.[3]

> But the query is: "Is any one lawfully a subject of the kingdom of

[1]*Ibid.*, pp. 5, 6.   [2]*Ibid.*, p. 367.   [3]*Christian Messenger*, Vol. IV, No. 7, p. 160.

Christ, before he is *immersed* into his name?" It is already seen that all those named above, agreed that none are lawfully subjects of Christ's kingdom, before they are baptized. But a great many receive even unconscious, unbelieving babes into Christ's church by sprinkling; and call sprinkling baptism. This, to me and many others appears to be unlawful, or not found in the law of Christ. I cannot therefore view such, as lawfully and properly the members of the kingdom or the church of Christ on earth.

Objection. You unchurch all who are not immersed.

A. If the Baptism instituted by Jesus be immersion, then any thing not immersion is not Christian Baptism. This from full conviction I believe, and must conclude that all who have not been immersed are not lawfully members of the church of Christ. The Pedobaptists do not admit the Friend Quakers, to be lawful members of the church, they do not admit that a pious man, who has not been baptized, and who has attached himself to no body of Christians, is lawfully a member of any church. Yet they esteem many of the Quakers, and others not baptized as Christians. So we view the Pedobaptists—there are many among them, as well as among the Quakers, who are bright examples of piety, whom we love and enjoy the fellowship of the spirit, and hope forever to dwell with them in heaven. In this as in other things, we believe such pious persons honestly err;—and who can claim infallibility?[1]

At this early date, the question above stated became one of the leading questions among the restorationists. It was to become an even more important deliberation at the beginning of the next period of the history of the restoration idea, at which time it will have a more complete analysis than is needed here. It should be mentioned, however, that Mr. Stone is here giving only his "hope" in the matter, in the last sentences of the statement. In other words he has expressed his opinion, which he would force no one to accept and which he certainly would bind on no one as a test of communion.

It was often claimed that Barton Stone was a Unitarian. He answers this accusation in the *Christian Messenger* in 1830. Says Mr. Stone:

You enquire what is a Unitarian? Various are the answers to this query. Bishop A. Campbell, of Bethany, defines a Unitarian to be "One who contends that Jesus Christ is not the Son of God." Such a one has denied the faith, and, therefore, we reject him.[2]

Mr. Stone was not one to deny the fundamental faith of the church of Jesus Christ, nor was he one to equivocate the least upon so important a question. His objection was to the traditional "trinitarian" theological terminology, but his denial of the "human speech" did not mean that he had also denied the "pure speech" of the New Testament. With Campbell, he would plead for a restoration of the latter, but an outright denunciation of the former.

In our day much is being written and spoken concerning the union of denominationalism, and it is the claim of some that such was the desire of the earliest advocates of the restoration idea. In the year 1832, this concept was considered by Mr. Campbell, who says:

Our essay on *the ancient order of things* was begun seven years ago the 7th of last month, under the conviction that nothing permanently

---

[1]*Ibid.*, pp. 162, 163.   [2]*Christian Messenger*, Vol. IV, No. 9, p. 203.

valuable, worthy of the name of reformation in the church—nothing permanently and extensively useful in the conversion of the world, can be achieved unless the citizens in the kingdom of Messiah do their duty first as individuals in all personal purity and excellency, and as congregations in all social co-operations in keeping all the ordinances and traditions of the Apostles. The union of present professors, called the union of Christians, is not worth an effort, if united they were to proceed as the Baptists and Christians, and Methodists and Presbyterians, now proceed. If there was no division among them, but all united in the order now prevalent in any one of these sects, I would, were it my last breath, say, 'Reform,' or 'Come out of her, you people, that fear God and wish to stand with Jesus in the New and heavenly Jerusalem.'[1]

Evident it is that Mr. Campbell is not interested in a mere union of the denominational forces. His interest is a complete change in principle and practice, a complete abandonment of all that is human in the church and a complete restoration of all that is divine. The duty of individuals and congregations alike, purely and accurately accomplished, according to the ordinances and traditions of the apostles is the thing for which he pleads and the thing for which the Restoration movement stands.

In this same year, Mr. Campbell had the following to say in regard to accepting the New Testament as the rule of reference:

The New Testament contains the constitution, laws, ordinances, and discipline of the Christian church, if such belongs to it at all. Hence the propriety of proposing this volume as the bond of union among the churches. But what avails a promise to be governed by this book, unless this promise be faithfully fulfilled? Why promise to submit to the constitution, laws, institutions, and rules of discipline found in this volume, and afterwards require submission to institutions and usages wholly human? . . . .[2]

The excellency of this question cannot be denied, and it throws additional light on the position of the New Testament in relation to the restoration idea as conceived by Mr. Campbell.

The unit in the unity proposed by Mr. Campbell is revealed in the following:

If the christians in all sects could be drawn together, then would the only real, desirable, and permanent union, of Christians be achieved. How to effect this has long been a question with us and many others. To us, it appears, the only practicable way to accomplish this desirable object, is to propound the ancient gospel and the ancient order of things in the words and sentences found in the apostolic writings—to abandon all traditions and usages not found in the Record, and to make no human terms of communion. But on this theme much must yet be said before all the honest will understand it. One thing, however, is already sufficiently plain to all, that a union amongst christians can be obtained only upon scriptural grounds, and not upon any sectarian platform in existence.[3]

If it is the drawing of all Christians together that is the desired object, as Mr. Campbell states it is, then the individual is the unit. The Plea would be proclaimed to the individual, but it would take two directions: 1) to the individual

[1]*Millennial Harbinger*, Vol. III, No. 4, p. 178.
[2]*Millennial Harbinger*, Vol. III, No. 5, p. 193.   [3]*Ibid.*, p. 195.

out of Christ to accept Him and to become Christian, 2) to the individual in the sects to complete obedience and to come wholly to Christ. The individuals, however, must be called to Christ and his gospel as it is recorded in the New Testament, and not to any sectarian or denominational platform.

The reasonableness of pleading to all to come to the church as it was established by the Apostles can perhaps be clarified by stating that we must have unity with the apostles as well as between Christians today. If we come to any other ground than apostolic ground, to any other basis than apostolic teaching and example, we cut ourselves off from the church of the New Testament. If they were in unity with Christ and with each other, thereby, then for us to plead for any other basis for unity than that in which they found unity would be to sever ourselves from them and from Christ. We would then have mere human union or co-operation and not essential Christian unity and fellowship. As Thomas Henley says, in 1833:

> To be united together IN THE ORDER OF THE GOSPEL, surely means that the examples of the primitive disciples and the precepts of the Gospel should *alone* be the bond of union among such as are BE-LIEVERS IN CHRIST. If any thing short of this, or more was intended, it could not be *"the order of the gospel,"* as every man of common sense must admit.[1]

In the *Harbinger*, in 1834, Mr. Campbell makes an excellent statement of the Plea, and, in introducing it, uses, in so far as is known, the term "Our plea" for the first time. He writes:

> Our plea has been, and still is, Burn all the Creeds in Christendom—abandon all their technical phrases—forget, as soon as possible, all that was ever learned from them—take the Book that God edited, the Creed which he inspired; and read, study, and practice it in the Spirit of Christ, in meekness, humility, and love; and then all christians must necessarily come together, because the walls and curtains of division would then be burned up. The more creeds the more parties. Let us have no human creed, in its ecclesiastical sense, and then we can have no sect, not so much as one Presbyterian from Nova Zembla to the Cape of Good Hope—from the head of the Ganges to the mouth of the Origon.[2]

In analyzing this statement, it is important to note that it advocates a subtraction, the elimination of everything human and divisive, and an addition, the practice of everything recorded in the word; also, that it is a plea for the unity of Christians and not of denominations. These facts, already previously pointed out, are well supported, and clearly so, in Mr. Campbell's statement.

The name of "Racoon" John Smith is well known among the advocates of the Restoration movement. He was a great Christian, a great preacher, and a sincere advocate of the Plea. In 1834, while on a tour to Alabama, he received a challenge to debate a P. S. Fall upon the proposition, "The Distinguishing Doctrines of the Reformation, are contrary to the word of God." In responding to this challenge, Mr. Smith wrote:

> The circumstance of receiving the information, while on a journey to a distant state, will account, why I have not, sooner attended to your

---

[1] *Millennial Harbinger*, Vol. IV, No. 3, p. 114.
[2] *Millennial Harbinger*, Vol. V, No. 11, p. 594.

invitation. I now inform you, that your challenge, is accepted by me; provided, the distinguishing doctrines, be definitely stated, previously to our public meeting. It is to be presumed, that you would not have given a challenge, to discuss the distinguishing doctrines of the Reformation, without knowing what they were, and therefore you can be at but little loss to present them. But in order to prevent this correspondence, running to a great length; and that, possibly, you in common with our opposers generally, may wish to oppose only *your inferences*, from our doctrine, and not the doctrine itself, I will here give a fair statement of the principal points of difference, which distinguish the people now called "Reformers," from the Baptists with whom you stand connected; as I presume you did not allude, to what distinguishes other sects, from whom, you differ yourself.

Then, 1st. We believe, and teach, that all men are sinners; that all have sinned, and come short of the glory of God etc.: But we neither, believe, nor teach, that man by nature, is totally and entirely depraved in a moral point of view. You do, and this is one point of difference.

2nd. We do believe and teach, that God so loved the world, (not a part of it) that he gave his only begotten Son, that whosoever believeth in him, may not perish, but have everlasting life.

3rd. We do believe, and teach, that the faith, which God requires, comes by hearing the word of God, and not by any operation of the spirit abstract from it.

4th. We do believe, and teach, that the first reception of the Spirit of Christ into our hearts, comes through faith in the word which God has given of his Son; and not, while we are in unbelief and disobedience.

5th. We do believe, and teach, faith, repentance, and baptism for the remission of sins: In other words—that believing penitent sinners, ought to be immersed in the name of Jesus Christ for the remission of sins.

6th. When persons are thus introduced, into the kingdom or church of Christ, we teach them, that they must walk in all the commandments and ordinances, of the Lord blameless, and that they, must be faithful unto death if they obtain a crown of life. Here I will remark, that every thing, which God requires of men, is essential in its place, and that nothing is essential out of its proper place in the divine arrangement, and

7th. Although we approve, and practice, supplications, prayers, intercessions, and giving of thanks, for all men, we have no confidence in the unauthorized prayers of any body; and therefore, when believing penitent sinners, desire the remission of their sins, we do not tell them to come, to an altar, mourning bench, anxious seat, nor around the feet of the preachers, that prayer may be made for the pardon of their sins.—No, you have just as much authority from heaven, to send them, in such cases to Roman Pontiff for pardon, as to any such places.

8th. When persons apply for baptism, we do not require them to tell their feelings, their foolish dreams, or what *you* call their christian experience, in order to entitle them to baptism, as in *your* custom.

9th. After they are immersed, we do not bring them under any creed, covenant, or decorum, of human composition or devise, nor into any baptist association, according to your custom. We are well assured, that all these things above named, which we do not teach, or practice, are as destitute of principle, example, or authority from the word of God, as Roman Catholic absolution, or the sand scrubbing of the Mohammedans, or even baby sprinkling itself.

10th. Our frequency in attending to the Lord's Supper forms another distinguishing point between us and the Baptists.

44

I do not now recollect any other distinguishing point of prominency between us and the Baptists, except

11th. Our denying, their divine call to the ministry, as you hold it.

I feel assured that every candid person, who is accquainted with our doctrine, will say, I have stated plainly, the most prominent points of difference, between us, and the Baptists, with whom you stand connected, and if you are in good earnest in wishing to show, that the "distinguishing doctrines of the Reformation are contrary to the word of God," you have only to select all or any, of the points herein named, and you shall have a fair opportunity of doing it.[1]

This statement, while of considerable length, is presented here as an illustration of Mr. Smith's conception of the position of the Restoration movement. While it contains more than might rightly be called a statement of the Plea, it does contain enough to enable one to understand that "Racoon" John was not one to drift very far from the Plea.

D. S. Burnet was another of the prominent leaders of the movement in the earlier days. In the year 1835, Mr. Burnet edited a reprint of the *Christian Baptist* in one volume. A good statement of the Plea is recorded in the preface to that book. Mr. Burnet writes:

EXPERIENCE is an effectual teacher. By the trial, persevered in amidst many difficulties, we have seen that effected, which was deemed impracticable,—an extensive religious reformation, founded upon the scriptural knowledge, personal holiness, and the constant sacrifice of all its abettors. Such an abiding, extensive and personal reformation, consisting in the knowledge and obedience of the sacred writings, differs largely from those hasty excitements of popular interest which issue in an ephemeral association, whose bond of union is some sectarian peculiarity. But this is not all. The reformation alluded to, and which this book pleads, differs from others in this important respect: it contemplates not the change of any one sect or system, nor the amalgamation of any number of all of them; but it claims as a right, and labors to attain as its object, the reformation of society by a restoration of primitive christianity, i. e. christianity itself, in its gospel, institutions and laws. A creed reformed is a dividing barrier patched, and a sect remodeled is but a daughter of the mother of abominations in a new dress. This reformation aims at the demolition of the creed and the sect, genera and species, reformed or unreformed, as purity is incompatible with corruption.[2]

That Mr. Burnet was in agreement with Mr. Campbell's writing is evidenced by his willingness to edit a single volume copy of them, but is certainly also revealed in this statement of the Plea.

Mr. Campbell's understanding of the church is clearly set forth in a statement appearing in the *Millennial Harbinger* in the year 1835. Says he:

The materials for a church or congregation of Christians must, in the necessity of things, exist before a church can be formed. We have the stones quarried before we put them together in the house. The Lord's house is built of living stones closely laid together and well cemented. Figure apart: the materials for a church are regenerated men and women—disciples

---

[1] *Christian Messenger*, Vol. VIII, No. 12, pp. 365-367.

[2] Alexander Campbell, *The Christian Baptist*, (Cincinnati: Edited and Published by D. S. Burnet, 1835), p. iii.

of Christ. By regenerated persons we mean those born of water and Spirit— those who, believing that Jesus is the Son of God on the proper evidence, the witness of the Spirit, penitent for their sins, understanding his blood as the only procuring cause of remission, and determined to obey the Lord in all things according to his word; such persons having confessed the Lord by being immersed into the name of the Father, and of the Son, and of the Holy Spirit, according to his commandment, are the proper materials for the congregation of the Lord.

But the simple existence of such persons, or their being thrown together by accident, does not make them a church or house of God. There is some form of coming together as a church. There must be an agreement expressed in some way. They pledge themselves to one another in the name of the Lord, that they will walk together as becometh saints in the relation of a christian congregation.[1]

Here again is a statement revealing the unit of the unity sought, as well as a clear-cut presentation of the New Testament concept of the church. It is not a highly organized system of ecclesiasticism or control; it is a simple structure, composed of individuals, "living stones," who have been born of water and Spirit. If it is the New Testament church restored which is sought, the only possible unity would be that of the individuals who compose the church.

One of the most significant books of the Restoration movement came from the presses in the year 1835. This book, written by Mr. Campbell, was called at first, *Principles and Rules of Christian Unity*, and was made up of writings which, for the most part, had appeared in the *Harbinger* in the form of "extras." The same book, in its later editions, was termed *The Christian System*, and is without doubt one of the most significant books ever composed. Several statements of interest are here taken from the book for consideration. In the preface, Mr. Campbell writes:

The object of this volume is to place before the community in a plain, definite, and perspicuous style, the *capital principles* which have been elicited, argued out, developed, and sustained in a controversy of *twenty-five* years, by the tongues and pens of those who rallied under the banners of the Bible alone. The principle which was inscribed upon our banners when we withdrew from the ranks of the sects, was;—*"Faith in Jesus as the true Messiah, and obedience to him as our Lawgiver and King, the* ONLY TEST *of Christian character, and the* ONLY BOND *of christian union, communion, and co-operation, irrespective of all creeds, opinions, commandments, and traditions of men."*[2]

This statement is clear in itself. Mr. Campbell, also in the preface, explains the procedure he expects to follow in the book.

This work, then, naturally divides itself into three parts. The first, *the principles by which the christian institution may be certainly and satisfactorily ascertained*: the second, *the principles on which all christians may form one communion*: and third, *the elements or principles which constitute original christianity*. Whether this arrangement be most in the order of nature, or of importance, is not the question; it is the order in which we have from necessity been compelled to consider these subjects.[3]

Concerning the problem of Christian unity and proceeding to a more definite statement of the Plea, Mr. Campbell asserts:

---

[1]*Millennial Harbinger*, Extra No. VIII, Vol. VI, pp. 491, 492.
[2]Alexander Campbell, *Principles and Rules of Christian Unity*, (Bethany, Va.: McVay and Ewing, 1835), p. 9.   [3]*Ibid.*, p. 13.

From Messiah's intercession above quoted, it is incontrovertible that union is strength, and disunion, weakness; that there is a plan founded in infinite wisdom and love, by which, and by which alone, the world may both *believe* and *know*, that God has sent his Son to be the Saviour of the world. And like all the schemes of Heaven, it is simple to admiration. No mortal need fancy that he shall have the honor of devising either the plan of uniting christians in one holy band of zealous co-operation, or of converting Jews and Gentiles to the faith, that Jesus is that *seed*, in whom all the families of the earth are yet to be blessed. The plan is divine. It is ordained by God; and better still, it is already revealed. Is any one impatient to hear it? Let him again read the intercessions of the Lord Messiah, which we have chosen for our motto. Let him then examine the two following propositions, and say whether these do not express Heaven's own scheme of augmenting and conservating the body of Christ.

First. Nothing is essential to the conversion of the world, but the union and co-operation of christians.

Second. Nothing is essential to the union of christians, but the Apostles' teaching or testimony.

Or does he choose to express the plan of the Self-Existent in other words? Then he may change the order, and say,

First. The testimony of the Apostles, is the only and all-sufficient means of uniting all christians.

Second. The union of christians with the Apostles' testimony, is all-sufficient, and alone sufficient, to the conversion of the world.

Neither truth alone, nor union alone, is sufficient to subdue the unbelieving nations; but truth and union combined, are omnipotent. They are *omnipotent*, for God is in them and has consecrated and blessed them for this very purpose.[1]

Concerning creeds and their effect upon the unity of the church, Mr. Campbell makes the following striking statement:

. . . . *No human creed in Protestant christendom can be found, that has not made a division for every generation of its existence. And I may add—* the more thinking, inquisitive, and intelligent the community which owns a creed, the more frequent their debates and schisms.

But the Bible will do no better, if men approach it with a set of opinions, or a human symbol in their minds. For then it is not the Bible, but the opinions in the mind, that form the bond of union. Men, indeed, had better have a *written* than an *unwritten* standard of orthodoxy, if they will not abandon speculation and abstract notions, as any part of christian faith or duty.[2]

The Bible and the Bible alone, not any written or unwritten opinion or qualification, is the thing Mr. Campbell proposes as a rule of faith and practice. Human creeds or human interpretations of the Word are divisive in the very nature of the case, whether the material they contain is right or wrong. Furthermore, the Bible itself is to be approached with an open mind, a mind willing to be taught the precepts therein contained, not containing a set of "opinions, or a human symbol." We must have neither a written nor an unwritten creed or formula, for one is as bad as the other.

Mr. Campbell next presents one of the most concise and, yet, most complete statements of the Plea in its history. It would be difficult to find the po-

[1]*Ibid.*, p. 103.   [2]*Ibid.*, pp. 105, 106.

47

sition of the Restoration movement stated in fewer words and with more pointed accuracy.

But that the reader may have before his mind in one summary view, the whole scheme of union and co-operation, which the Living Oracles and the present state of the christian religion in the world demand; which has been, at different times and in various manners, illustrated and sustained in the present controversy, against divisions,—we shall here submit it in one period.

Let THE BIBLE *be substituted for all human creeds,* FACTS, *for definitions,* THINGS, *for words;* FAITH, *for speculation,* UNITY OF FAITH, *for unity of opinion,* THE POSITIVE COMMANDMENTS OF GOD, *for human legislation and tradition,* PIETY, *for ceremony;* MORALITY, *for partizan zeal,* THE PRACTICE OF RELIGION, *for the profession of it,— and the work is done.*[1]

No doubt, if these "restoration substitutions" could be put into practice in the life of every Christian, the purposes of the Restoration movement would soon be accomplished.

The age old question, "who is a Christian?" is next answered by Mr. Campbell in his statement of the plan of the Restoration movement for the unity of the church. Says he:

. . . . The grandeur, sublimity, and beauty of the foundation of hope, and of ecclesiastical or social union, established by the author, and founder of christianity, consists in this, that THE BELIEF OF ONE FACT, *and that upon the best evidence in the world, is all that is requisite as far as faith goes, to salvation. The belief of this* ONE FACT, *and submission to* ONE INSTITUTION *expressive of it, is all that is required of Heaven to admission into the church.* A christian, as defined, not by Dr. Johnson, nor any creed-maker, but by one taught from Heaven, is one that believes this *one fact,* and has submitted to *one institution,* and whose deportment accords with the morality and virtue of the great Prophet. The one fact is expressed in a single proposition—*that Jesus the Nazarene is the Messiah.* The evidence upon which it is to be believed is the testimony of *twelve men,* confirmed by prophecy, miracles, and spiritual gifts. The *one institution* is baptism into the name of the Father, and of the Son, and of the Holy Spirit. Every such person is a disciple in the fullest sense of the word, the moment he has believed this one fact, upon the above evidence, and has submitted to the above mentioned institution; and whether he believes the five points condemned, or the five points approved by the synod of Dort, is not so much as to be asked of him; whether he holds any of the views of the Calvinists or Arminians, Presbyterians, Episcopalians, Methodists, Baptists, or Quakers, is never once to be asked of such a person, in order to admission into the Christian community, called the church . . . .[2]

The importance of this concept as expressed here cannot be over-emphasized. It relegates everything to the scrapheap of the ages which is human and of the nature of opinion or tradition, as having any value in conversion, and replaces the New Testament, the plan of conversion, as it is set forth in that volume, to its proper place. What the New Testament has to say on these points is of great importance to the sincere seeker of salvation, but what men have speculated in their theologies and creeds on these points is not to be considered authoritative.

[1] *Ibid.,* p. 106.   [2] *Ibid.,* pp. 118, 119.

One of the cries of the Restoration movement through its history has been an appeal to call Bible things by Bible terms. Mr. Campbell is the originator of this maxim. His plea, constantly, was for a restoration of a pure speech. This fact has been brought out previously, but his position in the matter is very clearly stated in the following:

> *We choose to speak of Bible things by Bible words,* because we are always suspicious that if the word is not in the Bible, the idea which it represents is not there; and always confident that the things taught by God are better taught in the words, and under the names which the Holy Spirit has chosen and appropriated, than in the words which man's wisdom teaches.

There is nothing more essential to the union of the disciples of Christ than *purity* of speech. So long as the earth was of one speech, the human family was united. Had they been then of a pure speech as well as of one speech, they would not have been separated. God, in his just indignation, dispersed them; and before he scattered them, *he divided their language.* One of the Prophets, who lived in a degenerate age, who prophesied against corruptions of his day, when he spoke of better times, of an age of union and communion, was commanded to say in the name of the Lord, 'Then will I turn to the people a *pure language,* that they may all call upon the name of the Lord, to serve him with one consent.' Purity of speech is here declared to be prerequisite to serving the Lord with one consent.[1]

The Bible in its doctrine and practice, as well as in its speech, is the object of his plea. He is very sincere in his appeal, believing that "nothing is more essential to the union of the disciples of Christ than purity of speech." Certainly human terms, used as expressions of divine truths, are presumptuous. The terminology God used in granting his revelation to man ought to be used in continuing that revelation through the history of men. The danger, potentially, in trying to present the gospel in the terms of men, of propagating an idea foreign to the gospel, is real and unavoidable. Mr. Campbell would call "Bible things by Bible Words."

For several years, D. S. Burnet edited a small publication which he called the *Christian Preacher,* in which were printed sermons of special note by men who were prominent in the Restoration movement. Francis W. Emmons, in 1836, wrote a sermon which appeared in the *Christian Preacher,* and which contains a statement of the Plea worthy of consideration here. Mr. Emmons writes:

> That the Apostles are, by divine authority, our instructors, appears, from the prayer of our saviour for them, and from his commission *to* them. In his prayer to the Father for them, he says: "I have given them thy word. I pray for them; and not for them only, but for those, who shall believe on me through their teaching; that all may be one"—And in his commission to them, he says: "Go disciple all of the nations, immersing them,—teaching them to observe all the things which I have commanded you."
>
> That we are to learn, and be governed also, by the conduct of the first Christians, appears from the fact that what the Lord taught the Apostles, and the Apostles taught the first Christians, on many subjects, and particularly on this subject of public worship, can only be learned from their conduct. And this further appears, from another consideration; that the

[1] *Ibid.,* p. 125.

first Christians not only enjoyed the personal instructions of the apostles, who had committed to them the word of the Lord; but larger measures also, of the Holy Spirit's influence, which guided them into all the truth: consequently, the primitive state of the Christian church was, certainly, its most pure, holy, heavenly, happy, and best state; by conforming to which we must be right, if right we can be.[1]

The statement is sufficiently clear that no comment is called for. It is a point that has been made before in this dissertation: that the apostles teaching is all sufficient and alone sufficient to the unity of the church, since the church as it existed under the teaching of the apostles was the church in its "most pure, holy, heavenly, happy and best state." To return it to the apostles teaching, and to that alone, would reproduce this state in the church today.

Another significant book produced by the advocates of the Restoration movement is Walter Scott's *The Gospel Restored*. The whole book is, in reality, a statement of the Plea or a statement of the position of the churches of Christ, but it cannot be reviewed in any length here. Some of the most characteristic statements, however, have been gleaned from the book in an attempt to present Walter Scott's conception of the movement in fair light. In the preface of the book, Mr. Scott has set down the following:

> The professors of our holy religion having unhappily strayed from the scriptures and true Christianity, there seemed to be no remedy in any thing but a return to original ground. This suggested itself to many, in different places, almost simultaneously, about the beginning of the present century, and numerous churches were formed about that time, both in Europe and America, resembling, more or less, the churches planted by the Apostles, or the church of Jerusalem instituted by the Lord Jesus himself.
>
> These churches, with few exceptions, adopted the holy scriptures as their exclusive guide in religion, and rejected the dangerous creeds and confessions of Christendom, which have operated so fatally on the unity of the church. This formed the first positive step towards that return to original ground, for which the present century is distinguished.
>
> In 1823 a plea for a particular ecclesiastical order was put forth publicly, by Brother Alexander Campbell. This for distinction's sake was called the ancient order. Others had, before this time, taken the scriptures alone; but this master-stroke gave a fresh impulse to religious inquiry, and, by a single expression, "Ancient Order," limited that inquiry to a very important branch of our religion as a first step.
>
> Presiding, at that time, over a church which had already attained the ancient order, or at least as much of it as seems even now to be attained, the gospel, or rather a uniform authoritative plan of preaching it, became more the object of my attention, as may be seen from a few essays published in the C. Baptist, cut short, however, by the then limited knowledge of the extraordinary topic which had been selected; in 1827 the True Gospel was restored. For distinction's sake it was styled the Ancient Gospel.
>
> The present century, then, is characterized by these three successive steps, which the lovers of our Lord Jesus have been enabled to make, in their return to the original institution. First the Bible was adopted as sole authority in our assemblies to the exclusion of all other books. Next the Apostolic order was proposed. Finally the True Gospel was restored.
>
> The above very general notice of the progress and order of the present

[1] *Christian Preacher*, Vol. I, No. 4, pp. 76, 77.

reformation, is deemed sufficient to make the reader feel whither it is we desire to bring him by this discourse, namely to the gospel; and not to a plea for any particular order, or to any discussion of the previous question concerning the supreme and exclusive authority of the holy scriptures.

A volume of unbroken discourse of the true gospel is still a desideratum. Since 1827, it has floated through our periodicals in essays and fragments of essays very unlike the living orations in which it was then set forth to the public for acceptance. Those are scattered over a wide field, and necessarily apart from each other; so that when a disciple would invite a friend, or fellow professor, or relative, to a perusal of what has been learned and written of the gospel since that time, he must needs invite him to the review of numerous volumes, a task by no means acceptable to readers in general.

In the tenth number of the *Millennial Harbinger*, for 1831, the restoration of the true gospel is referred to, in the following manner: "Brother Walter Scott, who, in the fall of 1827, arranged the several items of faith, repentance, baptism, remission of sins, the Holy Spirit, and eternal life, restored them in this order to the church, under the title of ancient gospel, and preached it successfully to the world—has written a discourse," etc. In the *Evangelist* for 1832 the following paragraph, of the connection between the above elements and sin which they are intended to destroy, occurs. "In regard to sinners and sin, six things are to be considered—the love of it, the practice of it, the state of it, the guilt of it, the power of it, and the punishment of it. The first three relate to the sinner; the last three to sin. Now faith, repentance, and baptism, refer to the first three, the love, and practice, and state of sin; while remission, the Holy Spirit, and the resurrection relate to the last three, the guilt, and power, and punishment of sin. In other words, brethren, to make us see the beauty and perfection of the gospel theory as devised by God; faith is to destroy the love of sin, repentance to destroy the practice of it, baptism the state of it, remission the guilt of it, the Spirit the power of it, and the resurrection to destroy the punishment of sin; so that the last enemy, death, will be destroyed."

On the original arrangement of the elements of the gospel then and on the analysis of sin contained in the preceding paragraph, the present volume is built. It comprehends a connected discourse of the true gospel of Christ, and has been written by request of some of the most intelligent among our brethren. The task might have fallen upon some one more able to perform it; but as none has yet appeared to occupy this ground, we have yielded to the wishes of those who were perhaps better judges in the case than ourselves, and have done the best we could—May the reader derive as much profit from reading it as the author has been gladdened while writing it.

A discourse on the elements of any science, admits of but little elegance, except so much as attaches to correctness of description and accuracy of definition. The reader, therefore, must not hope to meet with much of it in these elementary orations, which are of the didactic and demonstrative kind chiefly. With this monition to the reader, we commend the book to the protection of God, and to the patronage of the public and the brethren. WALTER SCOTT.[1]

Mr. Scott's analysis of the movement and the order of discovery in it is very interesting and very important. The New Testament was first adopted as the

[1]Walter Scott, The Gospel Restored, (Cincinnati: O. H. Donogh, 1836), pp. v-vii.

only text book, the only source of reference in Christian matters; then the apostolic order was proposed, Mr. Scott says, by Mr. Campbell in his essays on a "Restoration of the Ancient Order of Things"; then, finally, the "true gospel" was restored. Mr. Scott dates this final development in 1827, which, oddly enough, is the date of his election to the position of evangelist for the Mahoning Association. However, history will no doubt so credit Mr. Scott, too.

One statement of interest to us here concerns the importance of the restoration of the proper order of salvation Mr. Scott says:

> Suppose for a moment that the order, which those elements have in the scripture, was preserved inviolate by all; that all proposed first faith, then reformation, and finally obedience, that the converts might be pardoned and blessed and introduced to the hope of life eternal. What then? Why, in this manner all who are converted to God by the gospel, would come uniformly instructed first to believe, then reform, then obey the message of God by Christ. The proclaimers and ministers, who labor for the Lord, would not then oppose and contradict each other as they now do in all places. The people would cease to stumble over those blocks that professors have thrown in their way, and the gospel would have free course, would run and would be exalted in society.[1]

He continues to say that the restoration of this element of apostolic Christianity would leave but the "order" of the New Testament church and the "morality" enjoined upon apostolic Christians to be determined, agreed upon, and restored. It would limit the investigation that much, and would begin it in the proper place, at the beginning. This truth has been proposed previously in this work, and here has the backing of Walter Scott.

Mr. Scott has much the same thing to say concerning the point of essentials and non-essentials as Thomas Campbell in the *Declaration and Address*. Note:

> But these faithful men (the apostles) followed to the letter the directions which were graciously given them by their Lord. Essentials and non-essentials were unknown to them. The nice and dangerous distinctions of modern times, were not then invented. With them every thing was essential to be done, which Jesus had enjoined and they proved their love for for him, only by doing whatsoever he had commanded them.[2]

Maintaining the correctness of holding to the apostolic pattern, Mr. Scott says:

> Those, then, who follow the apostles, those who hold to the True Gospel, who walk in the ordinances delivered to the church of Jerusalem, the parent institution, and keep the morality of Jesus Christ purely, have an ancienter and more honorable origin than Rome, filthy Rome. We are of the "free woman," says Paul, the legitimate spouse of Jesus Christ, Jerusalem, the church of Jerusalem, who never was accused in the scripture for having departed from the faith of Jesus; but on the contrary is there described as having maintained the faith once delivered to her saints in a great fight of affliction, even after her Lord had been crucified, after Stephen had been stoned, Peter imprisoned, and James slain with the sword. In the midst of unspeakable afflictions she maintained her perilous station, as the mother of christian churches, till the destruction of Jerusalem; when agreeably to the prophetic instruction of her Lord and Master,

---

[1] *Ibid.*, pp. 96, 97.   [2] *Ibid.*, pp. 303, 304.

52

she fled from the abodes of the wicked, whom she could not convert to the faith, and from the city which was now, on account of its sins, destined to a protracted desolation.[1]

To pattern after the church of Jerusalem is to pattern after a church that has a history of faithfulness even in times of great persecution and trial. This is to have an "honorable origin."

Concerning the faith of the Jerusalem church, Scott maintains:

> The word Lord, as all understand it here, means the heir of all things, or Son of God. So that we see, the matter of faith in Jerusalem, or the the thing to be believed in christianity, was that Jesus is the Son of God and the Messiah. Behold, reader, the above verse which contains the truth; it is the word of God; it lives and abides forever; it cannot be erased; it has thus read, and thus spoken, for near eighteen hundred years; and it will continue to speak thus till time shall be no more; it may be overlooked, it may even be scorned when seen; still it cannot be blotted out; it will maintain its position forever, and calmly as now to us, so to ages yet unborn, will preach with unerring certainty, the true faith which was first preached in Jerusalem.[2]

The contention here stated is incontrovertible. The truth that was first preached in Jerusalem by Peter is still the faith of the church of Christ. Men have avoided and scorned it, but it will remain the same for all time.

Mr. Scott suggests that the primitive creed is a rule by which all preaching may be measured true or false.

> By ascertaining the primitive creed of the gospel, and the blessings which originally attached to the reception of it, we obtain a rule by which all subsequent preaching can be measured and determined to be either true or false, pure or corrupted, evangelical or unevangelical. The true gospel therefore proposes to mankind as a first step, the remission of past sins in baptism, suppose the following oracle of the Father to be received, "Behold my son, the beloved, in whom I delight." How beautiful for simplicity, then, is the true gospel of Christ! A single proposition to be examined, heartily received in the manner God directs, and having appended to it the most inestimable blessings.[3]

This must surely have the agreement of all who seriously consider it. The gospel, as it was proposed in the beginning, is the true gospel and is therefore the only test of the true gospel we know anything about. It would do for every man who preaches to measure the truth of the gospel he proclaims by the original gospel, as suggested by Mr. Scott.

Divisions among believers are to be expected when men continue to move as they have in the past, Mr. Scott suggests. In the following statement, he urges the solution to the problem of division and, in accord with other statements that have been mentioned in this history, brings to bear upon the minds of all the ultimate thing to consider in the schisms which pervade Christianity, namely: a world is lost and dying without Christ, and its conversion awaits the unity of Christians. Says Mr. Scott:

> How can protestants be anything but divided, how can the people be anything but religious partisans when each man must thrust forward into

[1]*Ibid.*, pp. 304, 305.   [2]*Ibid.*, p. 307.   [3]*Ibid.*, p. 312.

notice a creed, a matter of faith different from that of all the rest, and in almost every instance different from the Bible too. You are at fault in this grand matter.—Review your premises. I say review your premises. Get you down out of your pulpits, stand among the people, go abroad into the land; propose as "the matter of faith" to the people what the Divine Father proposed both to you and the people; labor to show them that it is true, that it is the word of God, that he did say this of Jesus, that he did recognize him as his Son, that the Spirit did identify him with Messiah, that the apostles did preach him both as Christ and as the Son of God, and that you also will do the same. And when you have spoken this with success and have by proper proofs carried the proposition to the hearts of the people, when you have by the truth pricked their hearts, and dying to sin they cry, as the people on the day of Pentecost cried "Men and brethren, what shall we do." Tell them what Peter told his auditors, "Repent and be baptized, every one of you in the name of Jesus Christ for the remission of sins, and you shall receive the gift of the Holy Spirit." If you will do this; if you will propose to the people the word of the Father, the matter of faith intended for us all, and if you attach to the reception of it the same blessings of remission and the Spirit, which belonged to it of old, when handled by the apostles, you will speedily see a change; counteraction, schism, and sin will soon be dissipated, the christians will come together on one faith, one Lord, and one baptism, as of old, and the parts and shreds, of the body of Christ, which now defile the land will come together and become one body in Christ.

Have you no pity, have you no bowels of compassion? Do you not perceive, that ninety-nine out of a hundred are dying in their sins, ignorant of the very first principles of our salvation, and falling from the midst of your assemblies into the grave wholly unilluminated, wholly unsanctified, unpardoned? Is it possible that you do not perceive that your divisions and oppositions have driven the most sensible portion of society to seek for pleasure in every thing but our holy and delightful religion.—You are wrong in telling the people, that the word of God is a dead letter, that they cannot believe, they cannot repent, they cannot obey without a special and preparatory operation of the Spirit. You do err, you err egregiously when you preach, that the Spirit must make men believe, repent, and obey. It is the office of the word of God to do all this; and you greatly dishonor it by thus thrusting it backward and downward as a dead letter, incapable of quickening and making men alive to religion and to God.

I have conversed with hundreds of the youth of this country, and of your congregations. They are full of infidelity and scepticism; and believe with Paine, and Hume, and Voltaire, and Volney, and Gibbon, and Rousseau, and other American, French, and British sceptics; they feel that you have taken for granted the very thing to be proved; that you have neither stated the christian proposition, nor argued it in their presence; that what you propose to them of eternal election, eternal decrees, eternal justification, is eternal nonsense and cannot and ought not be proved. I exhort you once more, begin at the beginning, take the Father of mercies for your example, and not John Calvin; take the Holy Spirit and not Luther; take Christ and not John Wesley; and the book of God, the scriptures, and not the other systems of divinity with which your libraries abound. And may God direct you by this holy word, and comfort you by his Holy Spirit in all things. To Him be the glory through all ages.[1]

[1]Ibid., pp. 477, 479.

54

Walter Scott the preacher is certainly revealed in these statements. The flow of the language, the emotion of the appeal, the logic of his premises all certainly make evident the reason for the greatness of the man and the success of his preaching. This statement is without question one of the finest statements of the Plea and of the position of the Restoration movement to be recorded. It is worthy of very careful perusal and of wide publication.

Mr. Scott next turns to a different sort of appeal, which is directed to the preachers of the Restoration movement or to those who professedly have accepted the original message of the church.

> To those preachers who have professedly received the original gospel, we would say, it will be a long time before the mighty masses of men, to which you address your proclamation, will sufficiently understand the elements of christianity of which we have been discoursing, it will be long before you can supply the public with more than a bare sufficiency of proof that God recognized Jesus as his Son. If, however, you do this, if you prove this proposition, you do well, and will have but little time to prove anything else. But see, the resuscitation of the true gospel is of recent date and perhaps you do not yet perceive in what this proof lies. Can you decipher numerically the several branches of evidence for the oracle of the Father? Do you know whether they are internal or external, or mixed; whether they are antecedent, or consequent in their nature, or both; moral, or miraculous, prophetic or evangelical, or all of these kinds taken together? Do you know what class of proofs are most in number, which most forcible, which of them direct, which indirect, which collateral, immediate or remote? Believe me, however, that the internal evidence of our religion is that to which you ought chiefly to apply yourself. All beyond the book is of small value, or at least cannot establish one saving fact in it.—We are wholly dependent on the original witnesses for the faith that saves us.[1]

His statement above, "If you prove this proposition, you do well, and will have but little time to prove any thing else," is very true. The whole system of Christianity hinges about this one proposition, and all of its parts relate to it. Preachers have proclaimed much upon the doctrines of men which have no relation to the central proposition of the church, and, realizing this, Mr. Scott makes this appeal to bring the preaching of the church back to or up to the standard of the New Testament, to the proof of the proposition which all preaching in the New Testament sought to establish. Everything beyond this is "of small value."

To the man who says that the proof of this one proposition will take so much time that he will have little time to moralize, Mr. Scott says:

> But our argument on the whole of modern preaching is this; it fails in moral effect, because God's words are not sufficiently honored by it. "If they had stood in my counsel," said God to the teachers of Jeremiah's day, "and had caused my people to hear my words, then they would have turned them from their evil way, and from the evil of their doings." But this they did not, but substituted their own words, for those of God, and taught the people righteousness by precepts merely human. This is the character of modern preaching, which in general aims only at approved maxim and elegance in composition, leaving untouched, unproved, and unbelieved,

---

[1] *Ibid.*, pp. 479, 480.

the great oracle of the Father, which he intended to be laid by all true builders as a sure foundation stone in the mind of every son of man; the people, therefore, are not "turned from their evil way, nor from the evil of their doings." It is then on account of its absolute moral tendency that we wish you, brethren, to allow the Father to stand on the foreground of the picture, when you could portray the gospel in full form and improve the world. You can, I protest, do nothing in establishing a permanent morality in any city, town, or neighborhood, unless you do this. Do you then want your work to remain when you are dead and gone? Preach what was delivered at the beginning, that "Jesus is the Messiah the Son of God."[1]

It is the word of God, the Gospel of Christ, fairly proclaimed and soundly preached that will bring about the desired moral effect. The thing God desires he will bring about through the preaching of his Word. We are under obligation to proclaim it, not to change it or to proclaim our opinion in its stead. Under the faithful performance of the former, the desired effect not attained, God is to blame; but under the latter, the desired effect not attained, the preacher is to blame.

Continuing upon this same theme, Mr. Scott relates the following:

. . . . Now, then, our holy religion, when contemplated as a unique and distinct institution, resolves itself ultimately into this fact, and is based upon it, viz: *"Jesus of Nazareth is the Son of God."* If this be false, christianity is false; if this be true, christianity must prevail, and earth and hell in vain assail it: for great is truth and mighty above all things, and must prevail. "Upon this rock," said Jesus to Peter when he publicly confessed this truth—"Upon this rock will I build my church, and the gates of hell shall not prevail against it." It was for confessing this truth that Jesus was condemned by the Jewish Sandhedrin—he died for this, and became the first martyr to it. The Apostles died for confessing this—men were pardoned of God for confessing it—and congregations which held it were styled the churches of Christ, whether they were in order or no; whether they had ordinances, oracles, or officers, or no; and it is on the confession of this fact that the church within these few years, has begun, according to the true gospel, again to admit sinners to baptism for the remission of their sins. Glory to God and to Jesus Christ![2]

Mr. Scott's book includes also a series of questions and answers regarding the work of the Holy Spirit. This, as history well reveals, was one of the foremost points of emphasis in this day. Traditional theology, basically Calvinistic, held that the Spirit of God works directly upon the sinner in conversion, while it has been the position of the churches of Christ that the Spirit of God works through the word in conversion. These questions are of value in determining Mr. Scott's thought in the matter. They read as follows:

1. Is not the word of God, or the Gospel, which is the meaning of the word, *a dead letter?* No; falsehoods alone, when known to be such, are dead letters; but truth is living, quick, and powerful.

2. Was the Holy Spirit, when he came, to make sinners believe? No; he was to convict them of sin because they did not or had not believed.

3. How can he do this if he enter not the mind of sinners? By preaching to them through the members of the church, the Apostles, Prophets, Evangelists and saints.

[1]*Ibid.*, pp. 481, 482.   [2]*Ibid.*, p. 532.

4. When we reject his teaching by the Scriptures and those who preach them, do we resist the Spirit? Yes; this is the way the people resisted the Spirit of old. *Neh.* ix. 30.

5. Can we believe of ourselves? This is not required; believe in Christ on the testimony of God and the Scriptures.

6. How does faith come? By hearing the scriptures.

7. Why then have not all faith? Because most men are in love with the world and care not for eternal life.

8. But the word is called the sword of the Spirit? That is because he made it; and, therefore, Paul bids us take it and use it in our own defense.

9. Is not the Spirit given to every man? Yes; to every man in Christ, but to nobody out of Christ.

10. The Lord opened Lydia's heart. Granted, and he will open your's too, if you read his holy book in order to know and do his will.

11. Did not Cornelius receive the Holy Spirit before baptism? Yes; but not, as Protestants teach, before faith.

12. Was not Jesus to grant repentance to Israel? No; God was to do this by exalting their Messiah, and thus grant them repentance by his exaltation to heaven, as he would grant them remission by his death.

13. If you receive the Spirit, why do you not work miracles? Because miracles are now unnecessary. Truth may need miracles to set it upon a footing with error established by law; as in the Apostolic times, when Judaism and Idolatry prevailed; but truth needs not and will not accept of the aid of miracles to triumph over error.

14. But some say they can work miracles. Do you watch them narrowly; and think it no miracle if you find them guilty of error and falsehood.

15 What now, is proof of a professor's having the Spirit? His joyfulness in obeying the Christian religion by a holy walk and conversation.

16. What difference is there between the ordinary and extraordinary influences of the Spirit? It is corrupted and not true Christianity that recognizes such a distinction.

17. Does the Christian religion consist in knowledge or in a right state of the heart, that is, in a moral bias of the soul? It consists in both and more too. The Christian religion lets us first know what is good, second do what is good, thirdly feel what is good. Blessed be God and the Lamb.[1]

Further light on this point in so far as Scott's thought is concerned will be noted in the following:

PROPOSITION 1. *Jesus Christ was personally a missionary only to the Jews, his mission terminated on that people, and the designs of it were to proclaim the gospel, and to teach those among them who believe it.*

PROPOSITION 2. *The Apostles were missionaries to the whole world, their mission terminated on mankind and its design was to proclaim the gospel, and to teach those among men who believe it.*

PROPOSITION 3. *The Holy Spirit was a missionary to the church, His mission terminated on that institution, and the designs of it were to comfort the disciples, glorify Jesus Christ as the true Messiah, and to convince the world of sin, righteousness and judgment.*[2]

[1]*Ibid.*, pp. 547, 548.   [2]*Ibid.*, pp. 522, 523.

With this statement of Scott, the statements of the Plea in this period are concluded. Thoughout the period there was, it seems, a gradual development toward a more definite position. It, as Scott says, began in a solid stand upon the Sacred scriptures, an appeal to the world to forsake all else and stand alone on the word of God. Alexander Campbell's series of essays on "Restoration of the Ancient Order of Things" stated an appeal for a return to the ancient order, the primitive order of the church. Walter Scott's appeal was for a restoration of the ancient gospel or the New Testament plan or order of salvation, centering in the one proposition which was central in the faith and practice of the church of the New Testament. The similarity in the appeal of Mr. Campbell, as shown from his *Principles and Rules of Christian Unity* to that of Mr. Scott in his *The Gospel Restored* seems at once apparent.

By the close of this period the movement had crystallized into more definiteness of intention. It was no longer a small group of people, with seemingly no increase or progress. The strides it was beginning to take were attracting attention. The movement was beginning to get before the people. The Plea was having its effect in bringing earnest seekers after the truth to the solid foundation of original Christianity. The evil of sectarianism had been noted. Two decades of groping had been concluded, and the means to correct this evil was being more and more clearly understood. As yet the movement had not reached its greatest strides. These were left for the future, and were yet to be attained before the downward trend was to set in. However, as coming events cast their shadows before, so, in the next period to be considered, the seeds of difficulties to arise were beginning to show themselves in questionings.

CHAPTER IV

THE PERIOD OF QUESTIONINGS: 1837 - 1900

In the normal course of events, questions are raised before action is taken. The period under consideration in this section of this dissertation is so named, because certain questions, foreshadowing important actions to come later, came to the fore in the Restoration movement. The first of these questions, arising immediately at the beginning of the period, concerns itself with the possibility of the existence of Christians in sectarian bodies or denominations. The second question is raised in regard to the scripturalness of missionary agencies. The third involves itself in the validity or nonvalidity of the use of instrumental music in worship. The circumstances surrounding the raising of each of these questions will be more adequately treated when they come to attention in the chronology of our considerations.

That these questions should be considered at all in a thesis such as this may be questioned at first. However, due reflection on the matter will, it seems, clear the matter for the intelligent inquirer. The three questions above mentioned have nearly wrecked the Restoration movement. In the light of the statements of the Plea which have been gathered in this research, this ought not to be. These questions do not at all involve themselves in the Plea itself. They are secondary considerations to be dealt with on the side while the great fundamental truths of the movement are parading in victory through the Christian world. Instead, men have placed them first in their thinking. Some have gone so far as to say that there are no Christians in the sects and have been guilty of condemnation of the whole, while others have gone to the other extreme and maintained that all are Christian and therefore should be welcomed into the fellowship of the church of Christ. The latter concept springs fully developed into the movement about the middle of this period, as we shall see.

It must be fully noted and adequately emphasized today that the Plea interests itself only in whether a man is a Christian in the New Testament meaning of the term. As Mr. Campbell noted, we must determine his status by inquiring whether he has believed the one fact and submitted to the one institution expressive of the fact. Beyond this we cannot grant salvation, nor pronounce condemnation.

The union of the movement has also been seriously affected by the music question. Is it permissable or not to use an instrument as an aid to worship? Some have said, "no," others, "yes," without regard to the fact that nothing is stated in the New Testament making either conclusion essential to a man's salvation. The statements of the Plea make our wonderings and quarrels about this question absolutely silly. The question is very prominent, but the music issue is seldom, if ever, mentioned in a statement of the Plea on either side of the problem.

No open breach of the union of the movement has been reached, as yet, upon the question of the validity of missionary agencies, though some have maintained that the music issue is merely the missionary issue in a new garb. Here, again, we must note, however, that the issue is beyond the realm of the Plea. The support or non-support of a missionary agency is not, cannot, and ought not be made a test of fellowship or of unity in Christ.

It must be shown clearly that these questions are beyond the Plea and are no part of it. If this can be done, then we must conclude that the persons who claim today to be advocates of the Plea and who, still, allow these issues to break the movement into many parties and jarring sects, are going beyond the Plea into a realm of opinion for a test of fellowship with which to exclude one who is really, literally, and inseparably a brother in Christ. It is certainly not our relationship to a denomination, nor to a musical instrument, nor to a missionary agency that determines our salvation, but our relationship to Christ, in faith and in obedience. With this much introductory consideration, we turn now to the various questions and their relation to the statements of the Plea of this period.

CHRISTIANS AMONG THE SECTS, LUNNENBERG LETTER

The year 1837 brought a 'bombshell' into the hitherto comparatively peaceful thinking of the Restoration movement. In that year, Alexander Campbell received a letter of inquiry from a lady, whose name is not given, who lived in the community of Lunnenberg, Virginia. The letter reads as follows:

Dear Brother Campbell—I was much surprised today, while reading the *Harbinger*, to see that you recognize the Protestant parties as Christian. You say, you 'find in all Protestant parties Christians.'

Dear brother, my surprise and ardent desire to do what is right, prompt me to write to you at this time. I feel well assured, from the estimate you place on the female character, that you will attend to my feeble questions in search of knowledge.

Will you be so good as to let me know how any one becomes a christian? What act of yours gave you the name of Christian? At what time had Paul the name of Christ called on him? At what time did Cornelius have Christ named on him? Is it not through this name we obtain eternal life? Does the name of Christ or Christian belong to any but those who believe the gospel, repent, and are buried by baptism into the death of Christ?[1]

The letter is dated July 8th, 1837, from Lunnenberg.

Mr. Campbell took considerable space in the September issue of the *Harbinger* to answer the inquiry of this lady from Lunnenberg. The answer he gave stirred up considerable comment and, evidently, opposition, and a second article was printed in answer to the query, this one in the November issue. Still the objections poured in, and Mr. Campbell printed a third and final answer to the question in the December issue of that year. It would, perhaps, be well to include the answers at this juncture, but it is not practicable so to do. Only portions will be quoted, and an attempt will be made to point out a grave injustice being done to Mr. Campbell in an evident misuse of his words.

Portions of Mr. Campbell's answers to this letter are often quoted as support for the practice of "open membership," which may be defined as the reception

[1]*Millennial Harbinger*, New Series, Vol. I, No. IX, p. 411.

into the fellowship and full privileges of the church one who has been a member of the denominational bodies but who has never been immersed for the remission of his sins. This practice of so quoting him we will see in fact in the next chapter of this thesis. The following statement is an example of such quotations:

> I cannot, therefore, make any one duty the standard of Christian state or character, not even immersion into the name of the Father, of the Son, and of the Holy Spirit, and in my heart regard all that have been sprinkled in infancy without their own knowledge and consent, as aliens from Christ and the well-grounded hope of heaven.[1]

Also often quoted is the following:

> There is no occasion, then, for making immersion, on a profession of the faith, absolutely essential to a Christian—though it may be greatly essential to his sanctification and comfort. My right hand and my right eye are greatly essential to my usefulness and happiness, but not to my life; and as I could not be a perfect man without them, so I cannot be a perfect Christian without a right understanding and a cordial reception of immersion in its true and scriptural meaning and design. But he that thence infers that none are Christians but the immersed, as greatly errs as he who affirms that none are alive but those of clear and full vision.[2]

These two quotations certainly seem to support the conclusions of those who use them so often, that unimmersed persons are Christian and therefore ought to be given the full privileges of fellowship. However, there are other sections of this answer to the letter from Lunnenberg, which are never quoted by these people, and which throw an entirely different light upon the subject. Says Mr. Campbell:

> But to conclude for the present—he that claims for himself a license to neglect the least of all the commandments of Jesus, because it is possible for some to be saved, who, through insuperable ignorance or involuntary mistake, do neglect or transgress it; or he that willfully neglects to ascertain the will of the Lord to the whole extent of his means and opportunities, because some who are defective in that knowledge may be Christians, is not possessed of the spirit of Christ, and cannot be registered among the Lord's people. So I reason; and I think in so reasoning I am sustained by all the Prophets and Apostles of both Testaments.[3]

Thus, we see that 'insuperable ignorance' or 'involuntary mistake' constitute the only basis upon which one might be saved without baptism, in the mind of Mr. Campbell. The willful neglect of the ordinance or failure to use all the means at ones disposal to ascertain the truth will not excuse him.

In the third answer to the question, found in the December issue of the *Harbinger* in 1837, even stronger language is used by Mr. Campbell, as he writes:

> It will require but a moment's reflection to perceive that those who care nothing for this opinion will not rejoice it nor abuse it; and that those who would, for their own sake, rejoice in it are not included in it. He that rejoices in such an opinion, for his own sake, has had the subject under consideration; and it is a thousand chances to one that he is obstinately or wilfully in error on the subject; and, therefore, in the very terms of the opinion, he is precluded from any interest in it. His joy, indeed, is strong presumptive evidence against him; because it is proof that

---

[1] *Ibid.*, p. 412.   [2] *Ibid.*, p. 414.   [3] *Ibid.*

he is one-sided in his feelings, which no upright mind can be—at least such a mind as is contemplated in the opinion; for it respects only those who have not had any debate with themselves upon the subject, and have, without any examination or leaning, supposed themselves to have been baptized.[1]

It cannot be too emphatically stated that he that rejoices for his own sake, that he may be accepted by the Lord on his infant or adult pouring or sprinkling, because of his dislike to, or prejudice against believer's immersion, gives unequivocal evidence of the want of that state of mind which is contemplated in the opinion expressed; and he has proved himself to be a seeker of his own will and pleasure, rather than rejoicing in the will and pleasure of God; and for such persons we can have no favorable opinion.[2]

Such statements, taken from the answers Mr. Campbell submitted to the query of the lady from Lunnenberg, ought to silence forever the notion that he had any intention of sanctioning the present day practice of "open membership." It is to be remembered that Mr. Campbell's opinion would not alter the truth in any sense, and even a categorical statement from him in favor of 'open membership' would not make the practice valid in the church of Christ. However, in fairness to Mr. Campbell, it needs to be shouted to the house-tops, that conclusions favorable to the practice are not to be found in his writings.

It is the business of the preacher of the gospel to be certain that those who hear him proclaim the message of salvation are not "ignorant" of its commands and promises. The willful neglect or rejection of those commands, when they are known, is the thing that will condemn, and the church has been commissioned to make them known "to all nations." The preacher who claims license to himself to proclaim less than the whole gospel or to fail to proclaim an element of the gospel, which he knows to be a part of the plan of salvation instituted by the Lord, simply because, in his opinion, some may be saved who "through insuperable ignorance or involuntary mistake" neglect or transgress that element, is certainly taking to himself more authority than the Lord has given to his preachers and is promising salvation upon conditions which are in contradiction to those set forth by the Lord himself.

Time and space forbid the discussion of this problem more completely at this juncture. Later in the period, other letters and further discussion may be found in the *Millennial Harbinger* for 1862 in a discussion upon the "Communion Question" entered into by Geo. W. Elley, W. K. Pendleton, Robert Richardson, Benjamin Franklin and others. The question has no doubt arisen at various times and places in the history of the Restoration movement, and is one of the most important problems still facing the church today. The issue is proposed here in order that the reader may see the extent of the discussion of a question which is, in reality, beyond the Plea and no part of it. We proceed now to record again the various statements of the Plea coming to us out of this period of the history of the movement, noting that the problem did not enter into the statements of the Plea, except those directly concerned with the discussion of the moment. The other questions arising in this "period of questionings" will be discussed as they arise in the chronology of the history.

---

[1]*Ibid.*, p. 563   [2]*Ibid.*

David Staats Burnet has provided his readers with some very stimulating food for thought in the following statement of "our position."

The father is exonerated,—he has glorified Jesus. The Messiah is exonerated,—he has "finished the work and gone to the Father." The Apostles are exonerated,—they have delivered "their word" and having proved it with "signs and wonders following," have sealed it with their blood. Is the church exonerated? If so why is the world not converted? Did the Redeemer assume a false principle in his prayer? Did he ask the means inadequate to the end he contemplated? Is he dissatisfied with himself, or with Christians? If the former, then the blame is thrown upon the Father, for Jesus "finished the work the Father gave him to do!" There is no escaping the conclusion; the Father, and Christ, and the Holy Spirit originated Christianity, and aided by heaven, the apostles established it in the world; but its prevalence is entrusted to its friends—"those who believe in Jesus through the Apostolic testimony." Oh Christian! Oh Sectarian! Measure your obligation and assay your task, for the time is short. This is not the work of a man nor of an order, but of us all.

But are not Christians united, and is not the world fast surrendering to Christ? To both questions we answer no! To the last we say, that should the millennium be postponed until the present ratios would give dominion to Christ's empire and annihilation to Satan's, in the interim the world will have grown gray, and the fires of the sun will have been extinguished. To the first we reply, that there is no visible union,—that if a few denominations in our country have established American Bible, Tracts and other Societies, this is not the union of the professed church, first, because only a small number of the sects are represented in these institutions; secondly, those engaged in them, confess this limited union partial, by remaining separate church organizations, and by each one having his own Bible Society and Sunday School Society. The name American is a misnomer.

Thirdly. These are not unions of fractional parts of the church, but unions of portions of the professed church with all such of the world, without distinction of sentiment or character, as have been persuaded, by their personal services, or their wealth, to co-operate with them in certain measures.

Nor is there an *invisible* union—for who has seen such a thing? An invisible union is not contemplated by the Saviour's prayer, as is obvious from two considerations; 1st. The union is to convert the world which would be impossible if that union could not be seen by them. 2nd. This union has for its basis the apostolic word. The Saviour prays for the union of none but those who receive that word. Then beyond it there is no union—it is the bond. It is visible—those illuminated by it are the light of the world—an organization built upon it is a city set upon a mountain, which cannot *be hid*, the union of all those would be galaxy brighter than the milky way. Nor will it do to say there is a union of sentiment—of feeling. The one would prevent error—the other subdue heart burnings. If any, or all these together, constituted the union the Savior prayed for, the result would have long since been realized. But we have had neither the cause nor the effect,—neither the church united nor the world converted.

What is the desired union? The royal petitioner said "May they be one, *as thou, Father, are in me, and J in thee,* that they may be one in us." Here is the measure and the definition. Jesus and the Father, contrary to the allegation of the infidel Jews were united in one religion, Christianity, unsectarianized, unchristened, unmodified Christianity, in favor of which every miracle was wrought, every prophecy spoken, every inspired word was written—not one of which predicates is affirmed of any denomination existing.

How shall this union be effected? Certainly by a restoration of the Christianity of the scriptures. To effect this we propose the following measures:

I. An Uniform DEFINITION of the technical terms of Christianity . . . .

II. An Uniform ARRANGEMENT of the terms and items of Christianity . . . .

III. THE DESTRUCTION OF PARTY NAMES AND PARTY ORGANIZATIONS . . . .

IV. That we may have ONE BODY, having one Lord, one faith, one hope and one spirit, we must have ONE (and but one) baptism. Eph. IV. 4, 5, 6 . . . .[1]

The appeal of this statement is without peer among those gathered in this research. Mr. Burnet's statement about the exoneration of the Father, the Son, the Holy Spirit, and the Apostles, narrowing it down to the church, is fine. The truth of the elimination and its stopping point would certainly not be overruled by any person of intelligence. His appeal for a "visible" union is also important, and his reasoning to the conclusion that such is necessary is good. Just what he means by "uniform definition of technical terms" and "uniform arrangement of the terms and items of Christianity" may be somewhat clouded. It appears that he intends to convey the idea that those terms and items of Christianity, the Christianity of the New Testament, which mark it and distinguish it, must be uniformly defined and held by all Christians. That the definition and arrangement of those items, in the plan as he states it here, is already decided upon and fixed, is indicated in his appeal for "a restoration of the Christianity of the scriptures."

In the year 1837, an article by Mr. Campbell entitled "Synopsis of Reformation Principles and Objects" appears in the *Millennial Harbinger*. The following statements are taken from that article, though, as will be noted, only the important points have been recorded:

CHAPTER I

For the healing of divisions among Christians and the better understanding on the Christian Institution, the following objects and principles have been proposed and discussed:—

1. The restoration of a pure speech, or the calling of Bible things by Bible names . . . .

2. The Bible must be proposed as a book of facts, not of doctrines, nor opinions; it must be understood and regarded upon the principles of cause and effect, or that action is to produce corresponding action . . . .

3. The Bible alone, instead of any human creed, as the only rational and solid foundation of Christian union and communion . . . .

4. The reading and expounding of the sacred scriptures in public assemblies instead of text preaching, sermonizing, and philosophizing . . . .

5. The right of private opinion in all matters not revealed in contradistinction from the common faith, without the forfeiture of Christian character or Christian privilege . . . .

[1] *Christian Preacher*, Vol. III, No. 6, pp. 122-126.

CHAPTER II
Principles and Objects of Church Reform

1. The church of Jesus Christ is constitutionally composed of those who have confessed their faith in the celestial proposition—THAT JESUS OF NAZARETH IS THE MESSIAH, THE SON OF GOD, and the only Saviour of the world, and have put him on by a baptism into his death . . . .

2. The administration of the internal and external affairs of the church is placed in the hands of bishops, deacons, and messengers extraordinary . . . .

3. The sanctification of the Lord's day by meeting in honor of the resurrection of the Saviour, and especially with a reference to the celebration of the Lord's supper, is essential to the edification, to the spirituality, holiness, usefulness, and happiness of the Christian community . . . .

4. The church not being of this world, cannot levy any contribution on those without for any religious or political purposes, neither ought she to go begging to the world for aid to support or extend Christianity . . . .

CHAPTER III
Principles Essential to the Proper Dispensation of the Gospel

1. The gospel is not a theory, a doctrine, a system of moral or spiritual philosophy; not even a theory of faith, repentance, baptism, remission of sins, adoption, the Holy Spirit, and eternal life . . . .

2. Three things are essential to a Christian—a peculiar disposition, state, and character. These must be changed from a preternatural or fleshly state to that which is spiritual and heavenly . . . .

3. The resurrection of the just, the coming of the Lord Jesus in his own proper glorified person, and eternal life, constitute the grand objects of the Christian's hope . . . .

4. No theory of spiritual influence in conversion is the influence of the Spirit. Therefore, to deny any theory, is not to deny the influence of the Spirit. . . .

CHAPTER IV
Personal and Family Reformation

1. As personal intelligence, purity, and happiness is the end of all public or private, theoretic or practical reformation, the present standard of personal knowledge, faith, piety, and morality being too low, must be greatly elevated. . . .

2. Family education and domestic religion must be, I need not say, greatly advanced, but begun . . . .[1]

The above rather speaks for itself. No comment is necessary upon the points elicited, for Mr. Campbell's position is really well stated, though not elaborately, in this series of propositions. It is, perhaps, worthy of a second notation that the year is 1837, the year of the query from Lunnenberg. The first proposition of chapter II is interesting, when considered in that light. Those who propose to put "open membership" into the mouth of Mr. Campbell should read that with care.

---

[1]*Millennial Harbinger*, New Series, Vol. I, No. XII, pp. 530-538.

The next statement, also one by Mr. Campbell, brings to light a very important concept. It deserves to be read with much care. Says he:

> The union of sects, and the union of Christians, are not identical propositions. Some of the sects must be united to Christ to make them Christians, before they could be a component part of a union of Christians. In one word, a sectarian and a Christian are not equivalent terms. A Christian adheres to Christ—a sectarian to his party. Now unless Christ would adhere to a party as such, a Christian could not.[1]

The union of sects and the union of Christians not being identical propositions is of much interest. The reason for this conclusion he states, "Some (individuals) of the sects must be united to Christ to make them Christian." Before this, there is no chance that they could have any part in a union of Christians, since the very term presupposes that there are Christians to unite. It is clear, therefore, from Mr. Campbell's expression in this statement, that the object of his efforts centered itself in individuals and not in churches or denominations. That a union of denominations could be achieved is probable. That it would be desirable is a question subject to debate. That it would be Christian union, in Mr. Campbell's conception, would be untrue. The uniting of the individual with Christ must be achieved, before union or co-operation with other Christians is possible.

In the year 1840, James Challen contributed something to the cause of the "current reformation" in the form of a short article in the *Harbinger*. He decries the spirit of sectarianism, insisting that the Christians of the New Testament day had far greater causes for division than do we, and then adds:

> In the New Testament we see a most attractive object presented before us in the church of Christ united and compacted in every part, like a well-formed, full-grown, healthy human body. The spirit of union and of brotherly kindness are among the most striking features; and nothing awakens so much concern and meets with so prompt a reprobation as the idea of schism or divisions in this divine institution. In all the Epistles this subject is adverted to, and exhortations of the most solemn and impressive kind are laid before the brethren. It must be obvious that the occasions for divisions in the primitive church were greater and of a far more serious character than those which exist in the present day . . . .[2]
>
> All the divisions that can obtain among us will have their origin in difference of opinion in relation to doctrine, form of government, discipline, or order of worship, or in matters of expediency. Let us, then, habituate ourselves to think and to speak in favor of union, as the only ground upon which truth can triumph over error, light can dissipate the darkness, and the church can save the world. Let this be our motto; and whatever we give up, let us not part with "the unity of the spirit." We may differ about things lawful and expedient, whether repentance precedes faith, or faith repentance; about standing or kneeling in prayer; about what we shall call our public speakers, preachers, teachers, or evangelists; or whether we shall have any such persons or not, or need them; or about how we shall raise funds in the congregation, or how much may be needed; or about the imposition of hands, if now necessary, and for whom; or about singing, whether grave or gay, the old tunes of our fathers or those of modern date, whether by note or by memory. We may differ about *the name* Christ-

[1]*Millennial Harbinger*, New Series, Vol. III, No. VIII, p. 344.
[2]*Millennial Harbinger*, New Series, Vol. IV, No. II, p. 66.

ian and Disciple, as the great patronymic of the citizens of the Kingdom of God. We may express ourselves with freedom upon all of these subjects, and may honestly differ; but "let all our works be done in love;" and no evil, but good will be the result.[1]

The appeal is evidently made to the advocates of the Restoration Plea. Mr. Challen seems to be concerned about the oneness of the people who are appealing for the oneness of all Christians. Had his reasoning and his solution to the problem been put into practice in the early day, the development of divergent elements would have been improbable, for in many instances a lack of love has been the root of division.

The next statement for consideration is by Barton W. Stone. The date is set, arbitrarily about 1840, for it cannot be accurately dated. Mr. Stone's regard for the Bible is clearly stated.

As man-made creeds have always divided Christians, and stood in the way of union—these must all be abandoned, and the Bible alone received as the only foundation and rule of faith and practice. On no other platform can all Christians meet. Here the Church rested in her best days. Here she would have rested, and remained in sweet union, had not human creeds been introduced and established as authoritative. From this period we may date the apostasy of the Church. From this period Christians were divided, and many inspired with the fury of hell, persecuted each other to death, fighting under their great leader the devil, "transformed into an angel of light." From this period the reign of darkness and ignorance commenced, called the age of darkness; for as the attention of the people was drawn to the creeds of the councils, it was of course drawn away from the Bible. They *might* believe the Bible, but if their belief differed from the creed, anathemas and death were their doom. Happy for the people, in a worldly point of view, that they were soon after prohibited entirely from reading the Bible! There was then no more danger of losing their lives; for they now believed the creed alone, because this alone they knew, or could know. All Protestants with one voice condemn this conduct of our fathers, and highly extol the reformers of the sixteenth century, for restoring to the people the Bible, and the divine right of reading and judging for themselves. But does not every Protestant see that the creed-making business is but the recommencement of the same tragic drama? Shall they plead for that which divides Christians, promotes strife, engenders hatred, impels to persecution, war, blood and death, and set up their own devices in the place of the Bible to judge and condemn a fellow Christian? Is not this like setting up the man of sin in God's judgment seat? Will any Christian plead for the life of his creed, when he must know that others can not unite on it without hypocrisy? No! No! Let it die the death . . . . The Bible, the BIBLE ALONE, is the only religion in which Christians can all unite. Not on the opinions formed by man of the truths and facts stated in the Bible, but upon the facts themselves.[2]

The implications of this statement are clear, and the reasoning is sound. Since abandonment of the Bible and the publication of creeds has been the cause of division among Christians, it follows that abandonment of the creeds and the restoration of the truth and facts of the Bible, not opinions about them, to belief and practice in the lives of Christians would be the solution to the problem of

---

[1] *Ibid.*, pp. 67, 68.
[2] James M. Mathes, *Works of Elder B. W. Stone,* (Cincinnati: Moore, Wilstach, Keys and Company, 1859), I, 315-317.

division among Christians. In the same article Mr. Stone goes on to remark that a second essential is the presence of the Spirit in the lives of Christians. The statement referred to follows:

As there can not be a union of righteousness and unrighteousness, of the spirit of Christ and the spirit of the world, therefore Christians must all have the spirit of Christ, and be holy as God is holy in order to be united according to the will of God. Any other union than this is no better than a rope of sand, useless and easily broken.[1]

To those who ask how such spirit may be obtained, Mr. Stone replies:

I know of no better way than to believe on Jesus through the word of the apostles; or to believe on him as the scripture hath said—through such faith united with obedience, the Holy Spirit is given, and all become one as the Father and Son are one. When men shall believe on Jesus through the word of the apostles, and not through the word of erring men; when they shall believe on him as the Scripture hath said, and not as fallen men have said, then they believe he is the Son of the living God, and Saviour of sinners, that he died for our sins, according to the Scriptures, that he was buried and rose again from the dead the third day, according to the Scriptures. Then they believe this whole teaching to be Divine; and humbly submitting to it receive the uniting spirit of God. This must be done in order to Christian union.[2]

Mr. Stone closes this statement with the assertion that all names but the one "given by Divine appointment" must be thrown out.

The heart of Barton Stone is revealed in the following statement:

Brethren of every name, help on this work by every means divine. For the want of this evidence—the Union of Christians, the world in thousands are daily dying in sin. Have you no sympathy—no bowels of mercy? Would you stop them from ruin? You have the means—be one, and they will be saved.

Let every Christian begin the work of Union in himself. Wait upon God, and pray for the promise of the Spirit. Rest not till you are filled with the Spirit. Then and not till then, will you love your God and Saviour—then and not till then you will love the brethren, who bear the image of the heavenly—then you will have the Spirit of Jesus to love the fallen world, and like him to sacrifice all for their salavation. The cry will then be, who will go for us, and bear the glad tidings to dying sinners that they may be saved. Everyone in this spirit would flow together, and strive together to save the world. The secret is this, the want of this spirit, the spirit of Jesus, is the grand cause of division among Christians: consequently, this spirit restored will be the grand cause of union. Let us, dear brethren, try this plan; it will injure no one. God is faithful who has promised—he has promised to give the Holy Spirit to them that ask him. With this spirit, partyism will die—without it anti-partyism in profession only, will become as rank partyism as any other, and probably more intolerant.[3]

The above was published in 1842, and reveals Mr. Stone's insistence again that the spirit of Christ in the lives of Christians must precede their union.

Also in the year 1842, the following appeared in the *Harbinger*, having been written by Alexander Campbell:

Am I too sanguine when I say to my brethren here assembled, that

---

[1] *Ibid.*   [2] *Ibid.*   [3] *Christian Messenger*, Vol. IX, No. 10, pp. 333, 334.

I think we have found the sure foundation on which all the Lord's people can be visibly and truly one people? We can have no better creed than the Bible. The sects pretend to be found on it: therefore the whole sectarian world acknowledges its excellency. We will not make it void by affixing to it the appendix of a human creed. We will build on the naked shoulders of the Apostles and Prophets, Jesus Christ himself the chief corner stone.

We shall begin with the Acts of the Apostles, and as they intimate the apostolic doctrine and practice we shall follow these. In Jerusalem the church began. To Jerusalem we must then look for a fair beginning. Whatever we have got in our faith and practice which they had not, we shall return to the rightful owners. What they had and we have not, we shall append to our inventory of Christian duties and Christian excellencies. Meanwhile, we shall assist each other in getting rid of our prejudices and errors, as soon as we can, and "whereunto we have already attained, we shall walk by the same rule and mind the same thing;" and if we live in peace, the God of love and peace shall be with us: for he has promised it.[1]

The recourse suggested is to the New Testament church as it is revealed in the first church history, the book of Acts. Whatever the church therein recorded had in faith and practice which we lack, we shall add to our agenda of Christian duties, and whatever we have in our practice which is not recorded in the record of the apostolic church, we will discontinue, subtract from our practice. As has been suggested previously in this dissertation, the Plea for restoration presupposes an addition as well as a subtraction, and again Mr. Campbell upholds this idea.

John Rogers is the author of the next statement, published first in the year 1844. He writes:

. . . . Among the first lessons taught me by our great and good father Stone, were the all sufficiency of the scriptures, as the only rule of the faith and practice, the only basis of Christian Union,—that all party names, and party creeds, are anti-scriptural, and schismatical in their tendency;—that all schisms in the body of Christ have grown out of a departure from the letter and spirit of the holy scriptures; and that, as a matter of course we can never be united but by an abandonment of our party names, creeds and spirits, and a return to the simplicity of the truth as it is in Jesus; that in order to church fellowship nothing more should be required than a credible profession of faith in, and love to Christ, and a course of conduct corresponding with such profession.

These and many other corresponding principles, I received most cordially into my heart, and rejoiced in them exceedingly. I had learned that God is love, and that he who dwells in love, dwells in God, and God in him— that love is the end of the commandment, the fulfilling of the Law—the soul of christianity. My young heart bounded with love to God, the church and the world. I wept over the schisms among christians. I sighed over a world lying in wickedness. And bouyant with hope and love, I resolved to devote my life to the advocacy of the great principles of christian Union. And though I have met with many difficulties in my onward course, I have never doubted that we took the true ground. I reasoned then, as I reason now: "If we are right in our religious views and practices, we have the only book in the world that proves us right—and if we are wrong, we have the only book in the world that can set us right."[2]

---

[1] *Millennial Harbinger*, New Series, Vol. VI, No. I, p. 12.
[2] *Christian Messenger*, Vol. XIV, No. 4, pp. 106, 107.

The simplicity of John Rogers is overwhelming, and his faithfulness to the word of the Lord could not be questioned when this statement is considered. He continues, expressing joy in finding Mr. Campbell advocating the same principles for which he contends:

> . . . . I admired the talents of brother Campbell, I found him with the talents of a giant, advocating many of the great principles for which Father Stone had been contending for near 20 years, I thanked God and took courage. I was peculiarly delighted, and instructed with his advocacy of the Bible as the only foundation of Christian Union—I regarded this as the great principle of Protestantism,—as the fundamental principle of our reformation. I longed to see christians united; for I had learned that the conversion of the world is based upon it.[1]

Something of his regard for Jesus may be seen in the following:

> That I may not be misapprehended in this communication and therefore subject to improper odium, permit me to say distinctly, that I am not a Unitarian or Trinitarian, in the Sectarian import of these terms—that if I have leanings to the *speculations* of either party, they are in favor of the Trinitarian side. I do believe there is more danger of making too little of Christ, than of making too much of him.[2]

It would be well for preachers of the gospel today to take inventory of their preaching in the light of John Roger's statement that "there is more danger of making too little of Christ, than of making too much of him."

One of the most common objections to the restoration of Biblical faith and practice is that each will interpret differently and everyone will come out with a different answer, Mr. Campbell, in 1846, published in the *Harbinger* some "Rules of Interpretation." Among them, he included one which should be published far and wide, and which seems to lie at the bottom of difficulties in interpretation. Mr. Campbell asserts:

> For the salutary and sanctifying intelligence of the oracles of God, the following rule is indispensible;—*We must come within the understanding distance.*

> There is a distance which is properly called *the speaking distance,* or *the hearing distance,* beyond which the voice reaches not, and the ears hear not. To hear another, we must come within that circle which the voice audibly fills.

> Now we may with propriety say, that as it respects God, there is an understanding distance. All beyond that distance cannot understand God; all within it can easily understand him in all matters of piety and morality. God himself is the center of that circle, and humility is its circumference.[3]

It is to be regretted that there is not sufficient room to include the remainder of the rules, but this one seems important, though perhaps not more so than the others. One wonders if Mr. Stone and Mr. Campbell do not mean the same thing when one advocates for the spirit of Christ and the other coming within "the understanding distance" which is humility.

Also, in 1847, Mr. Campbell had the following to say:

> From a full survey of the premises of ecclesiastical history, of human creeds and sects,—and especially from a profound regard for the wisdom and knowledge that guided, and the Spirit that inspired the Apostles of

---

[1]*Ibid.,* p. 107.   [2]*Ibid.,* p. 112.   [3]*Millennial Harbinger,* Series III, Vol. III, No. I, p. 23.

Jesus Christ, and that qualified them to receive his will, we have proposed an *Evangelical Reformation*—or rather, a return to the faith and manners anciently delivered to the saints—A RESTORATION of original Christianity both in theory and practice. The three capital points of which are:—

    I. The Christian Scriptures, the only rule and measure of Christian faith and learning.

    II. The Christian confession, the foundation of Christian union and communion.

    III. The Christian Ordinances—baptism, the Lord's day, and the Lord's supper, as taught and observed by the Apostles.[1]

The statement is short and to the point, and again Mr. Campbell's position is clearly stated. No one could mistake his position nor the goal toward which he sought to labor, if he were careful to read his statements, allowing them to speak for themselves.

MISSIONARY METHODS, THE AMERICAN CHRISTIAN MISSIONARY SOCIETY

As was previously mentioned in this dissertation, the question of Missionary methods, arising in this period, was one which created considerable stir within the movement. Since the statements of the Plea have brought our considerations to the year 1849 and since that is the year in which the first missionary agency was established, it seems appropriate to mention the circumstances surrounding its establishment and something of the effect it had upon the thinking of the people. Again, however, what may be said about this problem at this juncture is limited, by the nature of this study, to the barest remarks.

The problem of seeing to the spread of the gospel of Christ throughout the world has ever been one of the greatest facing the Christian institution. Various methods have been suggested and tried throughout the history of ecclesiastical efforts. That the Restoration movement should face this problem was inevitable, since the advocates of the Plea had their eyes fixed upon the conversion of the world. However, the question with them, as it had been with many others, was, "How is it to be accomplished? Who is to do it? Shall we organize, and what place shall the organization have in the life of the churches?"

This question came to a head, in so far as the Restoration movement was concerned, in the year 1849. In that year, Mr. Campbell published in the *Harbinger* a series of articles on "Church Organization," and there was much sentiment about the establishment of some sort of agency, pro and con. In October, 1849, a convention of the brethren met in the city of Cincinnati, Ohio, to consider the problem, and the American Christian Missionary Society was established. Mr. Campbell was elected its first president, though illness kept him from the convention.[2] D. S. Burnet was elected to the office of First Vice-President, and nineteen others were elected to the office of Vice-President, as provided by the constitution of the newly formed society. James Challen was elected Corresponding Secretary; George S. Jenkins, Recording Secretary; and Archibald Trowbridge, Treasurer.[3] Thus, organized missionary effort, so called, had its beginning in the Restoration movement.

[1] *Millennial Harbinger*, Series III, Vol. IV, No. IX, p. 487.
[2] *Millennial Harbinger*, Series III, Vol. VI, No. XII, p. 694.   [3] *Ibid.*, p. 691.

It may at first seem that no problem was involved and no question could be raised concerning the action taken by the convention at Cincinnati, but it remains yet to be said that organization of any form had long been strenuously opposed among the disciples. This organization, though sanctioned and brought into being by some of the most prominent men of the movement including Mr. Campbell, was no exception, and, as soon as the news of its beginnings had been published among the people, the voice of opposition began to rise against it. It appears that Jacob Creath, Jr., was the first to oppose its formation. In the year 1850, his opposition may be noted in the form of correspondence with Mr. Campbell published in the *Harbinger*.

Mr. Campbell answered Creath's objections that the organization was the beginning of ecclesiasticism by saying:

> The conventions, combinations, councils and decrees, of which he speaks are not plead, nor adopted, nor favored, by any one known to me in our ranks. Our associated meetings are wholly *executive*—neither *legislative* nor *judicial*.[1]

Later, Mr. Creath attempted to point out that the editor of the *Millennial Harbinger* had a different attitude toward the question involved from that of the editor of the *Christian Baptist*. To this, Mr. Campbell replied that there is a difference between scriptural and unscriptural conventions and organizations.

During the period in which the American Christian Missionary Society was formed, co-operative organizations also were formed in the various states in which the Restoration movement had progressed considerably. It would, perhaps, be well to include something of the organization of the efforts in each of the states and also something of the continued efforts at organization through the balance of the history of the movement. However, such is not the purpose of this thesis. The beginnings of organization and the beginnings of opposition to that organization are noted to show the tendency which has continued to exist.

The difficulties which have arisen in regard to this trend toward organization spring from two sources. From observation and experience, it seems, the opposition to organization has gathered its emphasis around opposition, and has made that its theme. The advocates of organization have centered their thinking and emphasis around organization, and have interpreted connection to the brotherhood in terms of relationship to the organization. Both groups have side-stepped the Plea, and have failed to remember that we have called for emphasis in essentials and plead for unity upon the basis of being Christians, not upon relationship or non-relationship to organizations. Unless both sides of this question can be startled back to original ground, another disruption is in grave imminence.

With this setting of the tendencies existing in this period following the year 1849, we begin again the consideration of the statements of the Plea in their chronological order.

In the year 1850, John Reis had the following to say:

> We are called on in our age, to restore to its primal beauty and symmetry the Christian religion. The rubbish of Paganism, with which we are

---

[1] *Millennial Harbinger*, Series III, Vol. VII, No. XI, p. 616.

surrounded, and we discover in every modification of Partialism, must be removed; and the foundation of the Gospel must be sought where it was originally laid, on the Prophets and Apostles, Jesus Christ himself being the chief corner stone: that is, the church must be founded, named, and disciplined, etc., according to the order prescribed in the New Testament. "For we are convinced from the Holy Scriptures, from observation and experience, that the Union of Christians is essential to the conversion of the world, and that no creed, or partizan establishment in christendom, can become the basis of such an union, communion, and cooperation, as will restore peace to a church militant against itself, or triumph to the common salvation. Hence, the falsity, absurdity and pernicious effects of the creeds and commandments of men must be fearlessly exposed; and the sublimity, simplicity and excellency of "the truth" as it is in Jesus, must be diligently proclaimed and defended.[1]

Mr. Reis' position, when this statement is carefully explored, could not be mistaken. He is pleading for the "primal beauty and symmetry" of the Christian religion, for the founding of the church "according to the order prescribed in the New Testament." There is little doubt as to the meaning of his words.

C. L. Loos, in the year 1851, stated in few words that the movement was not only one designed to eliminate the peculiarities of the denominational establishment but also to restore the faith and practice of the New Testament. Said he:

> The reformation we are pleading, is a reformation not of one idea, but one that shall be thorough and complete. We are calling for an entire restoration of Primitive Christianity, as well as an abandonment of everything unscriptural and traditionary.[2]

It has already been stated that the movement was not only a subtraction but also an addition, and Mr. Loos has supported the idea well in these words.

That Mr. Campbell's answers to the lady from Lunnenberg surrendered anything on the question of baptism, he answers for himself, in the year 1852, as he says:

> I say, then, that in order to *the union of Christians*, we must have a definite and unmistakable term, indicating one and the same conception to every mind. If, then, the Christian Church ever become really and visibly one, she must have one immersion, or one baptism; and, if she become not one, where is the hope of a millennium! It is a dream![3]

Certainly any idea that Mr. Campbell harbored hopes and dreams of "open membership" is refuted here. In his mind, immersion is not a hindrance to the oneness of Christians, as has become the conception of the modern mind, but it is an essential to the oneness of Christians.

Further clarifying the intent of the movement, Mr. Campbell writes in 1853:

> The restoration of Original Christianity, and not the reformation of Popery or of Protestantism, is the polar star of all our aims and efforts ecclesiastic.[4]

Mr. Campbell and Mr. Loos, as noted in his statement above, are in complete agreement as to the goal of the movement. Actually, these men affirm, the desire

[1]John Reis, *The Union of the Church of God*, (Near Cincinnati: Hygeia Printing Office, 1850), pp. 11, 12.   [2]*Disciple*, Vol. I, No. I, p. 1.

[3]*Millennial Harbinger*, Series IV, Vol. II, No. IV, p. 210.

[4]*Millennial Harbinger*, Series IV, Vol. III, No. II, p. 61.

of the advocates of the movement is to restore "original Christianity," and not simply to reform Protestantism or Catholicism.

Robert Richardson published, in the year 1853, a little booklet which he called *Principles of the Reformation*. As its title indicates, this booklet is designed to elucidate the intent and purposes of the Restoration movement, called "the Reformation" by Mr. Richardson. Much material could be included in this research from Mr. Richardson's work, but again we must include only sufficient to gain his point of view. He writes as follows:

. . . . the present Reformation proposes an immediate return to the broad and original platform of Christianity, as well as of true Protestantism; and urges, accordingly, the claims of the Bible alone, as the source of Divine truth for all mankind; and pleads for the exercise of man's inalienable right to read and interpret the Sacred Volume. It seeks to establish a *unity of faith* instead of that diversity of opinion which has distracted religious society; and to restore the gospel and its institutions, in all their original simplicity, to the world. In brief, its great purpose is *to establish* CHRISTIAN UNION upon the basis of a SIMPLE EVANGELICAL CHRISTIANITY.[1]

In our approaches to the Bible, Mr. Richardson says we should bear in mind:

1. That the Scriptures mean precisely *what they say*, when construed in conformity with the established laws of language.

2. That the Bible contains the only Divine revelations to which man has access; and that these revelations are perfectly suited, by their Divine Author, to the circumstances and capacity of man to whom they are addressed.

3. That true religious *faith* can be founded upon this DIVINE TESTIMONY *alone*.

4. That *opinions* are mere inferences of human reason from insufficient and uncertain premises, or conjectures in regard to matters not revealed and that they are not entitled to the slightest *authority* in religion, by whomsoever they may be propounded.[2]

In this reformation, however, it is a fundamental principle that every one shall take his religion directly from the Bible, without the intervention of popes or priests, councils or assemblies, or any of the creeds which they have framed. With us, every thing in religion must have a Scripture warrant, and human authority is regarded as wholly incompetent to the decision of any question which may legitimately arise in regard to the great matters of faith and duty. Whatever rests upon a Divine warrant is a matter of *FAITH*. Whatever subordinate and collateral questions may exist which have not this warrant are MATTERS OF OPINION, which each one is at liberty to entertain according to his own pleasure, and to which no one, from the very nature of the case, can attach any importance. Nor is it to be imagined that any doctrine or sentiment can be justly entertained under the title of an opinion which will conflict with or nullify any portion of Scripture. Where the Bible speaks, there is no place for any opinion; and if any one hold a view which contravenes any declaration of Holy Writ, this is not an opinion, but actual DISBELIEF of so much of the Word of God as is thus contradicted and opposed.[3]

The principle is clearly stated and is true. Certainly in advocating this posi-

[1]Robert Richardson, *The Principles and Objects of the Religious Reformation*, (Bethany: Printed and Published by A. Campbell, 1853), pp. 6, 7.
[2]*Ibid.*, p. 10   [3]*Ibid.*, pp. 21, 22.

tion, Mr. Richardson is in harmony with the statements we have examined thus far. If the movement is in difficulty today, it is in difficulty because it has departed from this fundamental principle and not because it has held tenaciously to it.

Mr. Richardson goes on in his discussion of the movement to deal more completely with the elements of the new institution, which have particular bearing upon the peculiar position of the Restoration movement. The first point he deals with is faith:

> The Christian faith, then, in our view, consists not in any theory or system of doctrine, but in a sincere belief in the person and mission of our Lord Jesus Christ. It is personal in its subject, as well as in its object; in regard to him who believes, as well as in regard to that which is believed. It consists of simple facts, directly connected with the personal history and character of Jesus Christ as the Messiah and the promised Lamb of God who takes away the sins of the world. It is personal in its object, leading to personal regard and love of Christ, and a personal interest in his salvation. It consists not in definitions; neither does it embrace the litigated questions of sectarianism. It contains not one, much less five cardinal points of speculative theology; nor does it inflict upon the believer, for his sins, forty articles save one. The gospel of salvation, indeed, were ill fitted, to be preached to every creature, illiterate or learned, if it consisted as some imagine, of those ponderous bodies of divinity, and intricate systems of theology, which have oppressed the energies and entangled the movements of the Protestant world.[1]

Mr. Richardson then goes on to remark, "the faith" is in reality this simple trust in Jesus, as will be found by anyone who carefully investigates the Word upon the subject. Then he adds:

> Christian faith, as we have seen, is simply belief in Christ, as he is presented in the gospel, and it is concisely engrossed in the great proposition that Jesus is the Christ, the Son of God. No one can comprehend the terms of this proposition, without having before his mind the whole Christian faith in its subject matter. The predicate, "The Christ the Son of God," if understood, implies a knowledge of God and a belief in him, and presents to view not only the official character of the Messiah as the *Christed* or *anointed* Prophet, Priest, and King of whom the prophets spoke, but also his personal character or divinity as the Son of God. The subject, "Jesus," is an expression which can be comprehended only as it involves an acquaintance with the personal history of Jesus of Nazareth, and, consequently, of the great facts which constitute the gospel. The whole proposition thus presents to us—Jesus as the Son of God—the Christ, or anointed One, whom God has appointed to be our Teacher, our Redeemer, and our King; to whose precepts we are to listen; through whose precious blood and intercession we are to obtain forgiveness; by whose word and Spirit we are to be sanctified, and by whose mighty power we are to be rescued from the captivity of the grave.[2]

This proposition, says Mr. Richardson, "was announced by the Father himself from heaven," "is the rock upon which Christ himself declared he would build his church," "is the 'good confession' which Christ himself 'witnessed' before his judges, and for which he was condemned to be crucified," and was the "confession which was made by those who, during the ministry of the apostles, were admitted to the institutions of the gospel and the fellowship of the church."

[1]*Ibid.*, pp. 26, 27.   [2]*Ibid.*, pp. 39, 40.

Some, however, will ask, as Mr. Richardson suggests:

> . . . . Do you propose, then, to receive persons into the Christian Church upon a simple confession of their belief in Christ as the Messiah, the Son of God, without repentance or change of heart, or even baptism?[1]

To this question, the following reply is made:

> I presume there is not a religious body in Christendom, which renders a more true and just honor to the Lord Jesus Christ, or receives with a more sincere faith, all that the Scriptures declare concerning him. With us, he is the Son of God, in the strict sense of these words. He is the Word which was in the beginning, which was with God and was God: the Word by whom all things were made; in whom was life, and who became flesh and dwelt among men, revealing his glory—the glory as of the only begotten of the Father, full of grace and truth. He is the brightness of the Father's glory, and the express image of his person. In him dwelleth all the fullness of the Godhead bodily.[2]

> With regard to the other inquiry, respecting repentance and a change of heart, we do certainly expect every one who presents himself for admission into the church, to exhibit satisfactory evidences of both. By the word repentance we here imply much more than a mere sorrow for sin, which may often exist without producing any amendment of heart or life. Judas is thus said to have 'repented,' and persons are often, in this sense, sorry for their actions, because they feel or fear the consequences which flow from them, or because of some transient and superficial impression, and not because they have realized the true nature of sin, the purity and perfection of the Divine character, and their own unworthiness.[3]

Enlarging his discussion now, to include those elements of speculation which lay behind the question propounded, Mr. Richardson continues:

> We have no fellowship with any theory which makes the word of God of no effect, or represents God as requiring to be moved with greater love for man than that which he has manifested in the gift of his Son; and we are accustomed to place far more reliance upon a willingness to hear and obey the Lord's commandments, as an evidence of a change of heart, than upon all those dreams, visions, and animal excitements, on which many are taught to depend for the proof of their conversion.[4]

Coming next to the question of Baptism, as it relates to Christian unity, Mr. Richardson asserts:

> . . . . Apart from the intrinsic merits of the questions which respect baptism itself, it will be seen that in adopting the action of immersion, which all grant to be valid baptism, and in admitting the believer, who is allowed by all to be a proper subject, we offer no impediment whatever to Christian union. We introduce no litigated or doubtful questions; we adopt that in which all are already agreed; we require no one to act contrary to the dictates of an enlightened conscience; we demand nothing more than what the word of God clearly and unequivocally enjoins. In this point of view, then, the position which the Reformation has assumed upon this subject, is eminently anti-sectarian and conciliatory.

> Nor, if we may regard the plain declarations of Scripture as worthy of universal acceptation, or the popular creeds as fair exponents of the views of the different religious parties, are we less catholic in the sentiments which we hold in regard to the design of baptism, viz. that is for the remission of sins.[5]

---

[1]*Ibid.*, p. 49.   [2]*Ibid.*, pp. 50, 51.   [3]*Ibid.*, pp. 51, 52.   [4]*Ibid.* p. 54.   [5]*Ibid.*, pp. 67, 68.

The question of spiritual influence in conversion and sanctification is the subject Mr. Richardson turns to in his discussion. The following is the crux of his statements on this subject:

The chief cause of misapprehension in regard to spiritual influence is, as it appears to me, to be found in the fact, that most persons confound the agency of the Spirit in the *conversion of the sinner*, with the influence he exerts as *indwelling in the heart of the believer*. Hence the vague and unscriptural notion, that the Spirit may be received before faith, and that faith itself is something wrought in the heart by a special and supernatural operation of the Spirit. This, indeed, seems to be with many, the beginning and the end of all spiritual influence, and they depend, accordingly, upon certain mental or emotional impressions, of which they have once been the subjects, for their evidence of conversion, their assurance of pardon, their means of sanctification, and their hope of heaven.

We regard, however, the conversion of the sinner and the sanctification of the believer, as distinct matters, accomplished, indeed, by the same Spirit, but in a different manner, and from a widely different position. We conceive the Holy Spirit to stand to the sinner in a relation very distinct from that in which he stands to him who is a member of the family of God. With the former, he is an outward witness for the truth; but the latter "has the witness *in himself.*" To the first he is an unknown visitant or stranger; to the last, he is an indwelling and cherished guest. To the sinner, he is as the rain which falls upon the surface of the earth to soften and subdue; to the believer, he is as a fountain *from within*, springing up unto everlasting life. In short, to bring the matter at once to issue, we deny that there is any scriptural authority for the notion that the unbeliever, or man of the world, can *receive* the Spirit of God. We hold this dogma to be in direct opposition to the Divine testimony, since Christ himself declares to his disciples that he would pray the Father, and He would give to them another Comforter, "even the Spirit of Truth," continues he, "WHOM THE WORLD CANNOT RECEIVE." (John XIV. 17).[1]

Perhaps it may be argued that we have included more than a statement of the Plea from Robert Richardson, and so we have. However, it has been done for a purpose, to show the appeal to the scriptures in each case of question or objection that might be raised. These early reformers were serious about their desire to see the church of the New Testament restored, and they were willing to allow the word to speak for itself.

Benjamin Franklin, in the year 1856, published a statement that is worthy of our considerations at this point. The approach he makes is somewhat different, though the same in substance. Writes Mr. Franklin:

We will not have a modern *form* of Christianity, some man's views of Christianity, or a system that some man has deduced from Christianity, but Christianity itself, as delivered by Christ and his apostles; the whole of it—nothing more—nothing less. We shall never be satisfied with anything short of being Christians, Disciples of Christ, in the New Testament import of those terms; and we are determined to add nothing to this. We desire the King of Kings and Lord of Lords for our Saviour, our Redeemer and our everlasting trust. We desire all the faith, all the hope and all the love he imparts to the children of men. We believe in him, and all he taught; we believe in doing all he commanded, enjoying all he gives now, and hoping for all he promises, both in this world and the world to come.

---

[1] *Ibid.*, pp. 74, 75.

In one word, we desire to put ourselves under his guidance, to be wholly controlled by him, to be like him, to imbibe his spirit, die in the faith of him, and dwell with him forever.[1]

It is all of Christianity, nothing more, nothing less, for which he pleads. Mr. Franklin's position is not in doubt.

In the year 1856, Mr. Campbell published what he termed "The Christian Platform of Communion and Co-operation by Divine Institution" which reads as follows:

The basis of this platform is full-orbed grace, in all its constituents. And what are its constituents?

1. The Divine Philanthropy, demonstrated in the *incarnation* of the WORD that was in the beginning with God, and that was God.

2. In the mission of this incarnate WORD as a *Prophet*, or Teacher, and also as a *High Priest* and a *King*.

3. The love of Jesus Christ exhibited in his life, death, and sufferings.

4. The Father's acceptance of his life and death, witnessed in his resurrection.

5. The Father's further acceptance of his voluntary sacrifice of himself, signified in his ascension into his immediate presence in the heavens.

6. His investiture with universal empire, and coronation as Lord of all.

7. The Mission of the Holy Spirit to be his voucher and the Guest of his church.

8. The Ordinance of a Christian ministry—Apostles, Prophets, Evangelists, Bishops and Deacons.

9. The ordinances for communicating his grace—faith, repentance, baptism, the Lord's day, the Lord's supper, mutual contributions for the poor, prayer and praise.

10. Contributions for the maintenance and extension of the blessings of the reign of heaven throughout the world, in all time.

Such, in substance, is the broad catholic basis projected in the Christian Scriptures, for the building up of the great institution of Christianity in the hearts and lives of all who embrace it; and such are the means of its diffusion, and spread, and triumph over all false, corrupt, and corrupting institutions.

This is no specific, or sectarian platform, submitted to any one for his assent, in order to church union or communion. It is a mere memento sketch, for posting up in our minds our studies of the Christian Scriptures; a sort of index, not to the Christian Scriptures, nor to the whole field of Christian learning, but to the demands which press upon us in reference to the materials for meditation, study, and enlargement of our conceptions on present emergencies and demands for light. We shall be obliged to any citizen of the kingdom of Jesus Christ, as now dispensed in Christendom, for any objections to this platform, or for any suggestions or emendations on the premises.[2]

Again, the statement is something more than a statement of the plea, as such, but it demonstrates the closeness to the scripture that characterized the thinking and writing of Mr. Campbell. His was an appeal for the scriptural order of

[1] *American Christian Review*, Vol. I, No. 2, p. 41.
[2] *Millennial Harbinger*, Series IV, Vol. VI, No. VIII, pp. 473, 474.

things, the practice of that for which there is no "thus saith the Lord" would have had no sanction in his mind.

Elder Jacob Creath, Jr., was a frequent contributor to the *Millennial Harbinger*, and his contributions were always to the point. The following statements, demonstrating the thinking of Mr. Creath, are no exception. In them he is discussing the "Three Great Religious Parties in Christendom."

BRO. A. CAMPBELL.—Dear Sir:—There are, at present in christendom, three religious *professedly*, Christian parties, to wit: The papacy, Protestantism, and Christianity, or the Christian religion, as taught and practiced by Christ and his legates. The Papacy is nominally predicated upon the Bible, tradition and the church, (or clergy), but *really* it is without the Bible, it is founded upon tradition. Tradition, with Papists, is above the Bible. The Bible, with Papists, is a mere ruse, a blind to catch the people. They prefer tradition to the Bible, Peter to Jesus Christ, and the Mass to the Lord's Supper, and infant rantism to Christian immersion. The Papacy is an amalgamation of paganism, judaism, tradition, and Christianity, a hotchpotch *mess*. Protestantism is an amalgamation of popery and the Bible, compounded of creeds, confessions, disciplines, traditions, and the Bible. Pure Christianity, as taught by Christ and his legates, stands single and alone on the pages of the New Institution,—as antagonistic to these two great powerful institutions . . . . [1]

Mr. Creath's analysis of the thing called Christendom is, indeed, interesting, and little question is there that it would stand the test of historical and doctrinal investigation.

To the charge that the Restoration movement possesses a creed in the form of some of the writings of Mr. Campbell, Mr. Creath asserts:

. . . . From the commencement of our reformation until now, one part of our opponents have labored to prove that we have a creed, that the Christian Baptist is a creed, the Harbinger, the Christian System, in short all your writings are a creed, all that we have spoken and written, is a creed. Now, at last, when they have failed to prove the charge, the Presbytery charges that we have no creed. We plead guilty to the latter charge. We glory in the Bible alone. We glory in the Lord, and not in men, nor creeds . . . . [2]

Taking this opportunity, Mr. Creath then attempts to prove the error of creed making. Says he:

. . . . The Apostle James says, *"there is one lawgiver."* Who is that one lawgiver to the Christian Church? The Westminster divines cannot be that one lawgiver. The Westminster Confession and the Bible cannot be one law. That Presbytery ought to have produced one passage of Scripture for their constitution. They ought to have proved that the ancient Christians had such a confession previous to the Nicene council, in the year 325; before condemning us for the want of such an one. Can you tell me what proportion of Protestantism is traditional and what Scriptural? Subtract their traditions from the Scriptures, and what remains of their religion? Is not a large proportion of the Turkish, Pagan, Papistical, and Protestant religion *traditional?* If the constitution is destroyed, can the government exist which is built upon it? If the constitution of the Presbyterian Church is destroyed, can that Church *exist?* If all the creeds in Christendom were destroyed, could the Christian Church exist on the Bible alone? Yes it could . . . . [3]

[1]*Millennial Harbinger*, Series V, Vol. I, No. XII, p. 715.   [2]*Ibid.*, p. 716.   [3]*Ibid.*

With much jockeying, Mr. Creath finally comes to the goal. The Christian church can exist, without the creeds and traditions of Protestantism, upon the Bible alone. This, as we have seen through this research, is a fundamental principle of the Restoration movement. One wonders, if it would not have been more beneficial to argue that the church of Christ, in reality, cannot exist where Protestant or Papistical Creeds or traditions are held to, cannot exist *except* upon the Bible alone.

Among the terms that have been bandied about by the advocates of the restoration idea are "union" and "unity." The movement, to this day, is in serious need of a clear definition of these two terms. Robert Richardson has defined them well, and his words, as quoted below, deserve wide publication today, in the interest of clarifying these issues. Says Mr. Richardson:

> . . . . We have found the edifice of modern Christianity to rest largely on human opinions; and, despairing of success in any effort to repair its separated and tottering walls, we have sought to build anew upon the rock—the true and firm foundation originally laid in Zion. We have found denominational union, without Christian unity; and Christian unity, without the possibility of Christian union; and we have sought to break down the partition walls which bigotry has erected, and to restore the Christian liberty and fraternity of the first and purest period of the church.
>
> By Christian UNITY, we understand *a spiritual oneness with Christ,* by Christian UNION, *an avowed agreement and cooperation of Christians with each other.* There can be no *Christian union,* unless there be first *Christian unity;* for, since oneness with Christ, is the very substance of Christianity, we must first have true Christians, before these can be united with each other . . . .[1]

This statement throws a brilliant beam upon many points in darkness. It identifies the Restoration movement more directly with the original form of Christianity. The purpose of the latter could certainly be stated as "the spiritual oneness with Christ" of every individual who would accept him. This, too, is the object of the reformation. It has a message for those who have been only partially united with him as well as for him who has yet to hear the message of salvation. Certainly, it is to be understood that both must be brought to oneness with Christ before any co-operation or common effort in his behalf may be expected. The aim of the Restoration movement is the complete conversion of every one to Christ. Therefore, its message centers in conversion, in Christian unity; and then in the need for co-operation of Christians in further efforts in Christ's behalf.

It will, beyond doubt, be agreed that there is a remarkable oneness demonstrated in the statements considered to this point in this research. All the authors have agreed that the Restoration movement has fallen upon the message which will effect the healing of the wounds of the body of Christ. It is not "our message" nor "our plea," but it is the message of the New Testament and the plea of the New Testament, a message and a plea not being proclaimed in its purity by the existing groups in Christendom. The evil of division and its hindrance to the cause of Christ is condemned again and again. The superiority of the Bible alone over the creeds and traditions of Protestantism is emphasized again and again. In short, the advocates of the Plea are conscious

---

[1]*Millennial Harbinger,* Series V, Vol. II, No. II., p. 65.

that they have much to offer the Christian world, and that, certainly, the evils of sectarianism will fall before the onslaught of pure gospel truth.

The year 1859, brings the first significant alteration in this oneness of thought. John Rogers reports a conversation with W. S. Russell in the following manner:

> I was determined to satisfy myself regarding his position. I said to him to this effect: 'Bro. Russell, while I think we are as good as others, I know we are far below our perfect standard. Do you not think we have greatly the advantage of the religious parties of the day, in that we have taken the word of God as the only basis of the union, communion, and co-operation of God's people, instead of human platforms?' Said he: 'I don't think we have any advantage of them at all; they all have some great truth to work out, and so have we.' This was and is placing us upon a level with the religious parties of the day, as a sect among the sects.[1]

It is well that this statement be allowed to stand on its own. No comment could clarify it or reveal the thinking behind it. It is, however, the first recorded off-key note in the research made to this period. Much reading was done and many channels investigated in attempt to locate further light on Mr. Russell's thinking. The most significant statements, though not specifically upon the Plea, were found in the *Harbinger* for the year 1860 in an epistolary debate over the question of Spiritual influence. Mr. Russell had taken a point of view out of harmony with that historically taken by the movement, and the editor of the *Harbinger* was attempting to reveal his errors. It is not well to stand in judgment against Mr. Russell and his opinions, but his statements do, without question, place him out of harmony with the movement of his day.

Elijah Goodwin, in the year 1861, made the following statements regarding the movement:

> I will now, for the sake of our young members, sum up, what may be regarded as our leading objects as a people.
>
> 1. To unite all believers in our Lord Jesus Christ, who love God supremely, and each other fervently, in one visible body, that there may be "One body and one spirit, even as we are called in one hope of our calling," as it was in the days of the apostles.
>
> 2. To restore the primitive order in the church of God; in name, in ordinances, in fellowship, and in the reception, or rejection of members.
>
> 3. To teach men the way of salvation more perfectly than it is often done by others, so that the poor trembling mourner may not be kept weeping between the porch and the altar, seeking rest and finding none, for long and anxious weeks and months; but that they may be taught to come to Christ at once, when convinced of the truth, and the necessity of a Saviour, and thus obtain salvation through the blood of Christ in obedience to the gospel.
>
> 4. Finally, that thus living in union, studying the word of God, bearing each other's burdens, and teaching one another, we may glorify God on earth, and afterwards be received up into glory.
>
> Christian reader, are not these noble objects? Are they not worthy of our warmest affections? Should they not call forth our strongest for their accomplishment? Let everyone who stands identified with us in church relation, remember that these are our professions; these are our objects,

---

[1] *American Christian Review*, Vol. II, No. 51, p. 204.

and O! let us labor and pray, and pray and labor for the accomplishment of these noble and heavenly objects. Then shall we know that our labor is not in vain in the Lord.[1]

It is worthy of note that Mr. Goodwin appeals first for "unity" and then for "union," bearing out the distinction made by Mr. Richardson. His final appeal to remember that these are the objects of our work is suggestive that perhaps some have forgotten that truth. The statement, in all, is clearly put, and the author's zeal for the movement is unquestioned.

In the same year the above statement was made, Isaac Errett wrote a series of articles entitled "Plea for Reformation" for the *Harbinger*. This Series was carried throughout almost the entire year. It is not possible to include much of the material, but the main points made in the articles are sufficiently significant to present at this juncture. Said Mr. Errett:

.... Our plea has ever been for the divine perfection of the Christian religion, as it came from its author, and as it was expounded by the apostles, and received by the primitive church. Our motto was and is: 'Stand ye in the ways and see, and ask for the old paths, where is the good way, and walk therein, and ye shall find rest for your souls.'[2]

We come now to speak of the features of the reformation which need to be developed, and which it is the object of the present movement to bring out.

I. The Bible, the Bible only, as the rule of faith and practice . . . .[3]

II. The second feature of the reformation we plead is *Faith in the Lord Jesus, and unreserved submission to Him*, the true test of conversion . . . .[4]

III. In the third place, we are peculiar *in referring to the word of God for the decisive evidence of pardon* . . . .[5]

IV. *The inauguration of the kingdom of Christ on the Pentecost succeeding his resurrection* . . . .[6]

V. Another prominent characteristic of this movement, is, *the effort to unite all baptized believers in "one body"* . . . .[7]

VI. With a view to promote this most desirable and scriptural scheme of union, it is proposed *to drop all theological technicalities which* are but the property of parties and speculatists—and return to a *pure speech*, even the language and diction of the Holy Spirit . . . .[8]

VII. The last feature of this plea for reformation, to which we now call attention is, *the common and universal priesthood of the members of the Church of God.*[9]

It will be seen at once that Mr. Errett has arranged the specific features of the movement into a connected series of statements, and that they are in harmony with the statements that have gone before. It may be construed that he has added three concepts, which have not been mentioned previously, at least not as clearly as stated here. They are: 1) peculiarity "in referring to the word of God for the decisive evidence of pardon," 2) "The inauguration of the kingdom of Christ on the Pentecost succeeding his resurrection," 3) "The common and universal priesthood of members of the Church of God." The entire series of articles is worthy of close examination.

[1] *Christian Record*, Vol. 5, No. 2, p. 52.
[2] *Millennial Harbinger*, Series V, Vol. IV, No. I, pp. 28, 29.
[3] *Ibid.*, p. 252.   [4] *Ibid.*, p. 312.   [5] *Ibid.*, p. 314.   [6] *Ibid.*   [7] *Ibid.*, p. 317.
[8] *Ibid.*, p. 446.   [9] *Ibid.*, p. 449.

The next statements are by James M. Mathes, who has an interesting approach to the problems faced by the Restoration movement. They date in the year 1861 and read as follows:

. . . . God has shown us the pattern of the "church of the living God." This divine pattern was the church constituted at Jerusalem, on the day of Pentecost, when the Holy Spirit came down, according to the promise of Jesus, and 'guided them into all truth.'

To this model we must always refer; and if we should find that in our honest efforts to build up the church of Christ, and "spread scriptural holiness over these lands," we have made a mistake, and have entirely failed to "make all things according to the divine model or pattern" shown us at Jerusalem, and that instead of "spreading scriptural holiness over these lands," we have been building up a sect of very recent date, and spreading Methodism, Presbyterianism, or Campbellism "over these lands;" I say, if we find that we have been thus engaged, no matter how honestly, we ought at once to acknowledge our errors, reform and set ourselves right.

For example, if we should find from an examination of the "divine pattern," as given to us in the New Testament, that in the Jerusalem church, and those organized under the eye of the Apostles, there were no "class meetings," "class leaders," "local preachers and exhorters," such as we find in the M. E. Church, placed over the congregation and between the members and the pastor, no "presiding elders" over the traveling preachers and between them and the bishops, to form the "bishop's cabinet," we should then be satisfied at once that we have not "made all things" according to the "pattern shown us" in the mount of God; and we should at once give these things all up, and abandon them as an excrescence upon the tree of life.

Or if we should find in our examination of the "pattern," that none were received into the primitive church without faith in Christ, as the Son of God, repentance, confession of Jesus Christ, before men, as the Savior of sinners, and immersion in the name of Jesus Christ, into the name of the Father, and of the Son, and of the Holy Spirit; and that this immersion was for, or in order to, or *into* "the remission of sins," we could then apply the divine pattern to our work, and see whether we have been working according to it.

And if we find that we have been working and "experimenting" upon rules and regulations of our own make, for a hundred years, under which we have taken into our church unconverted persons and infants without faith; and that we have changed immersion into the unmeaning rite of *sprinkling* or *pouring*, then we may know with absolute certainty that we are wrong, however sincere we may have been in our efforts.

And on the other hand, if in our examination of the divine pattern, we find that we have the same faith, the same divine regulations for receiving members into the church, and of withdrawing fellowship from unruly members; that we have the same immersion, and submit to it with the same design; that we wear the same name, speak the same things, and mind the same things; then we may know certainly *that we are right*, and *can not be* wrong. [1]

This statement really represents the application of the restoration principle. The marks of the church of the New Testament are the marks that should be found in the church of Christ today. The comparison of institutions claiming to be

[1] James M. Mathes, *Letters to Thomas A. Morris, D.D.*, (Cincinnati: George B. Bentley and Company, Printers, 1861), pp. 110-112.

churches with the divine pattern, admitted by all to be right, will inform us as to the correctness of the faith and practice of those churches. Mr. Mathes suggests that all should be sufficiently honest to remove or alter the marks of existing institutions until they coincide with the marks of the church of the New Testament. Only in this way, may we be sure that our efforts are right.

A statement by A. B. Green, in the year 1862, reveals the answer of the Restoration movement to the interpretations of Christian union as proclaimed by the prevailing establishments. Mr. Green records the following:

I listened to a discourse from John xvii. 21: "That they all may be one; as thou, Father, art in me, and I in Thee."

The subject was divided as follows:

1st. The Saviour prayed that His people should be one, *as* He and His Father were one. It was observed, first, that Christ and His Father were not one in person, neither did Jesus design that His people should be intellectually one, for that could not well be accomplished. People would have their peculiarities and there was no hindering it. It was impossible that men should see alike on a great many points of doctrine.

2nd. He did not design that His people should be denominationally one. While people from human frailty differed in sentiment, it was better that those of the same sentiment should be in a body by themselves. There would be more good done in that way, because there would be a state of emulation that would prompt to a great zeal and activity.

He also said it was better to have these intellectual and denominational divisions on another account. Religion would be kept more pure, and the Bible kept from being corrupted by having the different religious bodies to watch over one another with a jealous eye; and thereby the cause would be greatly benefitted, and God would be more honored, because this denominational jealousy and zeal would stimulate to greater efforts.

3rd. The true union of Christians, he said, was a union of feeling, a union of sympathy. We ought to love one another, and pray for one another, and rejoice in each other's prosperity. In so doing the world would be led to embrace the gospel, because they would be led to see its excellency, etc.

In reply, I would quote Paul, I Cor. i.10: "Now I beseech you, brethren, by the name of our Lord Jesus Christ, that you all speak the same thing, and that there be no divisions among you; but that ye be perfectly joined together in the same mind and in the same judgment."

How much more good Paul could have done if—instead of saying as in Eph. iv. 3 to 6, "Endeavoring to keep the unity of the spirit in the bond of peace. There is one body, and one spirit, even as ye are called in one hope of your calling; one Lord, one faith, one baptism, one God and Father of all, who is above all, and through all, and in you all;" he had said: let each maintain the unity of the spirit in his own bond of peace under which he has enlisted. For, brethren, this denominationalism of Saducees, Pharisees, etc., etc., is greatly to the advantage of the cause. Thereby we shall watch over one another with a jealous eye, and be stimulated to a holy strife to outstrip each other in our efforts to do good. Let each have his own faith, and be baptized by any action he may choose, and remember that true Christian union is a union of sympathy, not intellectual union, such as would lead to all speaking the same thing, or of being of the same mind, or of the same judgment; for this is impossible. But let us be one in sympathy, let us bear with each other's weaknesses, and be willing to "live and let live." Nay, more: let us pray for each other's prosperity, and that divisions may increase; for the holy emulation of diverse parties will stimulate to greater activity!

But I am one that cannot so believe nor so pray; but I can sincerely pray that the watchman on the walls of Zion may see eye to eye, and be of the same mind and of the same judgment.[1]

Mr. Green has used the logical process of *reductio ad absurdum* to good advantage in this statement. It would seem that many of the so called arguments of infidelity and sectarianism would fall as hard before the use of the same instrument.

A statement by Benjamin Franklin, published in the year 1863, is the next consideration. Having considered the negative aspects of the Plea, Mr. Franklin says:

This is sufficient for negative ground. Now for affirmative ground. What shall we have in place of all this? We must have the following:

I. We must be simply Christians, disciples of Christ, children of God—no more, no less—simply this, and nothing else.

II. We must have what Jesus calls "My Church," the Church of Christ, of God—no more, no less—simply this, and nothing else.

III. In this church, or body, we must receive the one foundation—the one rock—on which it is built, which is Jesus the Christ, and no other foundation; for other foundation can no man lay than that which is laid, which is Jesus the Christ. The man who will be received on this rock—this foundation—that Jesus is the Christ, the Son of the living God—by making the confession which he has explicitly appointed, and taking the other steps He has laid down in his law, and nothing else—no more, no less—we must receive, and no other.

IV. We must take the law of God itself for our creed, and nothing else. Nothing must be added or taken away. The law of God—no more, no less, nothing else—must be the supreme authority.

V. We must maintain the original designations of the church, as found in Scripture, and designate it in the same way now. In speaking or writing of the Church, style it "the Church of God," "the Church of Christ," or, in many instances, it is entirely sufficient to say, "the Church."

VI. We must speak of individuals in the Church in the same way, call them what they are, "Christians," "disciples," or "disciples of Christ," "brethren," or "the brethren," "saints," etc.

There is unquestionably but one religion from God on earth. All other religions are spurious, and the work of the genuine reformer is to separate that one out from all the others, describe it, advocate it, maintain, defend, propagate and perpetuate it to the extent of his ability. This is the work of the genuine reformer. There is but one Gospel of Christ.[2]

Such was the Plea as Mr. Franklin understood it. His words need no defense nor interpretation.

The next statement, published first in the year 1864, is from the pen of Moses E. Lard. It follows in harmony the statements that have preceded it in this dissertation. Mr. Lard writes:

. . . . The reformation proposed was to be marked, positively, by accept-

[1]*Herald of Truth*, Vol. I, No. 5, pp. 167, 168.
[2]*American Christian Review*, Vol. II, No. 4, p. 363.

ing, as matter of faith, what and only what, the holy Scriptures teach; practically, by doing every thing and only what they enjoin, and, negatively, by rejecting every thing which they do not sanction. Such was the reformation proposed by Mr. Campbell and his brethren.[1]

This brief statement, indeed, has much between the lines and is sweeping in its implications. Mr. Lard continues:

. . . . The reformation for which we are pleading consists, 1st. *In accepting the exact meaning of Holy Writ as our religious theory*. This is held as the doctrine of the Holy Scriptures, the thing taught in them, and hence the thing to be believed, or the matter of faith. Hence, human elements are absolutely excluded from our theory. Reason may determine what *is* said in God's word, not what *ought* to be said. We accept as our creed the contents of his word without enlargement, contraction, or modification. Such is the matter of our theory.

2nd. *In the minute conformity of our practice to the revealed will of Christ*. Such is the second feature of the reformation. Hence all practices having their origin in tradition, human reason, or expediency, are utterly eschewed. In other words, the reformation consists in an effort to induce all the truly pious in Christ to become perfectly joined together in the same mind, and in the same judgment, by accepting as doctrine, precisely and only what is either actually asserted or necessarily implied in the Bible; to speak the same things by speaking what the Bible speaks, and to speak them in the language of the Bible; and to practice the same things by doing simply the will of Christ. Thus it is proposed continually to construct the body of Christ after the divine model, to unitize completely its constituent members, to imbue them with a new, divine life, and to pervade them with the "peace" of Christ, and a warm, pure, fraternal affection. Such is the great and good work in which we are engaged. That it should ever have been opposed or spoken against by a single being possessed of mind enough to comprehend it, is certainly one of the mysteries of sin.[2]

To some the term "our religious theory" may be somewhat confusing. To them Mr. Lard says:

. . . . We do not mean that a mere resemblance shall exist between the elements or particulars of our theory and the contents of His word; but that these contents shall themselves constitute those elements or particulars. This is what we mean. The contents of that word must reappear in our theory, and compose it; otherwise it is false—it is no theory at all, but a mere vacant gaze of the mind.[3]

The assertion that the Plea has both a negative and a positive aspect is important and is well made here by Mr. Lard. His emphasis upon a "minute conformity" is interesting, having not been made in exactly those terms before.

John Smith sounds a warning note in the next statement, which is dated arbitrarily in 1865, three years before his death. He states as follows:

The friends of the Reformation may easily injure their own cause by giving to it a sectarian character; against which we should always be specially guarded. And in order to avoid this, and all other departures from the Apostolic order of things, we can not, we will not, knowingly sanction any tradition, speculation, or amalgamation, unknown to the primitive Christian congregations. On the other hand, we are determined, by the favor of God, to the utmost of our ability, to teach what the primitive disciples

---

[1]*Lard's Quarterly*, Vol. I, p. 11.   [2]*Ibid.*, p. 22   [3]*Ibid.*, p. 13.

taught; and in admitting persons into the congregation of Christ, we will require what they required, and nothing more. We will urge the practice of all the Apostolic commands and examples given to the primitive Christians, and thus labor for the unity of the disciples of Christ upon this one foundation. And wherever we find others—whatever they may have been called by their enemies—laboring for the same object, aiming at the same thing, we are bound joyfully to receive them, treat them as Christians, and cooperate with them. And such we believe are the Christian brethren about Lexington, Georgetown, Paris, Millersburg, and Carlisle.[1]

Those of like faith, whether formally associated with the reformation or not, are Christian brethren and ought to be treated as such, says Mr. Smith, otherwise we exhibit a sectarian spirit. His loyalty and faithfulness to the ideal of the New Testament church is here asserted again.

The importance of Christian baptism and the danger involved in willfully neglecting or rejecting it is the subject of the next statement, made by W. H. Hopson, in the year 1868. According to Mr. Hopson:

No man can prove to heaven or earth that he has faith in Christ, repentance toward God, or love to him in his heart, who knows that Jesus commands him to be baptized; that the command has not been repealed, and is, therefore, still binding; who stubbornly and willfully neglects it. The sinner, like the Christian, must "show his faith by his works." His persistent neglect of baptism is rebellious resistance to the authority of the Savior. Such a man, with such a stubborn will and unloving heart, can not be served.[2]

The proximity of the reasoning of Mr. Hopson to that of Mr. Campbell, in his third answer to the query of the lady from Lunnenberg, is striking. Neither would express any hope for the man pictured here by Mr. Hopson. As Isaac Errett has suggested, "Faith in the Lord Jesus, and unreserved submission to Him, is the true test of conversion."[3] The man possessed of such attitude will not question the matter of Christian immersion, when it is known to him; too, the man who has been immersed into the name of Christ will not fail to meet the balance of his obligations.

Commenting upon the unchangeable nature of the Christian faith, G. W. Longan wrote, in the year 1868, the following statement:

The principles which form the basis of God's moral government are as immutable as those by which he determines the manifold phenomena of the physical creation. Whatever is reducible to necessary principles is, therefore, in harmony with the highest wisdom. If, then, the Gospel of Christ, in all its provisions and in all its requirements, is based upon unchanging principles, and springs up necessarily from the very relations which subsist between God and men, for whom it is intended, then is God's wisdom in giving the Gospel vindicated, and our obligation to obey it certainly established.[4]

That Mr. Longan regarded Christianity in the light suggested above will be seen more fully later in statements to be presented.

[1]John Augustus Williams, *Life of Elder John Smith*, (Cincinnati: R. W. Carroll & Co., Publishers, 1870), pp. 469, 470.

[2]W. T. Moore, *The Living Pulpit of the Christian Church*, (Cincinnati: R. W. Carroll & Co., Publishers, 1868), p. 295.

[3]*Millennial Harbinger*, Series V, Vol. IV, No. I, p. 312.   [4]Moore, *op cit.*, p. 189.

Charles L. Loos, from whom we have heard before in this research, had something to say in the year 1868 which calls next for our attention. Regarding the notion that union does exist within the existing divisions or that union could be accomplished without eliminating the divisons, Mr. Loos remarks:

> The great fallacy of the ideas and the plea of these men for Christian union, is, that they seek to effect a union without destroying the party divisions. With the present sect-separations, no real, effectual union, least of all, such as the Word of God calls for and the Spirit of God sanctifies, can be brought about.[1]
>
> It is the boldest sophism to compare *these* divisions in name, doctrine, organization, and membership, this clearly defined, mutually repellent, separate life and action, to the differences existing and allowed in the apostolic church. No such divisions were known and sanctioned there.[2]

Continuing Mr. Loos remarks:

> . . . . The terms of admission into the church or body of Christ, can surely by no logical or theological fallacy or sophism be made a non-essential. What would that theological system be, that would so degrade the divinely ordained (and we know of no other) means of union with the body of Christ and with Christ himself? This shameful disrespect and depreciation of God's laws and ordinances in the New Testament, engendered by this desire to cover up the sins of sectarianism, cannot be too severely censured. It is a direct attack upon the divine dignity, authority, and essential value of the Word of God.[3]

Having recorded this much of Mr. Loos' writing to present his view and consideration of sectarianism, the following is included to bring to the fore his conception of the Plea, as an answer to the problem, and something of his notion of the relation of the Restoration movement to the sects.

> . . . . Our position on this point must be absolute and positive. We know very well there is in such matters as these a strong pressure and tendency to a charitable forbearance and yielding; and that in some few instances—rare indeed they are—we have observed a disposition even among us to compromise this great principle and feature of New Testament Christianity. It must not be done, and it cannot be done, without giving up the plea of original Christianity in doctrine, form and life. We say it here with all forethought, with all calmness and with a full knowledge of what it means, that *we never can recognize the party names, creeds, and organizations as Christian,*—NEVER! Need we, after all we have said, tell why? One answer must suffice,—because we are advocates of a return to Primitive Christianity. Is it a good or bad position for Christians to occupy?—is it right or wrong? Who dares say it is not right? If such an aim therefore is right, then all abandonment of sectarianism follows absolutely as a logical necessity.
>
> If any man will ask us,—Is it charitable?—we shall ask in return, Is it scriptural?—and the answer to our question is a sufficient answer to all others that are legitimate.[4]

The above statement is no equivocation. The reader is at once aware of the conviction of the author, and no doubt is left remaining. One wonders if many problems within the movement could not have been averted had the pen, the pulpit, and the press always sounded forth with such forthrightness and direct-

[1]*Millennial Harbinger*, Vol. 39, No. II, p. 111.   [2]*Ibid.*   [3]*Ibid.*, p. 114.
[4]*Millennial Harbinger*, Vol. 39, No. I, pp. 8, 9.

ness. Certainly no apology needs to be made for the gospel as it is recorded in the New Testament.

W. K. Pendleton, son-in-law of Alexander Campbell and his successor to the editorial chair of the *Harbinger*, recorded the following in the year 1868:

Is not the power of the church limited by the word of God? and in what passage, chapter or verse, has the power been conferred, of changing the terms and conditions of pardon, so as to put a court of clerical inspectors between the sinner and his Savior, by which he can be held aloof from the privilege of salvation at their judgment or pleasure. These innovators upon the freedom of the gospel, and the untrammeled liberty of the sinner to come to it upon Christ's invitation the same hour in which he believes and is ready to confess, are the loudest advocates for salvation by grace; but in the end, it turns out to be a grace of the clergy, rather than of God. It .... terms and conditions after all, and these of ecclesiastical diction, and erring, fallible human application. Between the grace of God and the salvation of the sinner, the court of the examining clergy stands, with a string of inquisitorial questions, never asked by an apostle, and some of which an apostle could not satisfactorily answer,— and by these the door of grace is barred, and the sinner kept from the pardon of his sins.

If the church may interpose some additional conditions to those which are prescribed in the word, why may she not interpose others? Who shall determine the limits of this assumption?—Once concede the right to transcend the express teachings of the Scriptures, and you open the floodgates for a boundless inundation of priestly tyranny. This has been the small beginning of that enormous structure of spiritual despotism, we call Romanism. From the Pope upon his throne, now artfully stretching out his hands for the prerogative of infallibility, to the smallest court of examiners, that presumes to add to the plain word of God, its own rules of spiritual inspection into the state of the heart of the professedly penitent,—the principle is the same. They stand in the place of God, and legislate for the divine mercy.—They shut where the Savior has opened. They mystify what the apostles, both by precept and example, made plain, and they exact for their own satisfaction, what the divine grace has left between the conscience and the Creator. This is one of the sins of sectarianism. It is the duty of every friend of spiritual freedom to *protest* against it. Let us assert the liberty of the gospel, and cry aloud for a return to its simple and divine propositions of pardon.[1]

Such was the condition existing in Mr. Pendleton's day, and such is the condition existing still today, in a large measure. Where the clergy has ceased to regard itself in the inquisitorial position described above, the bars are often dropped altogether, and freedom to the fellowship is allowed, regardless of faith or obedience. If the church today would allow itself to be bound by the limits of the New Testament in regard to this question, who could deny the rightness of the action?

The struggles of the Pope for "infallibility" in the year 1868, as mentioned by Mr. Pendleton, are very interesting, since it is known today that such he accomplished, in the eyes of the Roman church, not many years later. The men of the movement were aware of the actions transpiring about them, and were fully conscious of the implications involved.

---

[1]*Ibid.*, p. 26, 27.

L. L. Pinkerton had the following to say in the year 1868:

God has placed before a sinful world, for its faith, its love, and its obedience, a person wearing human nature, and bearing its infirmities, yet possessing divine and infinite perfections and attributes. Jesus of Nazareth is a historic personage, whose individuality, so to speak, is marked with wonderful clearness. His manner of teaching—the things taught, as well as his beautiful life, are altogether peculiar, single, alone. The New Testament is the miracle of literature. In the person and claims of Jesus our faith is demanded; for his divinely-beautiful character our all-trusting, adoring love is asked. The commandments of Jesus are not doctrines, but plain rules of life, of action, to which submission is required. These three things: faith in Jesus, the love of Jesus, and obedience to Jesus, as Lord of all, constitute the Christian religion, and are possible to the poor and to the unlearned, as well as to the wealthy and the wise. Not so with theology, with scientific Christianity, about which most religious controversies arise, and which constitute the foundations of religious sects, regarded as such merely. Touching the commands of the blessed redeemer, we may say, it is not easy for the honest-hearted seriously to mistake them. The general import of the whole is, as illustrated by his own beautiful, Divine life, "to do justly, to love mercy, and to walk humbly with God." This is orthopraxy, without which orthodoxy is but an impertinence and a cheat.

Complainings on all sides, of the want of earnest religious living have become chronic. The general tone of religious life will not be improved till God's people shall come to apprehend with greater clearness, and to feel with far deeper intensity, the claims of their Redeemer on their affections, until they shall love him more than they love wealth, and friends, and life— until the love of Christ shall *constrain* them. Religious partyism has long been the opprobrium of the Church. The Church will never be united in "doctrines" of any kind. She must be one in Christ Jesus, or divide still more, and remain divided till the Lord shall come.[1]

In many points the above statement is very fine. More complete submission to Jesus as Lord is certainly the answer to a multitude of problems in the church of Jesus Christ. However, there are some things about it that may create questions in the minds of some. If the word doctrine means simply teaching, then the commandments of Jesus are doctrines, for it was his instruction to "teach them to observe all things whatsoever I have commanded you." Thus, the assertion that "the Church will never be united in 'doctrines' of any kind," is not so true as might at first seem. Certainly, the Restoration movement has, through its history, as has been noted in this research, been pleading for unity upon the basis of the doctrine of Christ. It is not to be supposed that the church will ever have Christian unity apart from the doctrine of Christ. At the risk of the accusation that such is merely an interpretation of Mr. Pinkerton's statement, it might be said that his arguments make Christianity too much more a way of life than the way of redemption.

Perhaps Mr. Pinkerton's position can be more adequately revealed through the inclusion of the following statement, made by him in the year 1868 or thereabouts. The date is arbitrary, since no way of setting it exactly is possible.

For more than thirty years I have been annoyed by the following question: Would you receive into a church of which you were the pastor a good man without requiring him to be immersed? I used to answer the

---

[1]Moore, *op. cit.*, pp. 126-128.

question by saying that I would decide the question when the case should arise in the course of my ministry. I constantly felt, however, that the reply was evasive and cowardly; and never made it without feeling a certain contempt for myself. 'Why not,' some one may ask—'why not answer with an emphatic no?' Let the interrogator exercise a little patience and a good deal of manly candor, and it may appear, that, according to the 'principles of this Reformation,' 'no' is not the fittest answer to the question. Latterly I have answered the question affirmatively, giving the following reasons for my decision, and insisting on the following limitations:

1. My affirmative answer assumes that the unimmersed person applying for membership is a member of some Christian community, and of acknowledged piety—one known to do justly, to love mercy, and to walk humbly with God.

2. The proposed action in the case assumes that the congregation in which the unimmersed seeks membership is like-minded with the pastor. This second condition is made intensely emphatic, for the reason that very few questions of expediency will justify any one in so pressing them as to cause dissension, strife, and division in a congregation of disciples. However much a church may be suffering from unwise administration, it will be sure to suffer more from an attempt at change which can be effected only by strife, angry debate, and alienation of heart. The first may be disease, the last is, generally, death . . . .

3. By the proposed action in regard to one asking membership in the church without immersion, I would escape some serious embarrassments and inconsistencies.

a. I would not disallow the right of private judgment in a matter of conscience, that is to say, I would not make concurrence in my views of a positive ordinance essential to membership. The problem which I propose thus to solve, may not admit of such a method of solution. That it is pressed on all sides by grave difficulties, I frankly admit; yet, as long as I profess to believe in the divine right of private judgment in questions of religious faith and practice, I shall feel constrained to act consistently with that profession.

In receiving into a congregation of disciples one who had not been immersed, I should endeavor to deal very frankly with him. I should probably say to him something like this: 'I do not think you have been baptized, and when, hereafter, you shall hear me teach baptism you will hear me teach immersion, and when you shall see me baptize, you will see me immerse, for, according to my understanding of the Scriptures, baptism and immersion are the same. You think differently and tell me that, on the subject, your conscience is at rest. I will not, therefore, thrust my translation of a Greek word between your conscience and your God; for, like the rest of us, you stand or fall to your own Master. Receive the New Testament of our Lord and Saviour Jesus Christ as the word and will of God, and—take heed how you read.[1]

This is the first open advocacy of the practice of 'open-membership' in the record of the restoration writings, in so far as this research has been able to determine. It is worthy of note that the writer says he has had this question under advisement for thirty years, thus when Mr. Pinkerton first considered opening the doors of the church to the unimmersed the year was 1838 or thereabouts, at least, within the decade of the Lunnenberg questionings. It has

[1] John Shackleford, Jr., *Life, Letters and Addresses of Dr. L. L. Pinkerton*, (Cincinnati: Chase & Hall, Publishers, 1876), pp. 110-112.

already been pointed out that many faithful advocates of the restoration idea felt Mr. Campbell had not answered in the wisest manner. Now the question arises, could this statement of Mr. Pinkerton be traced to those answers?

One point in the position of Mr. Pinkerton is good. His honesty in practicing his conclusions only among those people and in that church which concur with them is commendable and is recommended to those preachers of this day who may be tempted to draw the same conclusions. The man certainly is without excuse who attempts to force such practice upon a congregation, by direct action or evolutionary propaganda, which through its history has held a position in direct opposition to such practice. It has been demonstrated again and again that such tactics lead to no good.

Mr. Pinkerton's implication that private judgment gives a man a right to conclude that baptism is not necessarily immersion is certainly infantile logic. The church would be forced to give sanction to a myriad of private judgments upon this basis. The various and sundry conceptions of baptism are certainly not all right. In the very nature of things, some of them must be wrong. Private judgment often errs. It is the business of the church to look diligently in God's word for the truth about this question, and then to teach men who differ from this truth, that, in their privacy, they have made an error in judgment of this question. To make men aware of the error of their private judgments and to bring them into conformity with the judgments of God and of Christ, surely should be the direction of the efforts of the church. These same arguments may be directed against the conception that, to do other than he advocated, Mr. Pinkerton would be thrusting his translation of a Greek word between the unimmersed person's conscience and his God. It is not Mr. Pinkerton's translation of a Greek word that makes baptism an immersion but the translation of scholarship through the years.

THE MUSIC QUESTION

This section, dealing with the question of instrumental music in worship, is placed here, not because of the introduction of the instrument at this time, but because L. L. Pinkerton is said to have been the first among the advocates of the restoration idea to bring the organ or melodeon into a worship assembly. This action by Mr. Pinkerton probably occurred about the year 1859.[1] At the time, he was ministering to the church at Midway, Kentucky.

It is no secret that considerable stir was created by this action. Manifold have been the debates orated and the pages written for and against the use of musical instruments in the worship services of the churches. It is not the purpose of this dissertation to review those arguments here, except to say that the group opposed to the introduction of instruments maintained that since the New Testament does not mention the use of musical instruments, God is therefore opposed to the use of them. The group favoring the use of musical instruments maintained that, since the New Testament makes no mention of their use, God has granted permission so to do. The one group denies that silence gives consent, while the other group affirms that proposition. Both should consider the recent logic of W. R. Walker that "silence of Scripture constitutes a command to be equally silent."

---

[1]Homer Hailey, *Attitudes and Consequences in the Restoration Movement*, (Los Angeles: Citizen Print Shop, Inc., 1945), p. 200.

It is an established fact coming out of the history of revelation that it has been God's purpose to inform men of their sins. Such was the purpose of the law, as Paul sets it forth in his comparison of the law and the gospel in his letter to the churches in Galatia. This is in harmony with common reason. It would be expected that he would so do. His people could not be held accountable for transgressing his will, when his will had never been revealed to them. An infantryman cannot be held responsible for obeying a command that was never issued by his superior.

In the light of this fact, if the use of instrumental music were sufficiently grave a sin to blight the efforts of a great movement for the restoration of the Christianity of the New Testament or to divide the body of Christ, God would certainly have made more effort to inform men of that fact than the simple omission of it from his revelation. The works of the flesh he has revealed; the sins which divide he has revealed, the use of an instrument he has not mentioned. Who dare step into the supposed breach and rule where God has not ruled either for or against the use of the instrument in worship?

The problem raised in the use of instruments in the worship assembly is beside the point of the Plea. It is to the shame of the Restoration movement for time immemorial that such a question should have claimed the attention of emphasis in the preaching, in the writing, in the publishing of a people who had rediscovered the ancient gospel in its purity and who had found anew the original plan of salvation, while a world corrupt in sin and a church corrupt in error longed for the truth. It has been, as the statements we have reviewed thus far unanimously testify, the purpose of the Restoration movement to bring God's people to oneness with Christ, through recognition of his person and office and through submission to his will by use of the "instruments of salvation" supplied by him. One who has thus been united with Christ is brother to him who also has been thus united with Him, regardless of whether or not one uses an instrument in worship and the other does not or both use the instrument or both refuse to use it. Who could suppose that a silence of scripture could break a unity accomplished through obedience to every positive expression of God's will?

Benjamin Franklin, long claimed by those who oppose the use of an instrument in worship, made a statement in the year 1879, which we take out of chronology in order to introduce its argument at this point. Said he:

> But may we not have a general division about the organ? Not at all. We have none among us that will exclude us if we will not *fellowship the organ*. This is all the difficulty there is. Some of us will not *worship with the organ* nor *fellowship it*. Will not that divide us? Not at all. Those who would rather have their organ in their worship, than those who will not, and can not worship with it, *will have it*, and let those who can not worship with it, *stay away*. Those who can not worship with it will seek some place where they can worship without it, and worship as they know to be according to Scripture. They know this to be safe.[1]

James M. Mathes said much the same in the year 1881, which also we include here:

> . . . . We have never regarded the organ in the worship as a test of fellowship. We recognize many good and true brethren and sisters among

---

[1]Benjamin Franklin, *A Book of Gems*, (St. Louis: John Burns, Publisher, 1879), p. 49.

those who favor its use in the worship. And while in our best judgment, nothing that is good, can be accomplished by the organ in the worship, that could not be accomplished much better without it; still I have always been opposed to division in the churches on account of the organ. There is no true test of fellowship, but the commands of God. Disobedience to the commands of God destroys the fellowship. And the apostle says, "Withdraw yourself from every brother who walks disorderly."[1]

Those things that unite one with Christ should constitute the basis of our oneness with each other as Christians, for, if one be one with Him, he can not be cut off from another who also is one with Him.

The circumstances under which the Restoration movement was divided or, perhaps it should be said, listed separately in the United States Census Records will be dealt with later. The above will suffice for an introduction to the problem. It is well to keep constantly in mind that between the two groups still exists the sort of unity sought by the original advocates of the Plea. The disruption in the union of the two groups has come as a result of the misapplication of the Plea and of the development of a sectarian attitude on the part of many in both groups. However, continuance of the review of the statements of the Plea takes our attention at this point.

Robert Milligan is the author of the statement next to be considered. Said he:

.... We are brought back to the Bible itself AS THE ONLY PROPER CREED OF THE CHURCH: *the only infallible and reliable standard of our faith and practice.* Our faith, subjectively considered, is always liable to be erroneous in many respects; and our practice is likely to be even more so. But the Bible is perfect, as its Divine Author is perfect. And hence it should be our constant aim and effort, day by day, to test our thoughts, our words, and our actions, by this Divine standard; and to bring them up as near to its requirements as possible, but never to go beyond it. All efforts to transcend this limit are attempts at reformation in the wrong direction: they are the bitter fruits of infidelity, come from what source they may.

Happy, then, thrice happy, would it be for the Church today, if she had always contended earnestly for the Creed delivered to the Saints by the inspired apostles. But the pride of the human heart is amazing. There is a constant inclination on the part of fallen man, weak, frail, and erring as he is, to make his own opinions the standard by which to judge of everything else. And hence, at an early period, the subjective faith of the Church, or rather of her aspiring Bishops and Presbyters, was reduced to writings, and in a great measure substituted for the inspired creed of the Apostles and Prophets. But the trouble did not stop here. Very soon different opinions were entertained respecting the meaning of the newly formed Creed; and hence the necessity of again correcting the objective by the subjective. A third Creed was formed, and a fourth, and a fifth; but every attempt at creed-making has only served to destroy the unity of the faith, to multiply sects and parties, and to lead away the minds and hearts of the people from the earnest and prayerful study of the Holy Scriptures, which alone are able to make us wise even unto salvation.

And hence it is evident that every attempt to unite the people of God on any human basis must ever prove utterly vain and abortive. The only possible way to accomplish this end is to throw aside all human Creeds,

[1] *The Evangelist*, Vol. 16, No. 13, p. 197.

and take the Bible, and the whole Bible, and nothing but the Bible, as our rule of faith and practice.[1]

The analysis of the problems involved and the solution to those problems, as stated by Mr. Milligan, is clear and accurate. Certainly his suggestions are in accord with the movement as a whole.

In the year 1869, Charles Louis Loos set forth the following warning and prophecy:

> . . . . Two things may be looked for now, in these 'movements' toward union.—We must rest perfectly sure that sectarianism will make a long and mighty struggle for its life and power and dominion; it will not yield easily.— It is wary, skillful and strong. If it must meet and yield to the rising plea for Christian union,—it will do it in such a manner as to lose nothing by it; and—that is, it will consent to such a union that will leave it in the full enjoyment of its sinful life and dominion. This is one of the things that we must expect, inevitably, to see. The other is this:—in the enthusiasm for union, men will hasten to reach their object by ignoring and throwing aside, as obstacles to the realizing of their wishes, often what is essential and positive in the doctrine of Christ, and what can never be yielded up without offending God, without destroying the integrity, and therefore the divine power, of the religion of Christ.[2]

It can be truthfully said that the Christian world is experiencing the coming to pass of the thing concerning which Mr. Loos sounded this warning. He certainly did not favor the surrender of any positive precept of God's word in the interest of union of denominational forces.

The next statement, the final one for this dissertation from Alexander Campbell, is included to point out Mr. Campbell's attitude toward baptism in the final years of his life.

> Every sectarian in the land, how honest and pious so-ever, ought to bury his sectarianism, and all his other sins of omission and commission, in the 'bath of regeneration.'[3]

It is clear that Mr. Campbell had not changed his mind throughout all the years that he pled the ancient gospel. His supposed 'open-membership' leanings are just not existent in fact.

G. W. Longan is the author of the following statement concerning the basis of affiliation of the New Testament church. Says Mr. Longan:

> Now we have here in the primitive church, and in the primitive churches, associations, fraternization, in one work, and for one object, standing before us so palpably, that we can not be mistaken. This is true of each local community, and not less true of the whole body. What is the basis of this association? What its bond of union? What its tie of affiliation and confraternity?—What makes the aggregate individual membership of each local community one local body? What makes the aggregate membership of these local bodies one general or catholic body? The answer to the question which we have now reached, will bring us near the heart of our subject. The answer indeed has been suggested, as I may say, already: but it is now proposed to be more explicit. The importance of something here, that is clear, tangible, scriptural—something that will

---

[1]Robert Milligan, *An Exposition and Defense of the Scheme of Redemption,* (Cincinnati: R. W. Carroll & Co., Publishers, 1869), pp. 468, 469.
[2]*Millennial Harbinger,* Vol. 40, No. IV, p. 183.   [3]*Ibid.,* p. 193.

pass the ordeal of the judgment day—can not be exaggerated. Humbly and reverently then but in the full assurance of understanding and faith, I proceed to say, that the basis of affiliation among the primitive Christians—the constitution, if you please so to call it, of the primitive church, consisted of just two short articles. Here they are: Art. 1st, Unfeigned faith in Christ. Art. 2nd, Hearty and implicit obedience to all his commandments. Everything is here. The man who believes in Christ, has power to become a son of God. The man who under the influence of this faith, does the will of Christ, obeys the commands of Christ, is, in fact, a son of God. *Agreement in this faith, and in this obedience, was the basis of affiliation in the primitive church.* This is the only basis that heaven recognizes now. Nothing else, my hearers, will stand the test when Jesus comes. Let no man deceive himself. Listen not to the prophets, that prophesy smooth things. It is a fearful thing to set at nought the arrangement of the living God, to ignore and set aside the very foundation upon which every church in apostolic times was built.[1]

Mr. Longan's statement is one of the clearest and finest considered thus far. This position, as he presents it here, is precisely the position of the Campbells and of the majority of those whose statements have been reviewed previously. "The basis of affiliation" in the church is the basis of unity. The problem can not be reduced to lower terms than this.

Clark Braden in a debate with G. W. Hughey on the Action of Baptism brought out the following in regard to the relation of the Bible to the Methodist Book of Discipline:

> But, says my opponent, the Discipline is based on God's word. Then why not go to that directly, and take that? But we do not understand it alike, neither do we the Discipline. We do not reach uniformity by laying aside the perfect word of God, and taking the imperfect work of fallible man. Look at the reflection on God and his word implied here. We can understand man's work better than we can the perfect word of God. Man has to supplement God's perfect word to save himself from error.

> But I deny the gentleman's position. The Bible is not the standard. The Discipline is not tested by the Bible. Your preachers are required to understand and interpret the Bible by your standard, the Discipline. Suppose a trial arises in your church, will you allow an appeal from the Discipline to the Bible? Did you ever? You know you never did. Then what is the standard? Which is the higher authority? This Discipline of which you, sir, are to mind everything, great and small, whether you read it in the word of God, or prove it thereby or not.

> We have now placed before you our reasons for arraigning the Discipline for containing statements of doctrine and enjoining church usages contrary to the word of God. Compare it with the word of God in these particulars and decide. If it contains more or less than what is in the Bible, we do not, and will not accept it. If it contains just what is in the Bible, we do not need it. It is a blasphemous usurpation, view it in what light you will.[2]

> In conclusion, let me exhort you to throw away such human devices. Go back to the perfect word of God, which shall abide forever, which is perfect, converting the soul, which is clear, enlightening the eyes, which will make wise unto salvation, and is given by inspiration of God, and is profitable

[1]*Ibid.*, pp. 367, 368.
[2]Clark Braden and G. W. Hughey, *The Action of Baptism*, (Cincinnati: Franklin and Rice, 1870), p. 558.

for doctrine, for correction, for instruction in righteousness, and by which the man of God is made perfect, and thoroughly furnished to all good works.[1]

Again we see demonstrated the logical process of *reductio ad absurdum* this time applied to the Discipline of the Methodists. His appeal, then, to the Bible is typical of the statements of the movement.

In the year 1872, Tolbert Fanning wrote the following:

Paul informs us that there is "One God and Father of all, one Lord, one faith." Eph. iv: 5-6. Are we to conclude that there is but one faith for all Christians? No doubt, this is what the Apostle intended. If it were true that all the saints are of the one faith, what disposition are we to make of the various creeds, called the faith of the different orders of the age? The creeds, though denominating the systems of faith of the respective parties adopting them, are mere speculative views or opinions, but rise not to authority of faith. We doubt if the teachers in the various parties feel full confidence in any of the fancies required, and we see not how it is practicable for an earnest man to believe the articles of the creeds.

The same testimony was furnished to all by the Spirit, and, as was predicted, all came to the unity of the faith in acquiring the perfect testimony near the close of the first century. This was when the testimony was closed, when the finishing lesson was given by the beloved John.

Romanism, Protestantism, Modern Spiritualism, and Universalism, are but speculations, and nothing can be of the faith which is not in the words of *the* faith. As to the truth of the Bible, God permits man to differ, but still, he who rejects the Divine record, does it at his own peril. But we have no right to differ with regard to the things written. Jesus prayed that "All might be one as he and the Father were one, who should believe through the Apostles' words." John xvii:20. We can see no room for differences amongst a people whose faith is bounded by the word of God. Calvinists and Arminians see eye to eye, and have the identical faith, when they see and believe through the words of eternal life contained in the Gospel. In fact, there can be no difference until one or the other disputant, ceases to be governed by the inspired oracles.[2]

That there will be "no differences amongst a people whose faith is bounded by the word of God" is a very large statement. None have ever so claimed, and such is not the claim of the Restoration movement. However, it is claimed that the differences will not be sufficient to cause a breach in the efforts of such a people. There will be oneness in essentials, at least. If Mr. Fanning has reference to this, no argument is involved.

One of the most comprehensive statements of the Plea is the following by Isaac Errett, which was published about this period of the history of the movement. Mr. Errett writes:

Let us now state the doctrine of Christian union as taught and practiced by us.

1. It frankly avows not only the folly, but the *sin* of sectarianism, and teaches that, just as any other sin, it must be abandoned. It proposes no compromise whatever with denominationalism, but insists that party names, party creeds, and party organizations, being in direct contravention of the teachings of Christ, must be forsaken. It distinguishes between sects going away from the Church of God into Babylon, and sects coming back

[1]*Ibid.*, p. 572.   [2]*Religious Historian*, Vol. I, No. 5, p. 140.

97

from Babylon, seeking to find the Church of God. With these latter it has much sympathy, and offers for their imperfect yet important and salutary movements in reformation, many apologies. Still it insists that the return from Babylon to Jerusalem is incomplete so long as rival and jarring sects are found in place of the one catholic apostolic Church of Primitive times.

2. It insists that unity and union are practicable; that in the first age of the Church our Lord and his apostles did establish one grand spiritual brotherhood, and did embrace in it men of all classes and nationalities, however diverse or antagonistical their sentiments, tastes and habits may previously have been; and that the Christian condition of society at that time presented much greater obstacles in the way of such a union than any that are found now among the professed followers of Christ. The difficulties should therefore be manfully met in the face and overcome.

3. It proposes simply a return, "in letter and in spirit, in principle and in practice," to the original basis of doctrine and fellowship. Seeking after this it finds—

(1) That all who put their faith in Jesus as the Christ, the Son of God, and for his sake left their sins and renounced all other lordships, were at once accepted as worthy to enter this fellowship. *Faith in the Divine Lord and Saviour was the one essential condition of entrance.* None could enter without faith—infant membership was therefore impossible. None who had faith could be refused admission—no other test was allowed but that of faith in and submission to Jesus, the Christ. We therefore proclaim, in opposition to all big and little creeds in Christendom, *that the original creed has but one article of faith in it, namely*: That Jesus is the Christ, the Son of God. All doctrinal tests but this must be abandoned.

(2) That all such believers were admitted into this fellowship by baptism, upon the authority of Jesus Christ, into the name of the Father, and of the Son, and of the Holy Spirit. We have said in a former chapter that there ought to be no stumbling here, if there is indeed a desire for union; since all admit that immersion is baptism, and nothing else is admitted by all. It can only be the stubbornness of the sect-spirit that prevents union in that which all can accept. The only real difficulty here in the way relates to those who have received pouring or sprinkling in adult years, and have conscientious scruples about repeating, as they would regard it, an obedience already rendered. These, however, are exceptional cases, and would soon adjust themselves if it were at once settled that nothing should hereafter be practiced but that which all agree to be sufficient.

(3) That among these baptized believers there was no ecclesiastical caste—no distinction of clergy and laity; but all were brethren, and none was to be called Master or Father. The order of the church must harmonize with this. Nothing must be insisted upon as of Divine authority, or be made a test of fellowship, for which there is not a *thus saith the Lord*, in express precept or approved precedent.

4. In all matters where there is no express precept or precedent, the law of love should lead us to that which will promote edification and peace.

a. In matters merely inferential, unanimity is to be sought, but not forced.

b. In matters merely prudential, the majority should rule, care being had, however, not to transcend the limits of expediency by contravening any Divine precept; and regard always being had to the prejudices and welfare of all.

c. Where Christ has left us free, no man has a right to judge his brother. The largest liberty is here allowed, limited only by the spirit of apostolic teaching: 'If meat cause my brother to stumble, I will eat no meat while the world stands.'

Such is, in brief, what we propose as a basis of union. We have no desire for mere organic union any faster than a supreme love for Christ leads to unity of spirit, and prepares men for the voluntary sacrifice of all but Christ.

We have no faith in the practicability of uniting sects on any merely sectarian basis, however liberal. It cannot be Christian union unless it is union in Christ—in that which Christ enjoins, neither less nor more. The present unwillingness, with all the prevalent union sentiment, to abandon sectarian names and interests, proves how unavailing all attempts at a union of parties, as such, must prove. We do not, therefore, propose the union of sects; but call on all the people of God in the various sects to come out from them and unite in the faith and practice taught in the New Testament. We propose in this way to subvert sectarianism—calling the lovers of Jesus out from the sects, and leavening those who refuse to come with the doctrine of the New Testament until they, too, shall be ready to give up the sect for Christ.[1]

Mr. Errett has stated the issues well and completely in this brief of the movement. The tract, from which this statement is taken, deserves wide circulation even today among the people who have taken over the advocacy of this great idea.

The one point in Mr. Errett's statement which may raise a question is his indication that the only difficulty involves those who "have received pouring or sprinkling in adult years, and have conscientious scruples about repeating, as they would regard it, an obedience already rendered." His solution seems to imply that such would be accepted but that new converts would be immersed in accord with the scriptural pattern and design. According to Mr. Errett, this practice would soon eliminate the problem. This is most certainly not the position which has been taken in the bulk of the statements we have considered. The objectives of the Plea, historically considered, would be to convince such persons that they had not rendered complete obedience and to require that such be met before fellowship be granted.

The year 1877 brings forth a statement by Nathan J. Mitchell. He says:

If, as is stated in terms in nearly all the creed books of the Protestant sects, the sacred Scriptures furnish an infallible rule of faith and practice, we may discard all rules made by men, and be guided in our action by the very same commandments which were heard and obeyed when the Christian religion was first introduced into the world. Turning away from all that is modern, and being guided solely by the New Testament, we secure, not only a *reformation* of any sect, or sects, but a *restoration of primitive, Apostolic Christianity*. There are many sects which declare their reverence for the Bible by affirming their confidence in what it teaches by devising and using other and different rules in their practice. The disciples of Christ would show to all men their confidence in the word of God by implicit obedience to its teachings, and by an unwavering repudiation of all it does not teach; and if our practice can be brought fully to correspond with this theory, there will, beyond a doubt, be a church existing in the world, differing nothing in faith and practice from that which ex-

---

[1]Isaac Errett, *Our Position*, (Cincinnati: The Standard Publishing Company, n. d.), pp. 22-25.

isted under the teaching of the apostles of the Lord Jesus. And those who compose this church can not, with any regard to a proper use of language, be called a sect . . . .

In short, whatever the apostles taught, the disciples re-preach and re-teach. We know nothing but what the apostles taught as constituting any part of the faith once delivered to the saints. Certainly no living man does; therefore, the disciples have no peculiarities. All hold to and insist upon these things and whatever else was taught by the apostles, without raising and teaching theories on the philosophy of the things taught by the authority of our Lord Jesus Christ. All who believe that the Bible is the Book of God must receive its statement on any question, whether capable of sounding their depths or not; and when the statements of fact it contains are believed, and the commands it teaches obeyed, all who so believe and obey become simply disciples of the Son of God, with all the obligations and glorious privileges of children of the Most High.[1]

The high reverence of Mr. Mitchell for the word of the Lord is worthy of special note. His again is an appeal to the teachings and commandments of the New Testament. Some have supposed that the churches of Christ today have two messages one for union and the other the gospel, but such is grossly in error. The message of the churches of Christ is the gospel of Christ, nothing more nothing less. It is an appeal to all men to accept Jesus Christ as Lord and Saviour, in the terms and manner prescribed in the New Testament, and then to co-operate with one another in gaining this same acceptance of all others.

In the following statement, Samuel Rogers reviews his relationship to and his regard for the Plea:

Having been in the bondage of Egypt, and having felt the scorpion lash of sectarianism, I know, as those who were free-born can never know, how sweet a thing it is to enjoy the light and liberty of the gospel of truth, both as to faith and practice. Our children think us in our dotage, and that we see ghosts and hobgoblins where no real danger exists. But I know what I am talking about, and would warn them against any, even the slightest, departure from the plain teaching of the word of God. I am willing to be a liberal, and will be as far as it is lawful; but I must not be liberal at the expense of the truth. We may be as liberal as we please with our own things, such as our opinions and speculations, for they are private property; but let us be careful how we touch the Ark of God . . . .[2]

In those days we were emphatically a Bible people. The Scriptures were our daily study; we attempted to do nothing as a church or as individuals, without the divine warrant. As we assembled together to worship on the Lord's day, we resembled more a school of children, with textbooks in hand, than a modern congregation of worshippers.[3]

. . . .Men can never agree on opinions—they have no binding authority, and should not have. But in matters of faith, tens of thousands have been united and millions more may be. All that is needed for the accomplishment of this end, is a high regard for the plain teachings of God's Word. On matters of faith, there would be but one mind and one voice, today, but for the fact that men have made void the Word of God by their

[1]Nathan J. Mitchell, *Reminiscences and Incidents in the Life and Travels of a Pioneer Preacher,* (Cincinnati: Chase and Hall, 1877), pp. 192-194.

[2]John I. Rogers, Editor, *Autobiography of Elder Samuel Rogers,* (Cincinnati: Standard Publishing Company, 1909), p. 124.   [3]*Ibid.,* p. 123.

traditions. Of course, so long as men cling to traditions, and boldly set at defiance God's holy Word, there can be no hope of union. But if the day should ever come, when the whole Christian world shall hold God's Word in greater reverence than they do human traditions and speculations, then the whole Christian world will be one. I may be charged with a want of Christian charity; but I shall die in the opinion that nothing but a criminal contempt for God's Word is at the bottom of all our divisions.[1]

So wrote Samuel Rogers, sometime before his death in 1877. Again the appeal is to the scriptures, this time for a high regard for the word. The picture set forth in the second paragraph above is certainly from a day long since past, but the ills of the church would certainly fall aside, like the bundles of burden from Christian's back in *Pilgrim's Progress*, if, again, the people would assemble more as childen with text-book in hand then as a modern congregation of worshippers. That division is based upon a "criminal" contempt for God's word may be rather strong, but that it is based upon a criminal neglect the thinking man would probably not deny.

In the year 1879, Benjamin Franklin had the following to say upon the subject before us:

IN WHAT are Christians to be united?

They are to be united *on Christ*—on *being Christians*. This embraces the entire revelation from God to man, all the truth uttered, the commandments given and the promises made by our heavenly Father. The truth must all be believed, the commandments obeyed, and the promises must be hoped for. This includes the entire faith, obedience and hope of the gospel. *In this* we must be united.[2]

Mr. Franklin goes on to say, in answer to the question "What are the essentials of Christianity which cannot be compromised?" that "Christianity itself, as a whole and in all its parts, is essential." He adds: "The wisdom of God gives us no non-essential." However, the most important expression here is that Christians "are to be united on Christ on being Christians."

Henry Russell Pritchard, about the year 1880, published a pamphlet in which he made the following remarks:

I have been associated with some of the men who were in the beginning when that "one rule" was made, have talked with Campbell and Scott about it, and never heard but one interpretation of that "one rule" till I had been preaching in the church thirty years. That was: We will teach for Christianity what the Scriptures teach, and do it in the words of the Scriptures, and make these things, and these things only, the tests of Christian fellowship, and the terms of union and communion among all Christians. Second, we will grant to our fellow-Christians the most perfect freedom of opinion; but we will not teach for Christianity any dogma, or church polity, as taught by the creeds of the times, and make such things tests of fellowship and terms of union among God's people. Hence, it was union upon what the Lord says, and perfect freedom upon what He does not say.[3]

The "one rule" of which Mr. Pritchard writes is the classic statement, "Where the Scriptures speak, we speak; where the Scriptures are silent, we are silent."

[1]*Ibid.*, p. 118.   [2]Franklin, *op. cit.*, p. 36.

[3]Henry Russell Pritchard, *Innovations, So called*, (Indianapolis: E. B. Schofield, n. d.), p. 5.

In the review as stated here, Mr. Pritchard has set forth very well his own position in the matter before us. He, too, would teach for Christianity the doctrine of the New Testament and let the creeds, disciplines, and dogmas of men "go to their own place."

W. Sumpter, writing in the year 1880, composed the following:

> Christian union is not an agreement simply, between Methodists, Baptists, etc., touching certain fundamental principles, yet, each party adhering to its own sectarian name, organization, etc., that would be sectarian union. The Book speaks not of Methodist Christians, Baptist Christians, or Presbyterian Christians; the followers of Christ were simply Christians in primitive times, and we think that we have no right to assume more at this day. The following principles must be observed, before there can be the Christian union contemplated by the great head of the church.
>
> 1. The union must be on the word of God alone.
> 2. The church must have its scriptural name.
> 3. The people thus united shall be called Christians.
> 4. Everything existing among professing Christians, which is not authorized by the word of God, must be set aside.
> 5. We must preach the same gospel; and that, the gospel of the Lord Jesus Christ.[1]

The fact that a union of denominations, continuing as they now are, would not be "Christian union" has been brought out before, but Mr. Sumpter brings it forth here again. There are still many persons who confuse denominational union with Christian union; the former is the co-operation of sects, while the latter is the co-operation of Christians. Clear thinking is very much needed upon this issue.

Also in the year 1880, F. M. Kirkham set forth this fine analysis of the ends or purposes of the movement. Mr. Kirkham writes as follows:

> The end, the proximate end, for which we plead has been and is, "the union of Christians," with the ultimate end in view, the salvation of the world in accordance with the prayer of our Saviour wherein he said, "Neither pray I for these (the apostles) alone, but for all them also who shall believe on me through their word, that they may all be one, as thou Father, art in me and I in Thee, that they also may be one in us; *that the world may believe that thou hast* sent me."—John 17:20-21.
>
> Thus our plea contemplates both proximate and ultimate results.
>
> But our plea for Christian union, and its legitimate and necessarily involved results, the salvation of the world and the glory of God, would be impotent if it did not set forth the means requisite for its accomplishment. Accordingly, with our plea for union, has been urged "the restoration of primitive apostolic Christianity in letter and in spirit, in principle and in practice," as the necessary and Divinely ordained means for its attainment.[2]

Again it is pointed out that the restoration of primitive Christianity is a necessary prerequisite both to the union of Christians and the conversion of the world. The phrase "union of Christians" presupposes that there are Christians to unite, thus, if a person is not a Christian, he must be converted to Christ before he can have any part in any co-operation of Christians. The conversion of the world, that is the conversion of the individuals in it, must be accomplished

---

[1]*Evangelist*, Vol. 14, No. 32, p. 517.   [2]*Evangelist*, Vol. 14, No. 41, p. 640.

through the means of conversion employed by the Christians of primitive times, for such is the only authoritative means known to man. The whole problem of Christian union and unity and world conversion is thus shown to revolve itself around the question, "What must I do to be saved?"

One of the most famous statements of the position of the Restoration movement is that of James A. Garfield, martyred president of the United States and formerly a preacher of the church of Christ. It was a long search, through many books and pamphlets, ending in failure, to find the original source of this statement. However, the statement was found in several works. The following is the account of Thomas W. Phillips:

> General Garfield was present at that meeting, the publication of the *Christian Standard* was decided upon, stock subscribed, and Isaac Errett, one of our ablest men, chosen editor.
>
> In this connection it seems fitting to quote Garfield's statement concerning the religious principles of the disciples.
>
> 1. We call ourselves Christians, or disciples of Christ.
>
> 2. We believe in God the Father.
>
> 3. We believe that Jesus is the Christ, the Son of the living God, and our Saviour. We regard the divinity of Christ as the fundamental truth of the Christian system.
>
> 4. We believe in the Holy Spirit, both as to his agency in conversion and as an indweller in the heart of the Christian.
>
> 5. We accept both the Old and New Testament Scriptures as the inspired word of God.
>
> 6. We believe in the future punishment of the wicked and the future reward of the righteous.
>
> 7. We believe that deity is a prayer-hearing and a prayer-answering God.
>
> 8. We observe the institution of the Lord's Supper on the Lord's Day. To this table we neither invite nor debar; we say it is the Lord's Supper for all the Lord's children.
>
> 9. We plead for the union of God's people on the Bible, and the Bible alone.
>
> 10. The Christ is our only creed.
>
> 11. We maintain that all ordinances should be observed as they were in the days of the apostles.[1]

The sentiments expressed above are worthy of a great man. Garfield was on no digression from the Plea. The statement dates about 1880.

J. W. Butler is the author of the following review of the movement and of the Plea. Says Mr. Butler:

> Our fathers in this movement made a new call, the noble call to *return*. A new plea was made, one that had never been distinctly made by any previous reformer, the plea to *restore* that which had been lost in the apostasy—to restore primitive Christianity. The makers of this new plea said: "Let us come firmly and fairly to original ground, and take up things just as the apostles left them." This was not to enter the arena of contending parties, and fight for the supremacy as a party. It was not to

---

[1]Thomas W. Phillips, *The Church of Christ*, (Cincinnati: The Standard Publishing Company, 1915), pp. 461, 462.

run the gauntlet of the doctors of divinity by defending this or opposing that set of human doctrines; but it was to refuse all human speculations. It was to go back over the intervening centuries, and take up Christianity where the apostles laid it down in the beginning. This was no ordinary blow at humanism; for it not only decapitated the great pope, but also all the little popes, and restored Christ, the absolute and practical head of the church. It restored the word of the living God as the only rule of faith and practice to the Christian. It took away the spirit of party adherence; and put into its place a holy life as developed by faith in God, and obedience to his commands, as the basis of Christian fellowship. It destroyed the foolish and weak distinction between essentials and non-essentials in religion; and put in its place the noble sentiment, that the human heart should reverently bow to the authority of God, wherever found.

Christian Union was inscribed high upon our banners in the beginning; and today, brethren, it still remains where our fathers placed it. Let no degenerate son be found among us, who can, with ruthless hands, erase these noble words, Christian Union, from our escutcheon. If any should claim that Christian unity is better than Christian union, with such we will not contend; but we say, give us *both*, unity first, and union is the heavenly result.[1]

Certainly this statement needs no interpretation. The statement itself is an analysis and a plea, in harmony with many that have gone before. It deserves careful attention by all who claim to be a part of the movement to restore the Christianity of the New Testament. The date of the statement is 1883.

John F. Rowe, in 1884, published a statement in which he listed the things believed by the Restoration movement or the churches of Christ. The listing is proof positive that Mr. Rowe considered the New Testament to be the only source of authority in matters of faith and practice. At the close of the list, Mr. Rowe says the following:

What we have now mapped out as the ground we occupy, we are thoroughly convinced is truly the apostolic ground, and a ground of unity about which there can be no intelligent controversy. The ground we occupy excludes sectarianism. All the people of God may occupy this ground. We invite all men to receive the same Bible we receive; to accept the same creed we accept; to honor the same Lord we honor; to obey the same gospel we obey; to bear the same scriptural titles we bear; to "walk by the same rules," to "mind the same things," to "speak the same things," to be "joined together in the same judgment," to contend earnestly for the same faith.[2]

Since the ground occupied is the same ground the apostles occupied, Mr. Rowe is convinced that the basis suggested is authoritative and will find acceptance in the minds of the people.

Reviewing a sermon he had preached, Samuel K. Hoshour, in the year 1884, says:

I made the twentieth, twenty-first, and twenty-second verses of the twenty-eighth chapter of Acts the basis of my discourse. The main point was: The "Sect everywhere spoken against." I showed that that sect was not any of the sects with which we are familiar in our day. That these

[1] *Christian Quarterly Review*, Vol. 2, pp. 401, 402.

[2] John F. Rowe, *History of Reformatory Movements*, (Cincinnati: G. W. Rice, Publisher, 1884), p. 204.

were all too young. I delineated that primitive sect in all its salient characteristics; its head or founder, *Jesus of Nazareth*, how the head was made manifest, namely, when he was baptized (John i:31); how the *sect* was formed by faith and baptism (see John iii:22, John iv:1, Acts ii:41, Acts viii: 30-39); what the sect believed,—that Jesus was the Christ, the Son of the living God; their name, Disciples, Christians; their nicknames, "Galileans," "Nazarenes;" why they were everywhere spoken against,—not because of any bad principles, for they embodied the purest morality in the world; but because they unwaiveringly believed that Jesus was the son of God,—the rightful sovereign of the universe; because they claimed that they alone had the true religion; because, the unbelieving Jews, their first opponents slandered them among the Gentiles,—raised bad reports of them, etc.[1]

The above signifies the position held by Mr. Hoshour. Like Mr. Campbell, he would be a member of no sect but the sect everywhere spoken against.

Some very important thoughts are expressed in the next statement, made by J. S. Lamar, in the year 1884. Says Mr. Lamar:

. . . . Looking abroad over the field of Protestantism, they saw that it was cursed by divisions, which embittered its spirit and weakened its in-influence. Then in the Bible they noted that this state of things was positively prohibited and denounced as carnal and sinful. But was it possible to correct it? Could any basis be formed or found upon which elements so heterogeneous and antagonistic might unite in peace and love? In answer to this question they were led to believe that the Bible was such a basis . . . . No amalgamation of parties is contemplated; no passing over of one sect into another; no breaking up of existing congregations; no suspension of any good work; no compromise of good conscience; no sacrifice of truth; and no loss of self-respect or Christian freedom.[2]

With this much to portray the setting and create interest, Mr. Lamar continues:

In order to set forth my idea with yet more definiteness and precision let me say in brief that I regard the true basis of Christian union as being identically the same as the true foundation of the church, namely, the Rock, the Tried Stone, which God laid in Zion. And all of every land and every name who are truly built on this, and are faithfully building themselves up on it, whatever their divergencies and differences respecting a thousand questions of New Testament hermeneutics, I regard as being in true and vital Christian unity. They are all *one* in Christ Jesus . . . .

Christians are united with each other just because they are united to Christ. In him they are gathered together in one. He is the bond of peace, and in him is the unity of the Spirit. The New Testament tells us *how* to get to him, and *how* to obtain this Spirit, and so, *how* to form and to perpetuate Christian union.[3]

. . . . Thus united, we also sustain and maintain a certain definite *relation* to the New Testament, which may be peculiar to us, but which, never-the-less, is not the relation of superstructure to foundation. It is rather that of submission to authority. This may be better expressed in two propositions: 1. That the New Testament is authoritative in matters of religion; and 2. That in these matters it *alone* is authoritative. According to the first of these propositions we are pledged and bound to submit

---

[1] Samuel K. Hoshour, *Autobiography - Samuel K. Hosbour,* (St. Louis: John Burns Publishing Company, 1884), p. 84.   [2] *Disciple of Christ,* Vol. I, No. 5, p. 130.
[3] *Disciple of Christ,* Vol. I, No. 10, pp. 294, 295.

to this authority; according to the second we are free from submission to any other authority. Neither proposition alone would express the whole truth of this relation.[1]

Mr. Lamar's position has been expressed before in other terms, but he has made it very clear in this statement. One thing of note is the second of his propositions describing our relationship to the New Testament. "We are free from submission to any other authority." To this, and the first proposition, attention is specifically called. We are free from all authority outside of the New Testament, including that authority self appointed who would make rules derived from inferences drawn from scripture premises to cover silences of the scripture. The person who says, "You must do this or that," when God says nothing is a little creed maker in his own right.

In the year 1885, Frederick D. Power made the following statement:

How then may spiritual, organic, and practical oneness be secured? One word is the key to it. Restoration! Not legislation, not confederation but restoration of the original apostolic New Testament church with its doctrine, its ordinances and its fruits. We must step up the stream of eighteen centuries and stand at the fountain head. We must go back to the spirit, the unity, the faith, the practice, the foundation of the early church. By returning to Jerusalem it is possible to take up the gospel just as the apostles left it, to receive the ordinances just as our Lord delivered them, to discover the church just as it existed in its primitive purity and simplicity, to establish ourselves upon the eternal rock just as did Saul of Tarsus and the thousands of that early time and to revive once more in the glory of its original beauty and splendor the Christian institution.[2]

Such precisely is the position of the Restoration movement, as has been demonstrated so many times already in this research. We have found but few stating otherwise to this time.

Publication of the following statement by F. G. Allen was made in the year 1866.

The primary object of the religious work in whose interests we are here assembled, was—

I. *To restore the Church to the world as it was when left by the Apostles* . . . .

(1) This work of reformation demands that we accept Christ as our only creed, and the Bible as our only rule of faith and practice . . . .

(2) Our work demands that we hold to the simplicity of conversion, and admission into the Church by Baptism, just as we find them in the New Testament . . . .

(3) Our work demands that we call Bible things by Bible names . . . .

II. *Our plea for Christian union* . . . .

(1) Our plea for Christian union implies that there are Christians to unite . . . .

(2) Our plea for the union of God's people implies that the Church of God includes more than those engaged in this work of restoration. In other words, that the Church of God is a more comprehensive term than those descriptive of our work . . . .

[1]*Disciple of Christ*, Vol. I, No. 11, p. 326.   [2]*Christian Evangelist*, Vol. 22, No. 24, p. 372.

(3) From this it follows that our work of restoration is wholly undenominational . . . .

III. *Unity of faith and diversity of opinion* . . . .

(1) From the distinction between faith and opinion it follows that nothing should be claimed as an item of faith that is not clearly expressed by precept, example or necessary inference . . . .

(2) From this it follows that we may make nothing a test of fellowship that Christ has not made a condition of salvation . . . .

(3) While our plea demands conformity to the precepts and examples of God's word, we should carefully mark the distinction between the essentials and the incidentals of that age of the Church which we have accepted as an example for our imitation.[1]

Mr. Allen has conveniently outlined "our plea" for our investigation. The simplicity of the whole proposition may be clearly noted here. There is not one premise in the group that is difficult to understand. This is one of the sources of the power of the Plea and an essential to its acceptance.

The year 1887 brought forth the statement below from the pen of W. L. Hayden. Mr. Hayden asserts:

This was not merely a reformation; it was a complete restoration of primitive Christianity "in letter and in spirit, in principle and in practice," in its pristine purity, its perfect unity and original power. In order to such a restoration we must go back to the "beginning of the gospel of the Son of God." Whatever can not be found *at* the beginning, sanctioned by inspired precept or precedent, is not *from* the beginning, and is therefore without divine authority.

Hence the grand men who became the great lights in this restoration movement went back of all reformations; back of the great apostasy that culminated in the Roman papacy; back of the age of ecclesiastical councils and of human formulated creeds, and planted their feet upon the primitive rock, upon which Jesus said: "I will build my Church." They stood in the ways, and saw, and asked "for the old paths, where is the good way," and walked therein and found "rest to their souls."

This led to the repudiation of all creeds of human formation as authoritative, or as terms of fellowship, and of all changes in ordinances by the Romish Church and its later imitators. It led to the first grasp of the plain precepts of the Word of God and its approved precedents as expressive of the will of God in respect to the terms of salvation, the worship of God and the discipline and deportment of the members of the church. That will thus expressed is the only and all-sufficient rule of faith and discipline in the Christian Church.[2]

This conception of going back of everything to the beginning of the gospel has appeared in several of the statements considered within the past few pages of this thesis. It is a precise statement of the thing sought to be accomplished by the advocates of the Restoration Plea. That which was established in the beginning of the church is binding upon all men who would call themselves Christians; the opinions of men or their speculations of the intervening centuries are not.

[1] F. G. Allen, *The Old-Path Pulpit*, (Covington: Guide Printing and Publishing Co., 1886), pp. 164-172.

[2] W. L. Hayden, *What Is the Christian Church*, (An address delivered before the Pennsylvania Christian Missionary Convention at Johnstown, Oct. 6, 1887), pp. 3, 4.

Pardee Butler, who labored many years in the state of Kansas, sought to establish New Testament Christianity in that state when settlers were first beginning to enter. The following is an excerpt from a sermon preached by Mr. Butler upon this very subject. Said he:

My friends and fellow citizens, I have the honor to represent to you a people that have said we will go back to that order of things originally established by Jesus and the apostles—we will make no vow of loyalty to any but Jesus, and we will have no bond of union save the testimonies and commandments of the Lord as given to us by the Lord himself and the holy apostles. Out of this we hope may grow such a union of God's people as Jesus prayed for when he prayed that all Christians might be one. We are striving for such an order of things that Protestants may present a united front against the world, the flesh and the devil, and against all disloyalty to Jesus.[1]

Mr. Butler's understanding of the intention of the Restoration movement is clearly made known in the above statement, and differs nothing from the main stream of thought as this dissertation has revealed it. The Year is 1889.

J. V. Coombs presents the following interesting statement:

The denominations *may* be right. They *may* be wrong. We are right, and *can not* be wrong. It *may* be right to make a human creed. It *may* be wrong. We take the Bible as our creed, hence *can not* be wrong. Human names *may* be right, or they may be wrong. All agree it is right to be called Christian. We can not be wrong in wearing that name. If you have a doubt, *you*, and not *God*, are responsible for that doubt. Sprinkling may be right (for argument's sake), or it may be wrong. All admit immersion is valid baptism. We are right, and can not be wrong in practicing only immersion. If you doubt your baptism, you can remove that doubt by being immersed, for all accept immersion.[2]

It is presumed that the argument, as presented, is designed to appeal to the desire of men for security. Any man of sound mind will take the surest way.

In a published sermon, in the year 1892, John S. Sweeney stated the position of the Restoration movement briefly but accurately in the following words:

Can we find that primitive Christianity and church? We have decided that we can, and that by the help of God we will direct all the people of God in the world to it. We believe that it is to be found in the New Testament and only there. This is generally conceded when the New Testament is said to be an all-sufficient rule of faith and practice. Then we must return to the New Testament; not through the creeds and churches, but directly. We will never get back if we undertake to go through all the creeds and churches in the order in which they came into being. Never in the world. The way to get back is to let go all creeds and parties, all humanisms, and go back. Let go just now, and right where we are, and return at once. That is the only way it can be done. Cut entirely loose, and at once, from all human creeds and parties, and return and take our stand with the apostles and first Christians. Can we do it? Certainly. The New Testament will afford us all the necessary light and means. If not, then it is not an all-sufficient rule of faith and practice. But we believe that it is, and to return to its teachings for our faith and practice, to make it,

[1]Pardee Butler, *Personal Recollections of Pardee Butler*, (Cincinnati: Standard Publishing Company, 1889), pp.57, 58.

[2]J. V. Coombs, *Our Plea*, (A Tract of a sermon preached by J. V. Coombs in the Christian Church, Noblesville, Indiana, March 30, 1890), p. 8.

and it only, authoritative in all things essential to salvation. This is our fundamental aim.[1]

It is again to be noted that Mr. Sweeney does not drift from the established position. His loyalty to God's word and his complete disregard for the creeds and councils of men is typical of the statements of the Plea of this day. The question of the rightness of the idea did not enter their minds. This was the way to the oneness of God's people, and they sought to follow in that way.

In a sermon published by John W. McGarvey in 1894, he sets forth the idea that the Jerusalem Church is the perfect model for the emulation of all churches today. He presents, then, the solution to the problem of a divided Christianity in the following manner:

> Let me say, that we have here in the Jerusalem church not only a perfect model of Christian union, but also the Lord's own method of working toward the universal unity of the people of God. God began by bringing into existence one church perfectly united in itself and in Him, and then went on to originate others that were called on to imitate this. Had they done so, there would have been universal unity as far as the faith in Christ extended. So now, if we would bring about unity once more, we must begin by having at least one perfectly united congregation. Do you know such a congregation? Would you not travel many miles to see a church of even a few hundred members, of whom it could be truly said that they are all of one heart and soul, and that not one of them says that anything he has is his own? But until we have some such churches as that, how can we possibly have Christian union? If we could today bring into union all the congregations in the United States without a material change of each within itself, we should not have the unity for which our Saviour prayed. It would be a jumbling together of many incongruous elements.[2]

Continuing this apeal, Mr. McGarvey says:

> Some of us are obviously looking in the wrong direction for a restoration of the unity which once existed. We must look backward to the church that was, and not forward to some imaginary church of the future, for the model of union, and the union must begin in the individual congregation. When you get one congregation united in the Lord, you have made the right start, the start which the Lord himself made. Then get another and another into the same condition, and you will have them united with one another as fast as they become united within themselves in the Lord. The man, then, who is doing the most today for the final union of all of God's people, is not the man who is making the most noise about it, and getting up the biggest conventions to consider the subject, but the man who is doing the most to establish the unity of the Spirit in the midst of some single congregation, and thus reproducing the model church of old. Why can not the church which I am now addressing be the one to first set an example in this direction? Here is your model. See that you work according to it.[3]

According to Mr. McGarvey, then, Christian union will be the result of the bringing to be of a world of local congregations, which have been established according to the model of the New Testament church by the accomplishment of the unity or oneness of the individuals of those congregations with Christ.

[1]John S. Sweeney, *Sweeney's Sermons,* (Nashville: Gospel Advocate Publishing Company, 1892), pp. 135, 136.
[2]J. W. McGarvey, *Sermons,* (Louisville: Guide Printing and Publishing Company, 1894), pp. 250, 251.   [3]*Ibid.,* p. 251.

The problem before us is the problem of making Christians, uniting persons with Jesus the Christ, or accomplishing the union of the efforts of those Christians locally, and, finally, the union of the efforts of the local congregations on a world-wide scale. So reasons Mr. McGarvey.

Attention should be called to the fact that the above solution presents a problem at the point of the co-operation of the local congregations. There are many questions that could be raised in regard to that relationship. Who is to direct the union of their efforts? In what is it to consist? Who is to do the work which such union would seek to accomplish? Christian union, it seems, must be kept a union of Christians and not of congregations. The New Testament recognizes no interlocking connection between congregations other than that of a common faith in Jesus as Lord. Some have asserted that the churches in Iconium and Lystra seem to have joined in recommending Timothy to Paul, but the word says that he "was well reported of by the *brethren* that were at Lystra and Iconium."[1] It was the union of the brethren of Lystra and Iconium and not of the churches that brought about Timothy's call to serve in the evangelistic party of Paul.

So, the local congregations are to see the accomplishment of the Lord's business through the co-operation of the local Christians; world-wide evangelism must be accomplished through the co-operation of Christians in that business, and not through a union of churches, over which someone could at once set himself up as head. Not one thing can be accomplished through a union of churches and the setting up of an authority over it, in so far as the effort of the local congregation is concerned, that could not be accomplished as well or better without it. Thus, the union of Christians in world evangelism should claim the attention of men and not union in the control of churches. Aside from this, Mr. McGarvey's statement pictures correctly the solution to the problem, as pled by the Restoration movement.

Earlier in this thesis, it was pointed out that the message of the Plea was to take two directions, to the heathen sinner, and to the incompletely converted. I. B. Grubbs also makes this point in the following statement of the Plea, published in the year 1896. Mr. Grubbs proclaims:

> Evangelism resulting in the utter destruction of denominationalism or sectism and in the complete recognition of Christ Jesus in all the fullness of his claims upon the human heart and life is the only way to effect the unity of Christians which the Scriptures require . . . .

> And as evangelism, or the faithful preaching of Christ Jesus to all men, is the only way to establish the union of believers, so the Christ who is thus preached is the only ground on which they can be brought to spiritual oneness. "Other foundation can no man lay" for the united church of the living God. The way to this blessed unity is not through denominational confederation based on a partial recognition of Christ as in Endeavor conventions and so-called "union meetings," but through the evangelistic presentation of Christ in all the fullness of his teaching and authority to the world religious as well as the world irreligious . . . .

> Moreover this evangelism must not stop with the unconverted. To much of the religious world it is needful to preach Christ in the fullness of his divine teaching and authoritative claims. Apollos knew more of Christ than

---

[1] Acts 16:2.

Cornelius and Cornelius far more than the Philippian Jailer; yet all these alike had to be instructed in "the way of the Lord" in proportion as each stood in need of enlightenment. It was in this way alone that all could come "in the unity of the faith and of the knowledge of the Son of God" to Spiritual oneness in Christ . . . .[1]

If the New Testament contains the record of the redemption of men and the means to be used by men in the appropriation of that redemption, then it cannot be truly said that men are converted until they accept the plan God has offered in the manner prescribed by him. Such is evangelism, which Mr. Grubbs describes as the "only way to effect the unity of Christians which the scriptures require." The requirements for salvation must become the *only* terms of fellowship, but they must become *the* terms of fellowship if unity is to be.

James A. Lord, in the year 1898, has the following statement to offer to our considerations here. Says he:

> The term, "our plea," is used much in the same sense in which Paul used the term, "my gospel." It is the plea that certain disciples of Christ who are simply Christians, make to the rest of their fellowmen. It is their plea not in the sense of ownership, but of trust. In fact, it is Christ's plea, and nothing more or less than the everlasting gospel of the grace of God.

> And first, this plea is an admonition to all men to forsake their sins and seek forgiveness through Christ . . . . . It is the invitation of our heavenly Father to his erring creatures to counsel with him with respect to their escape from the consequences of past sins. "Come now and let us reason together, saith the Lord; though your sins be as scarlet, they shall be as white as snow; though they be red like crimson, they shall be as wool."

> This plea, if heeded, would bring all men together in Christ, so that their fellowship with God and Christ and the Holy Spirit would also be the ground of their fellowship with one another. This means that, enjoying the same salvation, they are to be joined together in one saved body, called the church. Hence, toward men the two features of this great plea are first, the salvation of sinners; and, second, the unity of believers.[2]

Mr. Lord places a slightly different emphasis here, but essentially it falls into complete accord with what has gone before.

B. B. Tyler, in 1898, reviewed the Christian situation as follows:

> Pleas for Christian union are popular. Since the body of Christ was rent by schismatics, many efforts have been made by good and earnest men to heal the breaches. Their efforts, as all the world knows, have been ineffectual. The church is still divided. Believers are not "perfectly joined together in the same mind and in the same judgment." The suggested bases have not been practical. The methods have been, sometimes, utopian. The reasons for union have not always been Christian. The aims have not, in every instance, been lofty. The benediction of the Head of the Body has not, it is evident, rested on these efforts.

> The Christ himself founded his church. He gave it a creed. He appointed the conditions of admission. Its ordinances exist by his authority. They are to be observed with reference to him. Apart from him they possess no value. In connection with him they are significant and spiritually helpful. But out of this connection they are destitute of meaning and value. The purpose and work of Christ's church are not left to vague conjecture. The Church of Christ is not an evolution; it is a ceation. "I will build," said

---

[1] *Christian-Evangelist*, Vol. 33, No. 29, p. 454.   [2] *Christian Standard*, Vol. 34, No. 51, p. 1641.

Jesus; and he built. He built his church as he would have it. As he built his church in the beginning, so it ought to be today—in its creed, its ordinances, its life.

The only practical solution of the problem of Christian union is by a return to the Christ. "Back to Christ," ought to be the watchword. But this word ought to signify, "Back to the Christ of the New Testament."[1]

Attention is called to Mr. Tyler's statement that "the Church of Christ is not an evolution; it is a creation." This has, as we have seen, been the position of the movement all along, since it is the position of the New Testament. As will be seen later, some today would regard the church as an evolution. Also, it is well to call attention to the statement, "Back to the Christ of the New Testament." This has always been the cry of the Restoration movement, back to the Christ of the New Testament, not someone's interpretation of the Christ of the New Testament.

J. H. Garrison, in 1899, summarized the Plea in the manner and form below recorded:

This modern plea emphasizes several fundamental truths:

1. It is a plea or unity. Not a consolidation of sects into one huge ecclesiasticism, but such union with Christ, and such conformity to his teaching, as will bring all his followers into fellowship and co-operation with each other in the great work of converting the world. It is not uniformity of thought, or of opinion, or of modes of worship, or of organization, that is insisted on as essential to the fulfillment of Christ's prayer for the oneness of his followers, but oneness in faith, in submission to the sole authority and leadership of Christ, and in the spirit and aim of Christian service . . . . It is a union in Christ, with Christ, under Christ, and for Christ. This alone is Christian union.

2. It is a plea for liberty. No sooner had our fathers lifted their voices for unity among believers than they found the chief obstacle in the way of realizing it to be ecclesiastical authority, as that authority had embodied itself in the conflicting creeds of Christendom, and in competing organizations resting on these several creeds . . . . It was not the liberty of rejecting divine authority which they demanded, but the liberty of rejecting human authority whenever and wherever it came in conflict with the authority of God in Christ. In other words, it was Christian liberty for which they pled—the liberty not only to reject whatever error human authority had imposed, but the liberty to receive all truth, as God enables us to see it.

3. It is a plea for loyalty. The holy scriptures to which they made their appeal point unmistakably to Christ as the One possessing "all authority, both in heaven and on earth." They show, also, that the confession of Him as Lord and Christ is the true and divinely-given confession of faith on which the Church was to be built. Loyalty to Him, then, became the true test of fellowship . . . . Any idea of liberty or of liberalism which involves disloyalty to Christ, is at war with one of the fundamental principles of our plea, and is based upon a false conception of what constitutes true liberty . . . .

4. It is a plea for a return to New Testament evangelism. The plain, simple method of the apostles in preaching Christ to the people until they were convinced of sin, and then pointing out the way of salvation from sin, through faith in, confession of, and obedience to, Christ, had become ob-

[1] *Christian Standard*, Vol. 34, No. 34, p. 1085.

scured by human traditions. Our plea includes the restoration of the simplicity of the gospel, in its facts, commands, and ordinances . . . .

5. It is a plea for progress. The union of believers which should be is not yet. Knowledge of God and of His word and will is imperfect. Vast fields of truth yet remain to be explored. The world is not yet converted. We have only touched the outskirts of the pagan world. Wiser methods and deeper consecration are required. We have the Christian graces only in rudimentary form. How much remains to be done in us before we are even worthy to be used of God in carrying out His great purposes in the world! What abuses in Church and state remain to be corrected! What reforms await their consummation! In what an unfinished condition is God's work on this planet! We must go forward . . . .

Finally, it is a plea for love. No union is possible until love becomes the triumphant force. Look at the early church, made up of Jews and Gentiles, bond and free, differing in toto in a hundred things, but one in their passionate love for Jesus. Before that omnipotent love partition walls went down with a crash, and hearts long estranged by national and religious prejudices flowed together at its magic touch. Jesus, the crucified and risen Savior, was the bond of union. Loving Him they loved one another, and love spread its beautiful mantle over many faults and many differences. Our plea for union will never triumph until religious people of differing creeds shall learn to love each other more. "Beloved, If Christ so loved us, we ought also to love one another." So shall Christ's followers become one and the world be converted.[1]

Thus Mr. Garrison's keen mind envisioned the Plea of the Restoration movement for a return to the church of the New Testament. It is a plea for unity, for liberty, for loyalty, for New Testament evangelism, for progress, and for love. It is clear that, in so far as the above statement is concerned, the Plea centers itself in Christ, as he is pictured in the New Testament, and that the various elements of the Plea mentioned have meaning to the movement only in so far as they further the establishment of Christ's kingdom in the world. It is unity in Christ, liberty in those things outside of him, loyalty to Christ, the conversion of persons to Christ through use of New Testament evangelism, progress of Christ's work in the world, and love for one another centering in him, for which we plead.

M. P. Hayden explained the basis of union, in the year 1899, as recorded below:

Having ascertained that the Great Commission is the true basis of Christian union, let us examine it more critically, and ascertain what are the essential principles contained in it, principles that are vital, fundamental, and essential to Christianity. A careful analysis of the Commission reveals the following principles as embodied in it:

1. Jesus of Nazareth, the Son of God, having been crucified and raised from the dead, has all authority in heaven and on earth; he is "the blessed and only Potentate, the King of Kings, and Lord of Lords;" he possesses supreme and universal authority as ruler of heaven and earth.

2. The apostles, chosen, instructed, and commissioned by the Lord Jesus Christ, and clothed with divine power by the Holy Spirit, are Christ's authorized and infallible representatives on earth to set up the kingdom, to preach the gospel, and to declare the law of Christ.

[1] J. H. Garrison, *A Modern Plea for Ancient Truths*, (St. Louis: Christian Publishing Company, 1902), pp. 9-17.

3. The religion of Christ is an exclusive and universal religion, designed for all the nations: and therefore it calls for earnest, aggressive missionary activity in sending the gospel of Christ throughout the whole world.

4. Disciples of Christ are to be baptized into the name of the Father, and of the Son and of the Holy Spirit, thus bringing them into union with God in a holy and divine fellowship.

5. Christians are to be taught to observe all Christ's commands; and these commands are to be found in the teaching of his apostles.

6. The abiding presence of Christ continues with the apostles and the church to the end of the world.

These, then, are the vital and essential principles which are embodied in the basis of union. None of them is unimportant, not one can be omitted without setting at naught the authority of Christ and destroying the unity of the church. Some persons may be disposed to leave out the authority of the apostles, but a little reflection will show that to do this would be a fatal defect; others may want to shun the obligation to missionary effort but this can not be omitted; others may be inclined to dispense with baptism, but it is plain that the baptism which Christ enjoins in the Commission is of vital importance; and still others may desire to be relieved of the duty of observing all the commands of Christ, but this can not be permitted. All the parts of this Commission are vital and essential, and are necessarily included in the New Covenant, or the fundamental law of the kingdom of Christ.[1]

While Mr. Hayden asserts that the Great Commission is the true basis of union, he points out that this is so because it involves the carrying out of the purpose and plan of the One of all authority. Ultimately, then, it is for the New Testament plan of conversion that he pleads, and for the oneness of the individual in Christ which this plan will accomplish and for the union of all thus united in the observing of all Christ commanded the apostles.

The statements of this period have been many and some of those included have been rather lengthy, but each has its part to play in this research. The period was characterized by the questions that arose regarding the relationship of the Plea to certain items of attitude and practice or expediency, and, while the problems arose, the statements of the Plea continued to call for unity through conversion of all to Christ, and union through the co-operation of all in world evangelism. Christ claims a central place in the statements of the Plea, as we have seen. So important and so central is the New Testament Christ to the Restoration movement that J. H. Garrison was able to say, toward the close of this period, in the year 1899:

When men have broken with Christ and have proved disloyal to the divine creed, they have soon found that they had no place with us.[2]

[1] Christian Quarterly, (New Series, January, 1899), pp. 104, 105.
[2] J. H. Garrison, The Word's Need of Our Plea, (Chicago: The Oracle Publishing Company, 1899), Christian Tract Series, Vol. I, No. 2, p. 11.

Chapter V

THE PERIOD OF DIGRESSION FROM
THE PLEA: 1900 - 1948

While, as it has been pointed out, certain questions began to appear within the thought of the Restoration movement in the period from 1837 to 1900, those questions created no real disturbance until after the turn of the century. As the questions were brought to be, through consideration of points beyond the Plea, so the actions taken upon those questions are beyond the Plea, digressions from it. The first of these actions, over the question of instrumental music, was a relisting in the census bureau of the United States of a certain group of churches, making it appear that the Restoration movement had been divided and that the restored church of Christ had gone the way of division and sectism. The second of these actions is the beginning of a strong and open advocacy for the practice of "open-membership" allowing the free exchange of membership between churches of Christ and groups practicing sprinkling or pouring in lieu of Christian immersion. The latter action has as yet produced no breach in the movement in so far as census listing is concerned.

A potential action, which may well become third, though not nearly so well defined as yet, revolves around the question of missionary agencies. One tendency is to define the brotherhood in terms of relationship to the agency; while another tendency is to define the brotherhood in terms of non-relationship to the agency. Both, as has already been pointed out and as the original Plea loudly proclaims, are essentially beyond the scope of the Plea. For almost one hundred years, the churches of Christ had been pleading for unity upon a New Testament basis. Oneness with Christ, through the conversion of individuals to him, and the co-operation of Christians thus made in world evangelism, through the simple form of Christianity proposed in Christian scriptures, are the objects of the movement. The terms of fellowship are as wide as the terms of salvation and no wider. The relationship of a man to his Christ is the determining factor in whether or not he is a Christian, whether or not he may assemble himself with the congregation of Christians in any local community as a Christian brother, whether or not he may have any part in a union with other Christians in world evangelism.

The one proposition the Restoration movement has been attempting to establish before the Christian world is that only questions sufficiently serious to endanger one's unity with Christ are sufficiently serious to cause disruption in His church and disunion in efforts to convert the world. The questions that have been raised and the actions that have been taken upon them within the movement to restore New Testament Christianity must stand the test of this proposition or be cast into the background of our thought. Brothers are determined by common parentage not by whether they both wear brown shoes and gray suits.

This chapter will concern itself, in addition to the reviewing of the various statements in their chronological order as heretofore, with the incidents and backgrounds of the already mentioned actions, in their relationship to the restoration idea. The advocates of the various actions, it will be noted, will justify their position upon the ground that, after all, they are attempting to accomplish exactly what the advocates of the Plea have always been attempting to accomplish. However, the statements of such must stand on their own in comparison to those we have listed already. We continue now with the review of the statements.

In the year 1901, W. J. Wright wrote:

> The church divided on *opinions*, and will reunite on *facts*; it divided on *fancy*, and will reunite on *faith*; it divided on *speculation*, and will reunite on *revelation*; it divided on *non-essentials* generally, but will reunite only on *essentials*; it divided on things held by *portions* of the church, but will reunite on things held by the *whole church*.[1]

This statement sounds a great deal like much that has gone before, though it has never been expressed in these terms before.

Herbert L. Willett, in 1901, makes a comment as follows:

> Yet the question arises, What does this million and a quarter of people propose to accomplish? Where their voice is heard in the counsels of the church at large they are understood to stand for two principles: First, the unity of the people of God; second, the restoration of the apostolic teaching and practice as the ground of such unity . . . .[2]

In another publication, Mr. Willett remarks:

> It is not, however, to conferences and resulting platforms that we can look with much expectation of Christian unity, for it has been largely the history of such gatherings that they have magnified rather than covered the differences between the participants. Christian unity can never be realized as the result of formal declarations, except as these are the consummation of actual fellowship already enjoyed. There is a certain value, no doubt, in drafting plans for the unity of the church, such as those proposed by the Lambeth-Chicago committee, or by the Disciples of Christ through their committee on Christian union which had an existence for several years. But the real task of Christian union lies closer to the soil. It can only be realized through the active and sympathetic efforts of a people heartily believing in the idea and committed to its promotion. Such a people as our own, with the forces at our disposal, with our large and growing representation in all parts of the country, could take such active steps toward the promotion of this great end as would hasten by leaps and bounds the consummation of that union which constitutes the Apostolic ideal. It is not merely by preaching the doctrine of Christian union on the Apostolic basis that this end can be reached; for we secure only a very partial hearing, and too frequently our conduct gives a direct and sharp negative to all our pleas for the union of the people of God. It is not by proclaiming Christian union and acting as narrow and selfish sectarians, as is too frequently the case in our churches, that we can expect to influence the Christian world. If, in the cities where we exist, we would take thought to promote with our well-known zeal and enthusiasm all those unifying movements which lie at hand, we should compel the Christian world to take seriously our plea, where today it regards us too frequently as a sect as belligerent and polemical as any other, and yet strangely enough, insisting evermore upon Christian unity.[3]

[1] *Christian-Evangelist*, Vol. 38, No. 20, p. 620.
[2] Herbert L. Willett, *Our Plea for Union and the Present Crisis*, (Chicago: The Christian Century Company, 1901), p. 6. [3] *Christian-Evangelist*, Vol. 38, No. 14, p. 430.

In the first statement above, it is to be noted that Mr. Willett suggests that the message of the movement is "understood" to have two distinct compartments: one for unity, the other for restoration. Whereas the advocates of the Plea have always maintained that unity and the apostles doctrine were one, since neither could be without the other. In Mr. Willett's conception, it would be possible to accomplish unity and then, within the unified church, restore the apostles doctrine. Such, however, as has been established in the review of the history of the Plea thus far covered, is not the intention of the movement.

In the second statement, Mr. Willett says that "Christian unity can never be realized as the result of formal declarations, except as these are the consummation of actual fellowship already enjoyed." Does he mean that free fellowship will come first, then unity declarations as a result of that fellowship, and finally complete unity? It would seem so from the terms he has used. Again, the order of procedure is foreign to the conception in the minds of the first advocates of the Plea. It was unity first, the oneness of every person claiming to be a Christian, in Christ, accomplished through the use of the divine plan, and then oneness of fellowship and co-operation. There is no person, who truly knows the intent of the Restoration movement, who does not deplore the use of sectarian tactics in the propagation of the gospel of Christ, even though by one advocating the restoration idea, but that does not minimize the effect of the restoration of the apostolic doctrine in accomplishing the oneness of the Lord's people, for such cannot be had without that doctrine. Never has the Plea called for the co-operation with or the sanctioning of any ministry or group preaching anything less than the "simple original form of Christianity."

Also in 1901, the year of the above statements, Frederick D. Power wrote of the Plea in the words following:

> The restoration of the supreme authority of Christ is the plea we have urged upon the religious world. To be loyal to our Lord is our supreme duty. Christ did not exalt freedom, he exalted obedience. It was not liberty first and Christ afterward, but unconditional acceptance of Christ as the door to freedom. "If the Son shall make you free, ye shall be free indeed." And this authority of Christ found its expression in the gospel. The word, the teachings and ordinances of Christ, then, are authoritative. Christianity as set forth in the gospel is not subject to human liberty, but human liberty must be subjected to it. "He that believeth and is baptized shall be saved, but he that believeth not shall be condemned." Human reason is fallible and halting; the revelation of Christ gives the illumination of divine and infallible reason. Hence the Scripture is the supreme light, shining from the eternal temple for the guidance of humanity. Hence, when one co-ordinates reason with the Bible as a source of authority in religion, and another affirms that many have found God in the temple of their own souls when they could not find him in the Bible both are wrong. Hence, the claim concerning any of the positive institutions of the gospel that they are not essential, or that they may be changed to suit the demands of comfort and convenience, is going beyond the limits of human liberty . . . .[1]

The position of Mr. Power is supported by a long series of statements, as has been demonstrated in this research. The statement is from a sermon delivered at the Minneapolis convention of the year stated.

----

[1] *Christian Standard*, Vol. 37, No. 43, p. 1358.

From another sermon preached at that convention by I. J. Spencer the statement recorded below is taken:

I will endeavor to enumerate a few considerations which seem to me to need especial emphasis in setting forth that plea before the world:

1. A faithful declaration of the word of God only, as vital, in language easily understood, and in the spirit of Christ. That word, rationally and spiritually interpreted, as all sufficient for doctrine and discipline without the aid of human creeds and tests of fellowship.

2. The terms of admission into the kingdom of God, as given by Christ and his apostles, clearly enunciated without any human modification.

3. The observance of the divine ordinances of baptism and the Lord's Supper, according to both the spirit and the letter of the New Testament teaching and practice.

4. The restoration of pure, simple, New Testament names for New Testament things, preference being given for Biblical over theological terminology.

5. Speaking authoritatively only where the Bible so speaks; and forbearing so to speak where the Bible is silent.

6. The Church of Christ as a thorough democracy in all matters of expediency, but an absolute monarchy whereinsoever the King has revealed his will. The sole authority of Christ in the church—as its Foundation, Founder and Head.

7. The unity of all believers in the Father and in the Son, in order to the world's salvation, as pleaded for by the Saviour on the night preceding his crucifixion.

We strive to present fully all the other great truths of the Word of Life; but these just mentioned, are neglected or ignored by the great majority of religious teachers. We endeavor to give them only their proper emphasis and place, in the effort rightly to divide the word of truth.[1]

Mr. Spencer's statement is worthy of careful and intelligent perusal. It appears that his conception of the mission of the movement is clear.

The year 1901 also brought forth a clear and practical statement by Robert Elmore. Says Mr. Elmore:

There is one remedy, and only one. It is God's remedy. It is effective. It is attainable. We shall heap sin on sin if we decline it.

Here is the Bible prescription: Reject (a) human leaders, (b) human names, (c) human creeds, and (d) human inventions as of any authority; (e) restore Christ as head over all things to the church; (f) acknowledge the divine Word as the only final, complete and authoritative rule of faith and practice; (g) walk by this rule.

(a) *Let no one glory in men* (I Cor. 3:21).

(b) *When one saith, I am of Paul, and another, I am of Apollos, are ye not men?* (I Cor. 3:4).

(c) *Learn not to go beyond the things which are written* (I Cor. 4:6).

(d) *Why make ye trial of God, that ye should put a yoke upon the neck of the disciples?* (Acts 15:10).

(e) *God . . . . gave him to be head over all things to the church* (Eph. 1:22).

---

[1] *Christian Standard*, Vol. 37, No. 42, pp. 1321, 1322.

(f) *All scripture is given by inspiration of God, and is profitable for doctrine, for reproof, for correction, for instruction in righteousness, that the man of God may be perfect, thoroughly furnished unto all good works.* (2 Tim. 3:16, 17—Authorized Version).

(g) *We should walk after his commandments* (2 John 6).[1]

Notice is called to the fact that Mr. Elmore does not leave it to the person or reader to judge the solution to Christian division upon his own knowledge, but has a "thus saith the Lord" for each of his suggestions.

The following statement by F. M. Green is also from the year 1901.

Has any part of the Christianity of the New Testament been displaced or overlooked and lost. If so, what has been lost should be restored.

1. In the New Testament we find (Matt. 16:16) a simple and comprehensive confession of faith—"Thou are the Christ the Son of the living God"—on which Jesus the Christ said, "I will build my church." This confession declared the Messiahship and Deity of Jesus of Nazareth. This confession has been practically displaced by human formulas of doctrine more or less complex and elaborate which have been made the basis of denominational churches.

This simple, comprehensive and sublime confession should be restored to its proper place; and until it is restored there can be no unity in New Testament doctrine and practice.

2. That this confession is the only creed which divine wisdom has formulated for the faith of each person who desires salvation is manifest to all who study the great commission of Jesus as given to his apostles; and their preaching and practice as recorded in the Acts of Apostles. (See Matt. 28:16-20; Mark 16:14-18; Luke 24:44-49; John 20:21-31; Acts 2:32-39; Acts 4:10-12 and onward). This creed without addition or subtraction should be *restored*.

3. In regard to preaching the gospel, both in matter and manner, there have been serious and fatal departures from the New Testament teaching and practice. "Preach the word," said the apostle (2 Tim. 4:2), and "they so spake that a great multitude both of Jews and of Greeks believed" (Acts 14:1). See (I Cor. 15:1, 2). The gospel proclamation consists of facts concerning Jesus the Christ to be believed; of commands to be obeyed; of promises, to be *enjoyed*; and threatenings to be feared. These facts, commands, promises and threatenings are found in the great commission of Christ to his apostles and constitute the basis of all apostolic preaching and practice of all apostolic Disciples. (See Matt. 28:16-20; Mark 16:14-16; Luke 24:44-49; John 20:21-31.) The great commission embraces all the constitutional requirements of complete conversion from sin. As these requirements are constitutional they cannot be changed until the great law-giver changes them. No body of men, however gifted, no church court, however constituted, no human tribunal, however venerable, has any authority or right to change them. The apostles of Christ declared this gospel, preached this word and insisted on the "obedience of faith"— nothing more, nothing less, in order to salvation from sin and entry into the Church of God. In so far as this preaching has been varied from or perverted, to that extent it must be restored.

4. The memory ordinance of the New Testament is the Lord's Supper. In the realm of God's grace in which all Christians are to grow, divine wisdom has placed this ordinance at regular weekly intervals. In Acts 20:7 it

---

[1] R. E. Elmore, *Christian Unity*, (Cincinnati: The Standard Publishing Company, 1901), p. 75.

is written: "And upon the first day of the week when the disciples came together to break bread Paul preached unto them." Beyond seven days no Christian need go without being reminded of the fact that "Jesus died for our sins according to the Scriptures." And on the first day of every week—the resurrection day—every disciple who desires to honor his Lord will do so, if possible, by regarding the day and the ordinance. The weekly observance of the Lord's Supper should be restored to the place it occupied in New Testament times, for its observance was not to be temporary but "until he comes" (I Cor. 11:26). "For as often as ye eat this bread and drink the cup ye proclaim the Lord's death till he come."

5. If we study carefully the life of Christ and his true disciples as revealed in the New Testament, we will find that their main characteristics are universal kindness and beneficence or grace and love; purity in word and deed; real holiness or consecration to God; truthfulness and absolute sincerity; humility and lowliness. These are essentially Christian principles and are all represented in New Testament teaching and practice, and in so far as they have been overlooked or lost sight of by modern Christians should be restored.[1]

According to Mr. Green, then, the solution to the problems of the church will be solved through the restoration of: 1) the apostolic confession of faith, 2) the apostolic Creed, 3) apostolic preaching, 4) the weekly observance of the "memory ordinance," and 5) the Christian life. The "fatal departures" must be overruled by returning to the practice and preaching of the apostles.

James C. Creel, in 1901, lists the following eight propositions in an attempt to show the progression in the thinking of the original advocates of the Plea. He says that:

The fundamental propositions announced by the fathers as the basis of their matchless plea, were, in substance, these:

1. There has been a departure from the faith and practice of the inspired apostles of the Christ.

2. There must be a complete return in faith and practice to the faith and practice of the apostles.

3. The Holy Scriptures are all-sufficient and alone sufficient as a rule of faith and practice.

4. In faith and doctrine, "where the Scriptures speak, we speak; where the Scriptures are silent, we are silent."

5. All that the Scriptures would have one to be is to be a Christian only, and belong to the church of Christ only.

6. The church of Christ, or the church of God, is constitutionally and essentially one—one in Christ.

7. In all matters of faith and practice there must be an express command of the Scriptures, or an approved precedent, or a necessary inference.

8. A complete return in faith and practice to the faith and practice of the apostles will accomplish the union or oneness of all Christians, and the evangelization of the world to the Christ.[2]

The emphasis, it will be seen, is upon the finality of the Scriptures in so far as a rule of reference is concerned. This is the only record known of the life of Christ and of the carrying out of the commission by the apostles. To it we may

[1] *Christian-Evangelist*, Vol. 38, No. 13, p. 396.   [2] *Christian Standard*, Vol. 37, No. 51, p. 1636.

go in order to determine all things pertaining to the gospel and the church. There is no other record.

Coming now to the year 1902, we find W. K. Pendleton saying:

> Evidently, the work that is needed is a restoration in form and power of the apostolic church, a New Testament ministry that takes the word of revelation for its guide, and the spirit of inspiration for its impulse. To separate these in theory or in practice is to break up the bond of Christian unity and reduce Christianity to a theory, a philosophy, a mere scheme of salvation, without power of life.[1]

This statement is not altogether clear. Just what Mr. Pendleton means by the "spirit of inspiration" is somewhat confusing. It is supposed that the spirit of inspiration, so called, refers to the Word. The thing that is needed is the restoration of a ministry that will take for its guide the word of God and for its impulse the conviction that the Word is inspired, not merely a dead letter with no soul, no life.

W. B. Taylor, providing a statement for our consideration for the year 1903, writes:

> THE PLEA STATED.—1. Many of the answers to the one question, "What is our plea?" are stated, in substance at least, as "A plea for absolute personal loyalty to Jesus Christ, the Son of God." This I consider the generic, all-inclusive and catholic statement of "our plea." This is the only proposition the apostles tried to prove, and to which they demanded submission. Everything else was correlated to it. It was the proof and plea of Peter on the day of Pentecost. This was the logic of Stephen's discourse which struck the goad to Saul's conscience. The apostle to the Gentiles determined to know nothing else.
>
> PLEA IS CHRISTIAN.—1. We do not plea for an an infallible church nor an infallible book, but an infallible Christ revealing himself in both. Hence, we are a peculiar people without peculiarity; neither classed with Protestants nor Catholics and outclassing both. Our plea is simply Christian.
>
> 2. This evidently accounts for the growth of this movement, both in numbers and in grace; one manifested by the census enumerator, the other by our growth in missions, benevolences and life. It is of God. I admit that some of our denominational brethren may equal, or even excel, us in the latter, but must believe that the Church of Christ is more loyal to the Master than the ones bearing some other name, listening to any other teacher, obeying any other authority, or following any other standard.
>
> 3. This plea is liberal, but not lax. It is positive without being repulsive. Everything moves by positive impulse. It is simple enough for the child, yet profound enough for the sage. The good confession will never have to be revised. It is as high as heaven, as broad as God's love, and as deep as his mercy.[2]

It is true, as Mr. Taylor states and as we have seen, the Plea centers in the Lord Jesus Christ, just as the gospel centers in him. The foundation of the gospel and the foundation of the church is the foundation of the Plea. It is to the rock, to the foundation, to the fundamentals, to the first principles that the Restoration movement has called the Christians of the world. Unity here is essential. If anyone builds on any other foundation than that which has been

---

[1]Frederick D. Power, *The Life of William Kimbrough Pendleton*, (St. Louis: Christian Publishing Company, 1902), pp. 356, 357.

[2]*Christian Standard*, Vol. 39, No. 50, p. 1798.

laid by God, he builds something other than the kingdom of our Lord. However, the statement that we plead not for an infallible book must be regarded as a pendulum swing to an extreme in the interest of centering attention upon Christ. The Restoration movement has always sought to uphold the only infallible record of God's revelation to man.

James A. Lord suggests in the following statement that the Plea takes two directions, as it is sent forth into the world. In the year 1904, Mr. Lord writes:

. . . . The plea of present-day disciples for a restoration of the Christianity of the New Testament reaches two distinct classes: the people who have never confessed Christ, and our brethren in the denominations who need to be taught the way of the Lord more perfectly. In reality, the plea for restoration is primarily to denominational adherents, who are exhorted to leave their party folds and come together in the fold of Christ under the one great Shepherd. The whole plea is for union in Christ, and, when fully operative, sets believers free from the dominion of partyism as well as aliens from the guilt and power and penalty of sin.[1]

Thus, according to Mr. Lord, the business of the proclaimers of the Restoration Plea is not to admit all men to the fellowship of the local congregation, regardless of their failure to meet the requirements of ALL the gospel, but to teach them the whole plan and obtain their conformance to it. This has already been alluded to previously in this dissertation.

One of the greatest questions that have been bandied about by the preachers of the churches of Christ is over whether or not the movement is a denomination. To answer this question, Mr. W. O. Moore, in 1904, says:

Some insist that those known as the Disciples of Christ are a denomination. Is this true?

1. The apostles were told to go into all the world and preach the gospel to every creature. The Disciples of Christ at the present day are committed to this work. Is this denominational?

2. They were directed to so preach the gospel as to make disciples. Is this denominational? Those known as the Disciples of Christ will not take a denominational name. One can be a Christian and not be a Methodist, but he cannot be a Christian without being one of Christ's disciples. One can be a Christian and not be a Presbyterian or a Baptist, but he cannot be a Christian without being one of Christ's disciples.

3. They were told to baptize those discipled into the name of the Father, and the Son, and the Holy Spirit. Is this denominational? Is there a people who profess to baptize and do not baptize those discipled—those who believe in Christ with all their heart?

4. They were told to immerse believers. Is there a church that will refuse to immerse believers? The Disciples of Christ immerse believers. Are they denominational?

5. All believers who are baptized into Christ were instructed by the apostles to observe faithfully whatsoever he commanded. Can a church that does this work be called denominational?

6. Those known as the Disciples of Christ can say: "Christ is our Creed." They believe in their creed. They accept what their creed teaches and propose to follow him. Is there anything in this that can be pronounced denominational. Denominations began to arise when men formulated doctrine and called it their creed.[2]

---

[1] *Christian Standard;* Vol. 40, No. 3, p. 84.   [2] *Christian-Evangelist,* Vol. 41, No. 37, p. 1185.

122

The point Mr. Moore makes is that those people, who believe and practice precisely what the New Testament prescribes for the belief and practice of the New Testament church, do not constitute something parallel to the church of Christ but the church of Christ itself. Certainly, the church of Christ is no denomination.

George Darsie writes of the Plea in the following manner and form:

That plea may be briefly embraced in three propositions: First, to restore the New Testament gospel and church in all their essential features, and in all their simple beauty and power; second, to urge the union of all God's children on the basis of the restored gospel and church, the only basis on which it will ever come about, because no other commands the assent of all and the dissent of none; and, third, to aim at the conquest of the world for Christ on the basis of a united church. Our Saviour's prayer clearly indicates that this is the only hope for the world's salvation. A divided church of necessity means weakness and failure, while a united church of equal necessity means strength and victory. This is our plea, and, as I said, it is not narrow or sectarian, but broad and catholic. It is not a plea for any sect or party, but for the merging of all sects and parties into one mighty host for the overthrow of Satan and sin, and for the planting of the banner of Christ over all the world.[1]

Unity would be the result of the restoration of the New Testament gospel, since the acceptance of that gospel brings the individual into oneness with Christ. Union, then, would be possible among all those who were one with Him, and the grand result would be the conversion of the world. Mr. Darsie lists the items of the Plea in their proper order and importance.

W. T. Moore, in 1906, wrote of the Plea as below:

To sum up the Disciple position, it may be well to indicate specifically the comprehensive platform for which they contend. This will give a clear idea as to what they are trying to accomplish. Their aim, briefly stated, is as follows:

(1) To exalt Jesus, both as Lord and Christ; and, as Head of his body, the Church, that he may "in all things have the pre-eminence." They sum up everything in him. With them he is all in all. Without his light and love we perish forever. His divinity is our foundation; his life our example; his intercession our foundation of grace and mercy; his teaching our guide; his Church our school; his spirit our comforter; his Gospel our reliance for the conversion of sinners; his commandments our life; his promises our rejoicing; to that through faith and obedience, we are blessed with "all spiritual blessings in heavenly places in Christ Jesus." To trust in the Lord Jesus, to love and obey him—this is salvation here and life eternal hereafter.

(2) To reject human dogmas and human names as tending to division among the people of God, and to adopt that only as authoritative for which there is a clearly revealed precept or example in the New Testament.

(3) To turn alien sinners to Christ, according to New Testament teaching and example, and to build up these converts in faith, hope and love.

(4) To earnestly enjoin the obligation to observe the first day of the week as the Lord's Day, in commemoration of the resurrection of Jesus Christ, by acts of worship such as the New Testament teaches, and

---

[1] *Christian Standard*, Vol. 40, No. 6, p. 182.

by spiritual culture such as befits this memorial day; and to enjoin especially the obligation of the Lord's Supper, to be observed every Lord's day, in commemoration of the suffering and death of him "who was made sin for us, who knew no sin, that we might be made the righteousness of God in Him."

(5) To establish Churches without human names, ordinances, or creeds; Churches which are Congregational, because self governed and independent; Presbyterian, because administered by presbyters, or elders and deacons; Episcopal, because an elder, or pastor, in the New Testament sense, is an overseer; Baptist, because faithful to New Testament teaching as regards the ordinance of baptism; Methodist, because doing all things methodically; or to use the scriptural style, "decently and in order;" Catholic, because insisting upon nothing that may not be adopted by all other religious bodies without any surrender of conscience; in short, Churches that are Christian and Apostolic, because comprehending in their requirements all that Christ and his Apostles, in their teaching, make necessary in order to form that society which is called the Church, or the body of Christ.

(6) To illustrate in the life of the Churches the Christianity of Christ, which is something more than doctrinal orthodoxy; so much more so, indeed, that it is a Divine living, and much of it is living for others. Consequently, the spirit of missions must necessarily animate all who hope to be actively alive in the Churches, for the spirit of missions is essentially the spirit of Christ.

(7) To pray and work for the union of God's people, and to cooperate with all Christians, as far as possible, in all good works for the salvation of men and the glory of God.

Now it seems to me that every fair-minded person must regard the position of the Disciples, when taken as a whole, as eminently catholic as well as reasonable. It is also workable, whenever those who profess to be followers of the Christ will agree to be guided solely by his authority. But as long as men will continue to make their own conditions of fellowship, and insist upon these in order to Christian union, then it is highly probable that no kind of union will ever be practically realized, to say nothing of Christian union, the only kind that could be of much particular value. If, however, all who love the Lord Jesus Christ would adopt the principles and practices set forth in the foregoing considerations, I do not doubt for a moment that Christian union would no longer be a "hope deferred," but would be a joyful realization before the present decade shall have ended. The real difficulty in the way of such union is the additions which have been made by the respective denominations, while none of these additions are absolutely essential to the salvation of men.

The Disciple contention is not only catholic and reasonable, but workable also, from the fact that it makes the terms of fellowship precisely equal to the terms of Discipleship; or to put it in other words, the terms of fellowship must never be made to comprehend more than is necessary to make Christians and maintain Christian character. This being true, the Disciple position offers a comprehensive and practical platform on which every Christian can stand without surrendering anything that is necessary to the integrity of the Scriptures on the one hand, or the sacredness of conscience on the other.[1]

While Mr. Moore suggests that he is going to state "briefly" the principles of

[1] W. T. Moore, *The Plea of the Disciples of Christ*, (Chicago: The Christian Century Company, 1906), pp. 72-74.

124

the movement, the above is a comparatively comprehensive statement. It is included here in its entirety, since is is the only statement of Mr. Moore which will be considered in this thesis. It deserves a careful reading and a wide distribution. Only one thing is called to attention here. The use of the term "Disciple" is different or has a different emphasis than previously noted. "Disciple contention," "Disciple position," etc., are strange terms to this point in our research.

J. H. Garrison set forth a very important idea in the following statement made by him in the year 1906:

> What was the distinctive task which this Christian movement set for itself? It undertook the solution of that problem of all the Christian centuries, namely: the harmonization of Christian liberty and Christian union. How can we stand fast in the liberty wherewith Christ hath made us free, while standing fast also in the unity wherewith Christ hath made us one? Roman Catholicism secured union, of a kind, but it sacrificed liberty. Protestantism secured liberty, but at the sacrifice of union. Are these two principles, then, essentially antagonistic, the one to the other? Are they mutually exclusive terms, so that those who enjoy one must do so at the sacrifice of the other? This can not be, for Christ not only taught both union and liberty as principles of his kingdom, but he enjoined them upon his followers. How can they be reconciled?[1]
>
> Liberty *in* Christ and union through loyalty *to* Christ—that is the harmonization of these two principles of the Gospel. Loyalty to all that Christ has clearly commanded—that gives us unity. Loyalty to Christ *only* and a rejection of all human authority in religion—that gives us liberty. So far from there being any conflict between these two principles, each is essential to the other; for just as there can be no *Christian* union without liberty, there can be no real *Christian* liberty, in its widest and best meaning, without union. The vital relation of liberty to union is seen in the fact that all attempts to bind men's thought and conscience where Christ has left them free have resulted in division and strife, and that all steps in the direction of a reunion of Christendom involve the concession of liberty in matters of opinion, and the rejection of all authority that interposes between Christ and the liberty which the emancipated soul finds in him.[2]

The above represents some of the clearest thinking that has been done on the questions confronting the Restoration movement as well as those confronting the Christian world as a whole. The same solution will fit both cases. Indeed, Mr. Garrison has placed his finger upon the very center of the Plea.

The statement below, of which M. M. Goode is the author, was published in 1906 after having been preached at a ministerial conference in Northwest Missouri. Mr. Goode asserts:

> We may hold that God will accept to eternal life those who are honestly mistaken as to what constitutes baptism, and who faithfully walk according to the best light they have; but it does not follow that we are bound to receive them into the fellowship of the church. All we can do is to test every case by actual submission to the gospel. Revealed things belong to us. The gospel of Christ is our only guide. We must be loyal to our King. If we consent to disregard this initiatory ordinance, one of the divinely recognized essentials of Christian union and fellowship, and teach men so, then we preach another gospel. This settles the question for me. I cannot con-

---

[1] J. H. Garrison, *Christian Union*, (St. Louis: Christian Publishing Company, 1906), pp. 135-136.
[2] *Ibid.*, pp. 137, 138.

125

sistently consent to receive into the fellowship of the church those who have not been baptized.

So long as a man believes in Christ as the Son of God, accepts him as his Lord and Saviour, and lovingly and loyally obeys his commandments, no matter what opinions, notions and ideas he may hold concerning a thousand non-essential things, he is a Christian and entitled to fellowship in the church.

The basis of union herein set forth is the basis upon which the primitive Christian community rested. Upon this basis Jews, Samaritans and Gentiles were all united in one fellowship. Diverse opinions, national prejudices and hatreds all gave way before the all conquering power of heaven's King. The same result can, in the same way, be secured again.

This basis of union is divine. It has for its authority a no less personage than the beginning of Christianity, and it is sufficient for all now. No formulation of union theology in a creed, no decrees of councils, of conferences, can ever take the place of this divine basis of fellowship, or restore union to a divided Christendom. We can hope to realize Christian union only upon the basis given in the New Testament. It is for this we plead.[1]

Mr. Goode's reasoning on "open-membership" is sound. It is foolhardy for one to allow an uncertain opinion that some may be saved without baptism to overrule certain scriptural injunctions that baptism is necessary to salvation, and this is precisely what the practice of "open-membership" does.

Harry Minnick writes as follows in the year 1907:

WHAT WE HOLD IN COMMON

That which we hold in common is much more fundamental than that which holds us apart. Let me mention a few of the former:

We receive the Bible, and the Bible alone, as the inspired and infallible word of God, and our standard of appeal in religious thought.

We reject all human creeds, all formulated doctrines of men, as binding on the conscience, or as a basis of communion and fellowship.

We receive Jesus of Nazareth as the Christ, the Son of the living God, and the only Saviour of men.

We receive the Holy Spirit in his personal and perpetual mission. He is to "convict the world in respect of sin, and of righteousness, and of judgment." He is to abide in the church to comfort, strengthen and sanctify all who enter.

We receive the two ordinances, baptism and the Lord's Supper. Baptism, according to the Scriptures, is the immersing of a penitent believer in water into the name of the Father and of the Son and of the Holy Spirit, and a raising of the immersed to live the new life in Christ Jesus. The Lord's Supper is a feast of commemoration and a prophecy that Jesus is coming again.

We believe that the fullness and freeness of salvation is offered in the gospel of Christ to all who will believe and obey. These items of common belief might be extended, but they are sufficient to point out our oneness in many fundamentals. These agreements place upon us a heavy burden of responsibility. I most fervently pray it may not be said of us: "Ye can discern the face of the skies, but ye cannot discern the signs of the times."[2]

---

[1] *Christian Standard*, Vol. 42, No. 34, pp. 1267, 1268.

[2] *Christian Standard*, Vol. 43, No. 21, p. 869.

The above is an excerpt from an address delivered before the Baptist Association of Ministers of Worcester, Massachusetts, and published later. It represents the Plea in action. Mr. Minnick, as he says, is dealing with the points in common between the Christian Churches and the Baptists. It is a fine statement of the position Mr. Minnick holds in regard to some very important questions.

THE MUSIC QUESTION AND DISRUPTION

It has been mentioned previously in this thesis that the question which arose over the use of the musical instrument in the worship services of the churches finally developed to the place where the two groups were relisted as separate "churches" in the Census records of the United States, thus creating the impression that the Restoration movement had split and that the restored church of Christ had floundered on the rocks of division. Just what or who prompted this division on the census records is not known by many today, but the following statement should present the background of the situation to all who care to know.

We clip from the Nashville American "the following letters, the contents of which are of more or less interest to the members of all the churches:"

Department of Commerce and Labor, Bureau of the Census, Washington, June 17, 1907.—Elder D. Lipscomb, Editor Gospel Advocate, Nashville, Tenn.—Dear Sir: As you are aware, in accordance with the Acts of Congress approved March 6, 1902, this office is charged with the duty of collecting statistics of the religious bodies in the United States, similar to the collection made in 1890.

In carrying out these instructions, the office has found the religious press of great assistance. Among the papers that come to the office is the Gospel Advocate. Examination of it has resulted in a little confusion of mind as to its denominational connection. At times it seemed to be identified with the Disciples of Christ; at times to represent a distinct body. I was just upon the point of writing to ask you about the matter when a letter was received from Rev. William J. Campbell, of Marshalltown, Ia., speaking of over three thousand "churches of Christ," not now connected with the Disciples of Christ, though formerly belonging to that body. He also inclosed a list of preachers of the church of Christ, printed by the McQuiddy Printing Company, of Nashville, apparently the same company that prints the Gospel Advocate, and named the Gospel Advocate as a paper representing these churches.

A comparison of the list of editors with this list of preachers showed that all three are included in it. This seemed at once to solve the problem. A comparison, however, with the list of preachers in the "American Home Missionary," showed your name and Mr. Elam's name as belonging to the Disciples of Christ. The problem remaining unsolved, and the quickest and most satisfactory way seemed to be to go straight to headquarters.

I would like to know:

1. Whether there is a religious body called "church of Christ," not identified with the Disciples of Christ, or any Baptist body. Regular, Primitive, United?

2. If there is such a body, has it any general organization, with headquarters, officers, district or general conventions, associations, or conferences?

3. How did it originate, and what are its distinctive principles?

4. How best can there be secured a complete list of the churches?

You will, I am sure, realize the importance of the matter. It is the earnest desire of the Bureau of Census to make this enumeration complete and accurate, and not to leave out of it a single church organization, however small, much less to omit so large a collection of churches. It will, therefore, be esteemed a great favor if you will reply to these questions as promptly as possible, that the collection of detailed statistics may commence at an early date.

In replying, please mail in the enclosed envelope, which requires no postage.

Thanking you in advance for any information you can give, and trusting to hear from you at your earliest convenience, very respectfully,

S. N. D. NORTH, Director

To this letter Elder Lipscomb replied as follows:

Nashville, Tenn., June 22, 1907.—Dear Sir: Laying no claim to "headquarters," the movement that resulted in what is now known as the "Christian Church," or "Church of Disciples," began with the declaration and address of Elder Thomas Campbell, in Pennsylvania, about a century ago. The purpose, end, and means of this work are set forth in the following extracts:

"Our desire, therefore, for our brethren and ourselves, would be that, rejecting human opinions and the inventions of men, as of any authority, or as having any place in the church of God, we might forever cease from further contentions about such things, returning to and holding fast by the original standard, taking the divine word alone for our rule, the Holy Spirit for our teacher and guide to lead us into all truth, that by so doing we may be at peace among ourselves, follow peace with all men, and holiness, without which no man shall see the Lord." Again: "For the sole purpose of promoting simple, evangelical Christianity, free from all mixture of human opinion and inventions of men." Again: "Nothing ought to be received into the faith or worship of the church, or made a term of communion among Christians, that is not as old as the New Testament." They should follow "after the example of the primitive church as exhibited in the New Testament, without any additions whatsoever of human opinions or the inventions of men."

These show the keynote of the movement. The maintenance of these positions soon separated those holding them from those who did not accept the principle. The plea commended itself to many of the different churches and of no church, and the Christians or Disciples increased rapidly and the churches multiplied. As they increased in number and wealth, many desired to become popular also, and sought to adopt the very human inventions that in the beginning of the movement had been opposed—a general organization of the churches under a missionary society with a moneyed membership, and the adoption of instrumental music in worship. This is a subversion of the fundamental principle on which the churches were based.

Division of sentiment on these and the principle of fidelity to the Scriptures involved in them produce division among the disciples. The polity of the churches being purely congregational, the influences work slowly and the division comes gradually. The parties are distinguished as they call themselves "conservatives" and "progressives," as they call each other "antis" and "digressives."

In many places the differences have not as yet resulted in separation. There are some in the conservative churches in sympathy with the progressives, who worship and work with the conservatives because they have no other church facilities. The reverse of this is also true. Many of the conservatives are trying to appropriate the name "churches of Christ" to distinguish themselves from "Christian or Disciples' Churches." But the latter in all their publications and the proceedings of their conventions call themselves "churches of Christ"—moved, possibly, by the desire to head off the effort of the other party to appropriate the name as distinctive.

The progressives through their society organizations, gather and publish statistics that make a show. But they claim not over half of the churches—in all about twelve thousand—as working with them. They claim, and it is probably true, that a number who do not object to their methods fail through indifference to work with them. In a number of churches a few members work with the progressives, a larger number refuse to do it. Yet the church in which only a few members act with the society is counted as one of them. Their officials in gathering statistics magnify the number of members which work with them, minify those opposing them. So in Tennessee, where the churches generally oppose all innovations upon the primitive order, they report in their statistics about five hundred and fifty churches and fifty thousand members. I have a list of about eight hundred churches in the State, with thirty-five of the ninety-six counties unreported. These thirty-five counties are sparsely populated mountain counties, with not many churches, still there are near nine hundred churches in the State. The number of members would be a guess. Of these churches, about one hundred work with the progressives.

While the progressives oppose and refuse to have conservative preachers preach in their houses and to their congregations, and seek to divide and break up the churches they cannot control, and gain possession of their property, yet, for the sake of denominational show, they publish in their yearbooks all the members, preachers, and churches of the conservatives as one with themselves. It is just to say, too, that the conservatives discourage the churches having a progressive preacher to preach for them, as calculated to lead them from fidelity to the word of God and to introduce discord and division among them; but they never publish their preachers or churches as one with them, as the list of preachers you have shows.

With this statement, much of which you may think needless, I answer:

1. There is a distinct people taking the word of God as their only and sufficient rule of faith, calling their churches "churches of Christ," or "churches of God," distinct and separate in name, work, and rule of faith from all other bodies or peoples.

2. They are purely congregational and independent in their polity and work, so have no general meetings or organizations of any kind.

3. Their aim is to unite all professed Christians "in the sole purpose of promoting simple, evangelical Christianity as God reveals it in the Scriptures, free from all human opinions and inventions of men."

4. Owing to these differences still at work among the churches, there is more or less demoralization in many churches as to how they stand and what their numbers are. I know of no way to obtain the statistics desired other than to get the address of the different churches and address a circular asking the number of each church.

These disciples have separated from the "Christian Church" that grew out of the effort to restore pure primitive Christianity, by remaining true to the original purpose and the principles needful to develop it, while these churches have departed from this end and have set aside the principles of fidelity to the word of God as the only and sufficient rule of faith and practice for Christians. This seems to give as correct an idea of the facts concerning these churches as I can give. I will cheerfully assist in any way in my power in gaining correct information of these churches.

Respectfully,

David Lipscomb.[1]

As reported in a later number of the periodical edited by Mr. Lipscomb, Mr. North made a visit to his offices in Nashville. Blanks were sent to all the "churches of Christ" in an attempt to obtain the desired information,[2] and so the "division" came.

Later Mr. Lipscomb wrote:

Unity among the children of God is secured and maintained by all maintaining unity with and in God, and this can be gained and maintained only by doing the will of God. It requires no negotiation or arrangements among men to unite them as one in Christ. If we are in Christ, we cannot help being one with all who are in Christ. All in Christ are one with him and in him. His Father's will is his will. He has no other will than his Father's will. Doing his Father's will made him one with the Father. If we do his will, we do the Father's will, and in doing that will we are made one with him and with the Father.

Nothing can keep two persons in Christ separated. They will flow together and commingle into one as necessarily as two drops of water will flow into one, with all hindrances and obstacles removed. Christ Jesus came to remove all division walls and hindering causes and to make of the many families and nations of earth one new man in Christ. All human teachings, inventions, and institutions are occasions of discord, stumbling, and division. Two persons cannot be in Christ and not be one.[3]

Mr. Lipscomb has yet to reconcile the above statement with that contained in his answer to Mr. North. If the word of God is the rule, it must be demonstrated, by express injunction or approved precedent, clearly stated or implied, that instrumental music and missionary societies will divide between Christ and one practicing such things, all other things being equal. Mr. Lipscomb's rule based upon the silence of God on the question will not suffice for those who are ruled by the word of God alone. If the practice as above condemned by Mr. Lipscomb is not sufficient to divide one from his Lord, it is not sufficient to divide one Christian from another nor to cause one to be party to the listing of two groups in the census records.

The next statement strikes a note never before heard, in so far as the statements reviewed in this dissertation are concerned. It is from a published sermon by George H. Combs which was preached before the convention at Pittsburgh in 1909.

Mr. Combs says:

Our mission is not to the unchurched at home. No man in this midst believes in evangelism more than I, and yet even the supreme work of winning men to the Lord Christ must not, for one moment, turn us aside from the work to which we have been called. Great as is evangelism, let us bear in mind that our emphasis can not be here, but on the unity of the

---

[1] *Gospel Advocate*, Vol. 49, No. 29, p. 457.   [2] *Gospel Advocate*, Vol. 49, No. 45, p. 713.
[3] *Gospel Advocate*, Vol. 50, No. 3, p. 41.

130

Lord's people. Why? Because the unification of the churches is a necessary precedent to effective evangelism. A divided church can not evangelize our homeland. It is not evangelizing it. Protestantism is paralyzed by its disunion, and never shall we win the world at our doors until there shall be one church, even as there is one Lord, one Faith, one Baptism, one God over all.

Ours is not a mission to the heathen world. If, in this great missionary conventions it is difficult to present this proposition without danger of misunderstanding, the fault is with the conditions and not the speaker. Do we not, one and all, believe in the evangelization of the heathen world? Yes, it is because we believe in it so tremendously that we say this word. For we know that these nations beyond the seas can never be evangelized by a divided church. We have heard the Master's prayer, "Father, may they all be one as thou art in me, and I in thee, that the world may believe that thou hast sent me," and we know that only through a united church can the world be won. "First things first." And the first is unity, unity for evangelism; the unification of the church for the conversion of the world . . . .

What, then, is our mission? It has been already oft repeated—the unification of the churches of our Lord. Now, if our mission is to unite Christians, our message must be to Christians. If we were sent into the world with a message to Christians in all the communions of earth, we must somehow deliver that message. But are we? Before Almighty God, yes or no? Are we reaching the ear and heart of Christendom? Are we going as flaming messengers to the churches around us, beseeching them in Christ's name to be one? . . . .[1]

It is clear that Mr. Combs understands the Plea to be for the union of churches. This work must claim our attention, not evangelism, not missions, but the union of the churches. When that is accomplished, the united church will then be able to turn its power on the business of winning the world to Christ. It has already been pointed out that the Plea calls not for a union of churches, as such, but for the oneness of all God's people in Christ. It is a matter of uniting individuals, and this through evangelism, addressed to denominationalist and heathen sinner alike, but certainly the Plea has never sounded forth the cry of union first and world evangelism second.

E. V. Zollars, in the brief statement below, makes an appeal to hold fast to the Plea. Says he:

Let us continue to advocate our plea, our whole plea, namely, the union of the people of God by a return to the Christianity of the apostolic day; or, in other words, on the basis of the plain, explicit, unequivocal teachings of Christ and his apostles. In the meantime, let us exhibit the spirit of love and forbearance that should characterize those who make such a plea. Let us not invite people to come to us, but to take their stand with Christ and his apostles, and let us meet them there. Let us magnify the things wherein we agree, and they are many and vital, and let us discuss the things that divide courteously and lovingly . . . .[2]

Mr. Zollars would not surrender any item of faith, but he would meet all at the feet of Jesus and his apostles. Meanwhile, the problems confronting the Christian world should be discussed with Christian grace and poise. In this way and in this way alone, the goal can be reached. Unkindness and bulldog tactics are out of place in appeals for the oneness of God's people.

[1] *Christian-Evangelist*, Vol. 46, No. 41, p. 1305. [2] *Christian-Evangelist*, Vol. 47, No. 7, p. 221.

The statement of George H. Combs, above given, finds an answer in the statement below by I. J. Spencer, dated 1910. Says Mr. Spencer:

Put the cart before the horse, the house before the foundation, the stream before the fountain, the fruit before the tree, the effect before the cause, and you will do precisely what those are doing who urge that our plea is primarily a plea for Christian union.

On the contrary, the plea of the Disciples of Christ is primarily and essentially the Gospel—the pure, simple, complete Gospel. Jesus said to Pilate: "To this end have I been born, and to this end am I come into the world, that I should bear witness unto the truth." He Himself is "the Truth." He is the good tidings. We are his followers and are here for the self-same purpose—to bear witness to the Truth. The mission of the Old Testament Scriptures was and is to bear witness of Christ. The apostles and the church were called to the same mission. Even the Holy Spirit was given to testify of Christ and to glorify Him. The apostles had no plea but Christ. The true significance of baptism and of the Lord's Supper is found only in their relationship to Him. Prayer has no promise except in the name of Christ. The glory of the Lord's day is that it testifies to Him. All our preaching—if it be apostolic—is a preaching of Christ. Moreover, does not Christ say He is "the First" as well as "the Last?" To put first things first is not to put Christian union first. To put emphasis where it belongs is to put it upon Christ as both the First and the Last.[1]

Mr. Spencer has put the emphasis where the Plea and those who have voiced it have always placed it. The difference in emphasis, however, as seen here between Mr. Spencer and Mr. Combs, may be noted from time to time hereafter in the statements to be considered. The voice of the movement, in so far as the question of union is concerned, seems to split over this question: Is the Plea a plea for the union of churches or denominational parties or is it a plea for the union of Christians, individuals united with Christ and, thus, with each other, through conversion after the New Testament pattern? Is it a plea addressed to the denominations designed to accomplish the fusion of them all or is it a plea addressed to individuals belonging to the several parties designed to convince their severance from the party and from party loyalty and their attachment to Christ and to Him alone? The statements of the Plea which have been covered to this point in this research must answer that question.

Continuing the review of the statements, Finis S. Idleman writes in the year 1911:

. . . . This plea is not the peculiar shading or partisan statement it may receive from any center of theological utterance among us, nor yet by the offensive putting it has often endured. But it is the singleness of view in which we hold Jesus as the Son of God, as a personal Saviour, the ever-increasing Christ to an ever-enlarging experience. Its twofold aspect is loyalty to Christ and liberty in Christ. The loyalty of Jesus may be embraced in the inclusive words of Mary at Cana of Galilee: "Whatsoever he saith unto you, do it." Liberty in Christ is declared in the language of St. Paul when he said: "Stand fast, therefore, in the liberty wherewith Christ hath made you free." Who can set the boundaries of loyalty to Christ? Who has compassed the vast reaches of spiritual sovereignty which are the peculiar glory of our Lord? Who knows what new realms of loyalty may yet be unclosed to our holden eyes?

---

[1] *Christian-Evangelist*, Vol. 47, No. 17, p. 593.

If we should shrink from being self-appointed judges of all that loyalty may mean, much more should we hesitate to limit freedom in Christ.

Such a plea must be all-inclusive to all that may reasonably call itself Christian. He is our human Lord to the lowliest, the embodiment of God to the wisest. With no narrower limitations on the statement of faith all Christendom can unite. We are pledged both to preach and to practice such universality as the central fact in the plea prescribes. All other questions and practices included under the Lordship of Jesus find meaning and motive as they relate to him.

. . . . Loyalty to what is clearly ordained by Jesus must enter into the united church or it can never be the Church of Christ. Yet we must not categorically fix our apprehension of the plea as the bounds of loyalty and liberty.

But having once espoused such catholic faith we are pledged to catholic practice. To live and endeavor less than our central fact would indicate is to misrepresent that truth and hinder its acceptance. By so much as the plea we make is catholic to all—by so much is it our duty above others to practice catholicity.[1]

The similarity of the above statement to one previously listed by J. H. Garrison will probably be realized at once. Loyalty to Christ and Liberty in Christ is certainly the answer to the questions before the church. Mr. Idleman, however, would not attempt to define, with finality, the limits of either, though he is certain that "loyalty to what Christ has *clearly* ordained" must be a part of any unity that would be Christian. Meanwhile, we must practice what we preach in so far as our preaching and practice is universally held.

OPEN-MEMBERSHIP OR INCOMPLETE CONVERSION

It will be recalled that the first open advocacy of the practice of "open-membership" was made by L. L. Pinkerton about the year 1868. Since that time little was said upon the subject until the turn of the century and little more from the turn of the century until about the year 1911. At that time, the *Christian Century*, edited by C. C. Morrison and Herbert L. Willett, which had "always occupied a rather extreme, radical position,"[2] began an open advocacy of the practice. The *Christian-Evangelist*, in the year 1911, carried without comment the following statement by Ellis B. Barnes, associated also in the publication of the *Christian Century*:

"Who is a Christian? Answer, Everyone who believes in his heart that Jesus of Nazareth is the Messiah, the Son of God, repents of his sins, and obeys him in all things according to his measure of knowledge of his will. A perfect man in Christ, or a perfect Christian is one thing; a babe in Christ, a stripling in the faith, or an imperfect Christian is another. The New Testament recognizes both the perfect man and the imperfect man in Christ. I cannot, therefore, make any one duty the standard of Christian state or character, not even immersion into the name of the Father and of the Son and of the Holy Spirit, and in my heart regard all that have been sprinkled in infancy without their knowledge and consent as aliens from Christ and the well-grounded hope of heaven."

[1] *Christian-Evangelist*, Vol. 48, No. 31, p. 1091.

[2] W. T. Moore, *A Comprehensive History of the Disciples of Christ*, (New York: Fleming H. Revell Company, 1909), p. 700.

As long as these words stand, there can be no rational discussion among us as to the salvation of the pious unimmersed, no use of such a phrase when speaking of those who like ourselves honor Christ and his truth, as "the uncovenanted mercies of God," no hesitation when speaking of their destiny, no logical sleight of hand such as God's revealed way of salvation for the immersed, and another unrevealed way for those who misunderstood a Greek verb. There can be Christian union only by Christians, and the basis is already agreed upon—the Bible. What differences remain must be adjusted by time, and in the spirit of brethren in Christ.[1]

The opening quotation by Mr. Barnes is from Mr. Campbell's first answer to the query of the lady from Lunnenberg, as referred to earlier in this thesis. Mr. Barnes has not quoted all that Mr. Campbell says, and has taken his statement from two paragraphs of the letter, leaving out much that was written between the quotations he uses above. Among the statements omitted is the following: "Paul commands the imperfect Christians to 'be perfect,' (2 Cor. iii:11.) and says he wishes the perfection of Christians." However, in spite of this, Mr. Barnes is certain that Mr. Campbell has forever settled the question for disciples of Christ.

The basis of the difficulty seems to be a misconception of the true nature of the union for which the Plea calls. In the above case, the union is thought to be a union of churches, basically, and, since the question has already been settled that Christian union can be had only by Christians, the open and free admission that ALL members of denominational bodies are Christians is necessary and a free exchange of membership obligatory, if union is to be. While Mr. Barnes promises salvation to the "pious unimmersed" upon the basis of Mr. Campbell's statement, Mr. Campbell, in all three of his letters, promises salvation to no particular unbaptized person whatsoever. However, even when misinterpreting Mr. Campbell, it is to be remembered that he has no authority whatsoever to decide, upon his own premises, who is or who is not a member of the church of Christ.

In the *Christian Century* for 1912, Charles Clayton Morrison, published a series of articles entitled "The Essential Plea of the Disciples." It is sincerely regretted that the whole series cannot be included here, but sufficient excerpts have been chosen to present the central points of the argument. The series is an attempt to justify the practice of open membership upon the ground that, after all, the movement has been guilty of drifting from the original ground laid down by Thomas Campbell, who was free to admit that all members of the denominations were Christians and their churches, churches of Christ. Mr. Morrison writes as follows:

> To correct this evil (the evil of division) Mr. Campbell pleaded with Christ's people to restore the lost unity of the Church, and he bade them look two directions to find this unity, first to the pages of the New Testament, and secondly, to the actual Church of Christ existing underneath the denominational order.[2]

It should be called to attention that this is Mr. Morrison's interpretation of the *Declaration and Address*,[3] and not necessarily what Mr. Campbell really in-

---

[1] *Christian-Evangelist*, Vol. 48, No. 51, p. 1811.

[2] *Christian Century*, Vol. 29, No. 16, p. 368.

[3] Compare the treatment of that document on pp. 17-28 this thesis.

tended to say. Mr. Campbell does not say, "We are hereby making an appeal to the living church and an appeal to the church of the New Testament." He speaks simply of the abandonment of "innovations" and the putting into practice of only those things which are "expressly enjoined by the authority of our Lord Jesus Christ and his Apostles upon the New Testament church; either in expressed terms, or by approved precedent."[1]

If we regard his call for the abandonment of innovations as an appeal to the "living church," we must keep in mind that he appealed to it, not as illustrating anything right about it, but as exhibiting innovations and expediencies which it has adopted which make it foreign to the church of the New Testament. One important point should be noted especially: the determination of what an innovation is may be made only by reference to the New Testament church. It is in Mr. Campbell's appeal to the church of the New Testament that his true intent must be seen for there the faith and practice of the church as originally established may be determined. Thus, he appeals to the "living church" to reveal what the church should NOT be, and to the church of the New Testament to show what it should be.

Mr. Morrison, however, continues:

These two approaches to unity, one through the New Testament Church, the other through the living church, are not contradictory, but mutually interpretative. The New Testament Church is not one thing and the living Church another—they are identical. The historic appeal of the Disciples to "the Book" is a true appeal. The church in the Book is the true Church of Christ. The living Church in no sense supersedes the Church in the Book. It cannot supersede it; it is it.[2]

The concept of the church, as Mr. Morrison presents it above, may be illustrated as follows: if one were to gather sufficient string, twine, and rope to stretch from Los Angeles to New York when all tied together, and were to tie and stretch the string, twine and rope, as indicated, beginning with the smallest and ending with the largest, and were to stand in New York, pointing to the last piece of three inch rope to be tied in place, and say, "This is the piece of string in Los Angeles," he would hold about the same position in regard to the rope and string as Mr. Morrison does in regard to the church. It is the notion that the church is a development, beginning at Pentecost, changing and developing within the New Testament itself and on through the centuries until today. From this point of view, anything that has evolved from the original church must be regarded as it, regardless of how dissimilar it may be.

The analysis continues:

Of these two principles which were woven into the fabric of the Declaration and Address, the appeal to the Scriptures has, throughout our history, absorbed the mind of the Disciples to the practical exclusion of the appeal to the living Church. The Disciple mind forgot the living Church. It became engrossed in the academic, apriori method of finding out what the primitive Church was, and failed to reckon with the living Church of today.[3]

What, too, is the explanation of the apparent failure of our appeal to the Scriptures to produce in us, the Disciples, a typical people illustrative of the unity for which we plead and for which Christ prayed?

[1]Campbell, "Declaration and Address," op. cit., p. 16.
[2]Christian Century, Vol. 29, No. 16, p. 370.   [3]Ibid.

The explanation lies here: the Disciples have allowed their principle of appeal to the Scriptures practically to swallow up its twin principle, the appeal to the living Church. We have shut ourselves apart with our Bible to find the outlines of the primitive Church and have failed to check up our interpretation by contact with the living Church of today. The fault was not in the Scriptures—God forbid! The fault was that we put ourselves in a position apart from the living Church where it was possible to see things in the Scriptures that are not in the Scriptures at all. We searched the New Testament for the Church of Christ and allowed ourselves to forget that this Church of Christ described in the New Testament is a living Church *now*, that all its members are members one of another.[1]

Attention should be drawn to the fact that Mr. Morrison says that the living Church, as he calls it, is the New Testament church, through historical connection without regard to oneness of faith and practice.

Reviewing the rediscovery of baptism, Mr. Morrison says that the reformers adopted a practice that "would have shut out Thomas Campbell himself had such a test been made at the time he wrote the *Declaration and Address,*"[2] thus making Thomas Campbell's own action following the writing of the *Declaration and Address* out of harmony with the principles advanced therein. Mr. Morrison analyzes the events as below:

> As Alexander Campbell and his followers conceived it the New Testament clearly commanded them to be immersed and to practice immersion only. But it did not occur to them that the New Testament gave them not an iota of authority for adopting the Baptist practice of closed membership against members of the Church of Christ who had not been immersed.[3]

> The Brush run church under the guidance of the masterly leadership of the younger Campbell seized upon one of the substantive norms of the Declaration and ignored the other. It seized upon the duty of conformity to the New Testament Church of Christ and ignored the duty of practicing unity with those who were now in the Church of Christ. As a result it fell into a practice thoroughly repugnant to the New Testament.[4]

In Mr. Morrrison's mind, as expressed here, the strict conformance in practice to the exact meaning of New Testament Scripture on the subject of Christian Baptism is "thoroughly repugnant to the New Testament." Just how one becomes a member of the church of Christ without baptism, which Mr. Morrison categoriecally asserts, he does not explain, except upon his own authority. He appears to be confused over the order of certain terms. He assumes that because a man is a member of the church, he is a Christian and therefore is saved; whereas, the New Testament indicates that by comformance to the plan of salvation handed down by our Lord a man is saved, therefore a Christian and a member of Christ's body, the church. Thus, if one wishes to be a Christian and a member of the church of Christ, he must comply with the terms of salvation as appointed by Christ. A congregation does not have the right to overlook imperfect compliance with those terms, since they were given by the Lord Himself. This is certainly the conclusion to which Alexander Campbell came. It is interesting to note that the adoption of this practice did not shut out Thomas Campbell, for he accepted the truth about baptism when he learned it.

Mr. Morrison concludes with the following statement on the task of the Disciples:

[1] *Ibid.*   [2] *Christian Century,* Vol. 29, No. 17, p. 393.   [3] *Ibid.*, p. 394.   [4] *Ibid.*

This is the great task of the Disciples: to restore the norm of the living Church of Christ, the true New Testament Church, which lies underneath the denominational order as the common denominator lies under its fractions—to restore this normative magnitude to a focal position in their own thinking, first of all, and then in the thought and conscience of the Christian world. In this principle lies our genius and distinctiveness as a Christian union movement . . . .[1]

The solution to the problems of divisions among Christians, then, as Mr. Morrison conceives it, is to call the attention of denominationalists to the fact that underneath the denominational order lies the true New Testament church, hidden by the peculiarities of sectarianism. The true New Testament church, thus, is that which all denominations have in common, just as the common denominator is that which all of its fractions have in common. To bring all peoples to the elimination of everything but that which all have in common is to accomplish Christian unity. The difficulty is that this conception does not take into consideration variances from actual New Testament practice which would still be in existence even if this were accomplished.

Mr. Morrison has gone to the other extreme and has based his appeal entirely upon the living church, and has abandoned altogether the appeal to the church of the New Testament. Certainly no such conception as this can be detected in the previous history of the statements of the Plea. Mr. Morrison has come up with some ideas foreign to the Plea and attempted to reconcile them to it. It is not the purpose of the Restoration movement to ignore the "living church," but it is to take from its present practice those things foreign to New Testament faith and doctrine, and add to its practice those New Testament elements now lacking.

The difference again is a difference in the conception of Christian union. Mr. Morrison views it in terms of church union, or denominational union, making it necessary to admit that all members of such groups are Christian, since no Christian union is possible without Christians to unite. The refusal of the fellowship of the local church to one who has never been immersed to Mr. Morrison, is equivalent to saying that he is not a Christian and that he is condemned. This he refuses to do, since such action would void the appeal for Christian union, as he conceives it.

It is not sound logic to suppose that what exists is right, simply because it exists. The existence of something that people call a church, the members of which they call Christians, in itself, does not constitute the thing a church nor its members Christians. If the movement began with an appeal to the living church, so called, the swing to the appeal to the New Testament church resulted from their observation that the living church and the church of the New Testament were almost contradictory terms. The only way in which one can determine the meaning of the *Declaration and Address*, aside from a more careful reading of it, is to search history for the action it produced in those who followed its direction.

In another article in the *Christian Century*, Mr. Morrison attempts a further clarification of his views:

"Was it the aim of our movement in behalf of Christian unity to construct a platform broad enough to take in all the members of the exist-

---

[1] *Christian Century*, Vol. 29, No. 18, p. 10.

ing churches—or to return to the New Testament conditions of church membership as the true basis of unity?"

It was the aim of our movement to construct a platform broad enough both to take in all members of the Church of Christ, AND to return to the New Testament conditions of church membership as the true basis of unity. These two are not alternatives—they are identical. A platform broad enough to take in all members of the Church of Christ and none others IS the New Testament basis of unity. The New Testament conditions of church membership are identical with the conditions by which a Presbyterian, for example, became a member of the Church of Christ. If we know how an unimmersed Presbyterian became a member of the Church of Christ we will know what are the New Testament conditions of membership in the Church of Christ—for there is no conceivable way by which he could have become a member save the New Testament way. To admit that he is a member is to admit that he became such in conformity to essential New Testament conditions. To admit that he is a member of the Church of Christ is equivalent to denying that immersion is a New Testament condition of membership in the Church of Christ.[1]

According to this logic, one would not search in the New Testament to determine the New Testament conditions of membership in the church of Christ, but he would look to the "living church." Mr. Morrison's conclusions may be sound, granting his major premise: that the determining factor as to whether or not a church is a New Testament church is in historical evolvement or mere chronological contiguity from the original church established on Pentecost, A.D. 30. However, it cannot be admitted that such is the case; certainly the testimony of the statements of the Plea thus far contradict this position.

The identifying factor of the New Testament church is the continuance of the faith and practice handed to the early church by the Apostles. In the matter of Christian baptism, which is the point at issue here, the Apostles handed down an act which they had obtained from Christ. This act cannot evolve and become sprinkling or pouring, and still remain in historical sequence from the original. Therefore, the continuance of the act is essential to the identity of the church of Christ. This is the position the Restoration movement has sought to hold.

Considerable space has been given to Mr. Morrison's conception of the Plea, and it will be necessary to give more space to it later. However, so well does he portray the conception he advocates, along with others, that it was thought well to deal in some detail with his thinking and reasoning. The interpretation of the movement, as he sets it forth, has gained considerable prominence and numbers at the present day and represents a distinct group in the movement. It is essentially beyond the Plea, a digression from it, for it brings into being the practice of receiving unimmersed persons into the fellowship of the local church and of granting promise of salvation to all unimmersed members of the sects, a practice wholly unknown in the New Testament and repugnant to the Plea for unity, union, and world conversion.

Continuation of the statements of the Plea is begun through consideration of a statement by S. S. Lappin, which was made in 1912. Mr. Lappin says:

In terms of theology the plea teaches that men are to become sons of God through faith in the Lord Jesus Christ. In terms of sociology it

[1] *Christian Century*, Vol. 29, No. 27, p. 615.

provides for the union of believers on the foundation of the apostles and prophets, with Jesus Christ as the chief corner-stone. In its completeness it involves the restoration of the Christianity of the New Testament: its doctrines, its ordinances and its fruits. Eliminating all incidentals, it presents just the gospel of the grace of God without the incumbrance of Calvinism, Arminianism or other human systems. In figure it is the proffer of the water of life unmixed with any denominational tincture whatever.[1]

. . . . For this we have been pleading for more than a century, and when we cease pleading thus we surrender our plea, and should become a "disappearing brotherhood." But this plea does not require unity in the domain of speculative opinion. It allows freedom here, and only forbids individuals to make trouble by attempting to enforce their opinions upon others, either from the pulpit or through the press. Disregard for this cardinal feature of our plea for the unity of the church has caused us all the trouble that we have experienced for nearly half a century now, but especially in the last twenty years. We have a glorious plea, and we should adhere closely to it, and not render it nugatory by foisting upon it matters that do not inhere in it.[2]

So Mr. Lappin reviews the movement in the year stated. His conclusions that all the trouble the movement has had is a result of digression from the Plea is precisely the conclusion drawn previously in this thesis. Speculation as to the salvation of the unimmersed and as to whether or not instrumental music in worship is valid and as to whether missionary agencies are permissable, all are questions about which private opinion may be held, but the basis of unity is the apostle's doctrine.

W. R. Warren, in 1912, states the situation thusly:

For a hundred years the Disciples of Christ have been pleading that the gospel be cleared of human additions, cleansed of traditional corruptions and exalted above party divisions. Except for scattering and occasional voices, there has been only the one John in the wilderness of sectarianism . . . .[3]

The conclusion is supported, as we have seen, from a consideration of the statements that have been made through the years.

One thing that immediately comes to mind when one considers the fact that the Plea was being abandoned by some who claimed yet a connection with the historical course of the movement is the effect such action was having in the minds of younger men. It is not possible to go into detail on this point or to consider a number of statements concerning the matter, but the statement below is included for reasons that will be known when the statement is read. The statement is by Harry F. Burns, and it appeared in the *Christian Century* in 1913. Mr. Burns writes:

I was cradled in the faith of the Disciples; my parents being active members of the Christian Church and myself attending its Sunday School and church services. My college days were spent in a Baptist school, from which I graduated, but during this time I was a member of and regular attendant upon the services of the local church of the Disciples, and many was the time that I urged the need of Christian union upon the attention of the young Baptist theologs. Then came a year in "The Bible School" of

---

[1] *Christian Standard*, Vol. 48, No. 37, p. 1491. [2] *Christian Standard*, Vol. 48, No. 43, p. 1292.
[3] *Christian-Evangelist*, Vol. 49, No. 8, p. 256.

Drake University (where I went for special ministerial training), and a brief pastorate during which I began to read theological books representing a point of view decidedly at variance with the fixed system of thought to which I was accustomed. This led to my determination to enter the Divinity School of the University of Chicago, where I found a spirit of free, earnest scholarship, of earnest inquiry, which was to me like the light of a new day. After graduation I went to the pastorate of a church of some importance in a city of one hundred thousand population; and with enthusiasm, for I believed the church to be free and open minded. I even dreamed of soon being able to admit the "unimmersed Christians" into the church, as one of the ways of promoting Christian union, which seemed to me the fundamental plea of the Disciples, and an end greatly to be desired.

But three years' experience taught me that for the majority of people not only in that church but in the state, there was no road to Christian union except the basis of a fixed dogmatic statement of faith. And I further found that to preach the gospel without putting it in terms of that definite statement was to fail of response from many good people in the church. Now I had come to believe that this fixed and well-known statement of things was not adequate and implied an artificial definition of salvation. These were the bitterest hours of my life, for I had come to see that the Disciples' plea for union was not to be taken at its face value in many instances for it rested upon a narrow, dogmatic basis, upon which its realization was impossible; and I had come to believe that in most churches of the Disciples one would find most people unprepared to appreciate any statement of religious truth which did not contain the fixed phrases to which their ears were accustomed.[1]

For this reason, Mr. Burns says, he left the Disciples. Clear reading will reveal that Mr. Burns considered Christian union as simply good natured accommodation, a matter of church union and denominational confederation, and not the co-operation of Christians in world evangelism, who had been made so through acceptance of the apostolic form of Christianity. The above, of course, does not establish anything but the opinion of one man, but it shows a tendency in the thought, which may have been more wide spread than imagined.[2]

The year 1913 brought forth the following statement from George P. Rutledge:

But what is the plea? From the writer's viewpoint there are two extreme interpretations of it abroad in the brotherhood. The "very conservative" insist upon the rule of addition, while the "very liberal" insist upon the rule of subtraction. At the risk of being accused of departing from the exactness of literary rule, this writer will assert that, if the brotherhood really has two mental wings, some clippings ought to be done on both sides—especially the sides of the plea. With an occasional exception the questions that trouble our Israel are foreign to the plea. Brethren may think and preach on the majority of these questions as they please or as their temperament dictates, yet it is possible for the entire brotherhood to hold the plea in its beak and fly straight.

We frequently hear it said that the plea is union. It is; but the word "Union"—capitalized and writ large—is not sufficiently specific. Also, the Lordship of Jesus is sometimes suggested as our one great message. Amen! This phrase is comprehensive and splendid, and every sermon should be vitalized by its heart-throbs. But it can not be depended upon to reconstruct the present-day church, because it neither specifically condemns the

[1] *Christian Century*, Vol. 30, No. 49, p. 887.   [2] *Ibid.*

things that divide nor outlines a plan of union. The fathers pleaded for union and emphasized the Lordship of Jesus. But they recognized the futility of depending upon a word and a phrase, and incessantly pointed out the only possible basis of union.

Their plea proclaimed faith in Jesus Christ, the Son of the living God; repentance; a publc confession of the Saviour, and baptism as the only scriptural plan of conversion. It specified immersion as the only Scriptural baptism. It argued that the church should wear only the names mentioned in connection with it by the New Testament writers. It claimed that the Lord's supper was for all the Lord's children, and that it should be celebrated every Lord's Day. And it demanded that the church, as a whole, cast aside its authoritative ritualism and be guided, in its faith and practice, entirely by the New Testament. They preached these things as Scriptural, and, furthermore, declared that the union of the Lord's people could never answer the Saviour's prayer upon any other basis. Had they not preached as they did, our brotherhood, while it might have lived, would never have become the great world-power it is today, and the union spirit would not have assumed the proportions we now contemplate with such delight.[1]

Mr. Rutledge suggests that the proclaimers of the Plea should specify those points of New Testament doctrine in which union is to be based, that to say the Plea is "union" or "the Lordship of Jesus" will not suffice aside from these specific teachings of the Word. Essentially, however, as in the case of conversion, two attitudes must be developed in the mind of one whom we would desire to accept the doctrines specified: 1) a definite attitude toward the Word of the Lord, 2) a definite attitude toward the Lord. Submission to Jesus as Lord and the acceptance of the church of the New Testament will not be difficult to obtain once these two attitudes are developed.

In the year 1914, M. M. Davis summarized the Plea as below stated:

The principle involved was one of the loftiest that ever animated men —it was an unselfish attempt to restore primitive Christianity. At great cost, and with no material reward in view, these brave men, despite the greatest difficulties, began the search for the old paths. They would see just where Christ and his apostles trod, and, faithfully following their footsteps, they would give to the world of today the church of the first century.

The points emphasized in their search were numerous and vital. The principle ones were:

1. The proper division of the Bible . . . .
2. The deity of Jesus . . . .
3. Faith and opinion . . . .
4. Faith not doctrinal, but personal . . . .
5. Rule of faith and practice . . . .
6. Conversion . . . .
7. Bible names for Bible things . . . .
8. The Holy Spirit . . . .
9. Restoration of the ordinances . . . .
10. Bible schools . . . .
11. Christian union. An attempt to restore the apostolic church necessarily involved the plea for union, for that church was united. The Saviour taught and prayed for the union of his followers, and the apostles preached and practiced it. The restoration movement began as a protest against

---

[1] *Christian Standard*, Vol. 49, No. 21, p. 827.

division, and its great battles and splendid victories have been fought and won under this banner. "United we stand, divided we fall," is a maxim not less true in religion than in the family and the nation. "We must all hang together or we will hang separately," said one of the signers of the Declaration of Independence.[1]

It is regretted that not sufficient space is available for the complete listing of the principles named by Mr. Davis. Enough has been given, however, to establish his train of thought. Mr. Davis is thinking of Christian unity in terms of individuals and not of churches or denominations.

J. J. Haley presents the following statement on the "Catholicity of our plea:"

Catholicity of Our Plea

1. The catholic creed of Christendom, "I believe that Jesus is the Christ, the Son of the living God, the Saviour and Lord of men."

2. The catholic rule of faith and practice, the Word of God, written in the Old and New Testaments.

3. The catholic ordinances, baptism and the Lord's Supper.

4. The catholic name, Christian.

5. The catholic life, the ethics of the kingdom of God, "Whatsoever things are true, whatsoever things are honest, whatsoever things are just, whatsoever things are pure, whatsoever things are lovely, of good report, if there be any virtue, if there be any praise, think on these things."[2]

It is supposed that Mr. Haley is not suggesting that these are points universally held, but points which could be universally adopted by all without a surrender of conscience. It is an attempt at deciding upon the doctrines to be specified, as suggested by George Rutledge in an above statement.

In the year 1915, Thomas W. Phillips composed the following statement:

This basis of union, then, is the word of the apostles, the Scriptures of eternal truth. Christ is the rock on which the Christian institution is built. Every church founded on any other basis, or built on any other foundation, will perish from the earth. "Every plant which my heavenly Father hath not planted shall be rooted up." Is not this basis broad enough, deep enough, large enough, to unite the believing world? "This institution, unlike any other, is perfectly adapted to the genius of human nature. Not to the people of one part of the world, nor one race or age, but to all parts of the globe, to all races of men and to all ages of time. It contemplates man in the light of his whole destiny, as he was, as he is, and as he shall hereafter be." Christianity contemplates the completion of one great family gathered out of all families; built upon one foundation, having "one Lord, one faith, one baptism," one spirit, one inheritance and "one God and Father of all." Everything in it is unity and harmony. Divisions are denounced and oneness is everywhere taught. It presents one book, one Savior, one worship, one Judge, and one heaven. This, then, is the only basis for the union of believers, the only constitution for the Christian church.[3]

Mr. Phillip's appeal is to the word of God and to the Christianity therein revealed, in all its teaching and fruit.

---

[1] Christian Standard, Vol. 49, No. 4, pp. 124, 125.

[2] J. J. Haley, Makers and Molders of the Reformation Movement, (St. Louis: Christian Board of Publication, 1914), p. 22.   [3] Phillips, op. cit., pp. 377, 378.

The statement recorded below is from Willard Mohorter, dating about 1915:

> The yearning for some satisfactory solution of this problem is Christianity wide. Christians separated by denominational lines experience great loneliness of heart and soul.
>
> One hundred years ago, our fathers in this reformation, proposed a return to the church of the New Testament as a basis for the union of all God's people. They pled for the all sufficiency of the Bible as a rule of faith and practice. They advocated the observance of the New Testament ordinances of Christian baptism and the Lord's Supper as practiced in the apostolic church. They contended that we ought to use Bible names for Bible things. They repudiated all of creed or canon and stood together in simple faith in their risen Lord. They wore his name and exemplified his beautiful life among men.
>
> It is no marvel that this simple plea of the fathers has swept through our country and gained a million and a half devout adherents. The faithful preaching of these simple truths guarantees the continuance of this rapid growth. Shall we be faithful to our opportunity and obligation?[1]

The above is an appeal for the Restoration movement to remain faithful to the position and plea which it for one hundred years had maintained. The review as stated, does not reveal any digression from the original idea.

P. H. Welshimer, in 1916, states the issues as below:

> *The plea is the unity of God's people, the plan is RESTORATION, the purpose to be accomplished is the redemption of the world.* Jesus prayed in the garden that they might all be one as he and the Father were one, and he gave as the reason that the world might believe that God had sent him. The biggest curse today to the extension of the kingdom is the division of the forces. It weakens the forces that are at work, makes unbelievers, chills the ardor of Christians and causes the world to look on with' derision. Division breeds contempt and causes strife. The only salvation of the world lies in unity, and unity can not come without restoration. The followers of Christ are not asked to unite upon non-essentials. All are not asked to have the same opinion. In matters of essentials we are to speak the same thing. "Where the Scriptures speak, we speak; and where the Scriptures are silent, we are silent." We form opinions only where the Book does not speak, but where it speaks we will listen to the word of God, and opinions are to have no weight. God's word always must take preeminence over the opinions of men.[2]

Thus, the advocates of the Restoration idea are a people with a plea, a plan, and a purpose, which Mr. Welshimer sets forth, in order, as unity, restoration, and world conversion. Unity and restoration go together, and world conversion follows upon them. It is interesting to note the similarity between Mr. Welshimer's statement and the concept as set forth in our Lord's prayer in John 17 in which the oneness of the Disciples, the apostles teaching, and the conversion of the world are mentioned in that precise order.

Frederick D. Kershner sets forth the Restoration Plea in the manner and form following:

> The chief features of the Restoration plea are the following:
> 1. The acknowledgment of the New Testament Scriptures as the only authoritative rule of faith and practice for Christians.

---

[1] *Christian-Evangelist*, Vol. 52, No. 11, p. 324.　　[2] *Christian Standard*, Vol. 52, No. 7, p. 200.

2. The renouncing of all human creeds and the acceptance of Jesus as the Christ, the Son of God, as the only creed binding upon members of the church of Christ.

3. The restoration of the apostolic or New Testament church, with its ordinances and life as originally practiced in apostolic times.

4. The union of all Christians upon the basis of the platform laid down in the preceding propositions. The plea has sometimes been regarded as primarily a plea for Christian union, but it was only upon the basis mentioned that union has been advocated.

It may be well to outline a little more fully the four features suggested above:

I. *The First Feature—Authority of the Scriptures.*

The idea of the New Testament, and the New Testament alone, as the only rule of faith and practice for Christians is now accepted much more widely than it was some years ago. It is a position which cuts the ground from under the theory of Roman Catholicism that the church has authority to change or supersede Scriptural teaching. It also does away with the addition of man-made rules or tests to the word of God. It is in reality the core of the Protestant position as originally advocated by Wyclif, Hus, Luther and the Reformers in general. The only ultimate authority in religion, according to this position, rests in the inspired word of God as it has come down to us in the Bible. The advocates of the Restoration are, therefore, of necessity staunch defenders of the integrity and inspiration of the Holy Scriptures.

II. *The Second Feature—Christ the Only Creed.*

The assertion of the divine creed formulated in the confession of Peter (Matt. 16:16), as the only creed of the church of Christ, follows naturally from the acceptance of the Bible as the only seat of authority in religion. There is no other creed known to the Scriptures save this "good confession." It was enough creed to make people Christians in the apostolic days, and if we accept the Bible as our sole authority, it is enough today. This creed means an acceptance of the living, personal Christ as our Saviour and Lord. It is for this reason that ministers of the Restoration have frequently used the slogan, "No Creed but the Christ."

III. *The Third Feature—The New Testament Church.*

The restoration of the ordinances and life of the apostolic church means the discarding of all man-made innovations and of every practice which cannot be fully sustained by an appeal to the Scriptures. Early in the history of the movement the Campbells, who were then pedo-baptists, were forced to give up infant baptism because they could not find Scriptural authority for it. Because they could find no warrant for affusion in the New Testament, they were also forced to accept immersion as the only apostolic form of baptism. In every case, their appeal was to the Bible and to the records dealing with the church of Christ as contained in the New Testament.

IV. *The Fourth Feature—Christian Union.*

The plea for Christian union upon the basis of a complete restoration of the original church of Christ was a prominent feature of the movement from the beginning. The position taken is logical and simple. The original church of Christ was one (John 17:20, 21; I Cor. 1:10-13; Eph. 4:1-6), and when this church is restored all Christians will be one again. The denominational theory is an error and sectarianism is a sin. Christ founded but one church, and Christians are separated today because they have failed to remain true to the church which he founded. The only way to unite them permanently is for them all to come back to the original foundation. Human schemes for union will never prove effective because they do not go deep enough to touch the root of the matter.[1]

The statement above dates in 1918. Taken as a whole, it represents one of the most complete statements we have considered and portrays an accurate picture of the movement and its plea. The appeal to the scriptures is strong. The conception of Christ is Scriptural, and union pled for is the union of Christians, who have been made so through conformity to the Christianity set forth in the New Testament.

W. J. Shelburne, in 1918, asserts that the position held by the movement is simply Christian. Says he:

Is there not a position which may be rightly called Christian—a position clearly differentiated from humanism and sectarianism? Give a man a Bible and let him study it. Finding Christ to be the fulfillment of the Old Testament, let him carefully study the records of the gospel by Matthew, Mark, Luke and John. Becoming convinced that Jesus is the Son of God, let him further read in the book of Acts what the apostles commanded the inquirers to do on the day of Pentecost; what Philip commanded the Samaritans and the Eunuch to do; what Ananias told Saul to do; what Paul told the Philippian jailer to do. Were he to do as they did, he would not be a Campbellite, Methodist or Presbyterian, but a Christian. This is the position we try to teach and interpret—a position undenominational, unsectarian; just Christian.[2]

The above is a description of the putting into practice of the Restoration idea, to make Christians according to the pattern of the New Testament, and not according to the pattern of the opinions or theologies of men. Only the former can make Christians, uniting them to Christ and to each other.

B. J. Radford records the following review of the movement and its principles:

Luther and his co-reformers, having rebelled against both pope and council, necessarily turned to the Scriptures, the inspired word of God, as infallible and of supreme authority. But neither they nor their immediate successors could entirely break away from episcopal traditions and from persistent phases of ecclesiastical despotism. The resort to creeds was semi-recognition of counciliar infallibility, and the power of the Protestant clergy was rooted in the soil of long-continued Papal despotism. Although it has been more than a hundred years since the Campbells and Stone pushed this movement to its logical end and abandoned all "party standards" for the Scriptures, many of the denominations are yet held in these man-forged ecclesiastical bonds.

Having abandoned the fallible standards of uninspired men for the standard set up by Christ, and His apostles (whom he had endowed with spiritual guidance into all truth), and having abjured allegiance to popes, councils, and all other claimants to monarchical or oligarchical authority in the church, our fathers were driven to the only safe refuge from these enemies of the liberty with which Christ makes men free—the utterly democratic apostolic church. And here they struck the Restoration trail. They say that, while the Scriptures were the only repository of infallible

[1]Frederick D. Kershner, *The Restoration Handbook*, (Cincinnati: The Standard Publishing Company, 1918), pp. 7-9. [2]*Christian-Evangelist*, Vol. 50, No. 45, pp. 1472, 1473.

teaching—the truth as it is in Jesus, the truth that makes men free—the pillar and stay of that truth was the church; that it was through the church that the wisdom of God was to be manifested to principalities and powers in the heavenly places. So they set about the restoration of the apostolic church, seeing that this, if successful, would secure all their reformatory ends—unity, liberty and sound teaching. They had found their mission.[1]

The date of Mr. Radford's statement is 1919, a date with a familiar ring in the history of the movement. It is an accurate statement, in harmony with the impact of the movement as a whole.

THE UNITED CHRISTIAN MISSIONARY SOCIETY

It has already been pointed out in this history that the question of missionary organization has been a problem within the Restoration movement since the formation of the American Christian Missionary Society in 1849. The organization of the United Christian Missionary Society continues the dispute and raises again the issues involved. This section is so titled, not because the position of the United Society in regard to the Plea is to be considered herein, but because it was deemed wise to consider the formation of the Society, analyze somewhat the issues involved, and consider some of the statements of the Plea which were being recorded in the publications of the movement during that time and following. Thus, the United Christian Missionary Society and its formation are merely a background for the section.

By the year 1919, the organizational life of the movement had grown to considerable proportion. Some of the agencies by that date were: the various state missionary associations, the American Christian Missionary Society, the Foreign Christian Missionary Society, the Christian Women's Board of Missions, the Association for the Promotion of Christian Unity, the Board of Ministerial Relief, the Board of Church Extension, the National Benevolent Association, the Board of Higher Education, and in addition certain regional organizations set up in the interest of education and benevolence.[2]

It is clear to see that the multiplicity of boards for mission and benevolent work, appealing to the churches for support, would create something of a problem in the manner of appeal and response. This brought forth the suggestion from some preachers and leaders of the churches that to combine the boards into a united society was becoming a necessity. Furthermore, they suggested, each of the boards operating independently of the others made necessary a greater outlay of funds than would be necessary, if a common appeal and a united effort could be made. Still others suggested that, since we were pleading for Christian unity, it would be well to give a demonstration of our plea through the unification of the various agencies.[3]

In October of 1919, the United Christian Missionary Society was formed. The new organization was the unification of five of the above mentioned boards, namely: the American Christian Missionary Society, the Foreign Christian Missionary Society, the Christian Women's Board of Missions, the Board of Church Extension, and the Board of Ministerial Relief.[4] There has been

---

[1] *Christian Standard*, Vol. 54, No. 44, p. 1071.
[2] Dean E. Walker, *Reformation of the Nineteenth Century*, (Indianapolis: Class Notes Taken May, 1943).   [3] *Ibid.*   [4] *Ibid.*

some rearrangement of the boards today, but the original idea still remains. It was the centralization of the missionary and benevolent efforts of the movement. Unified Promotion, instituted later, is another attempt on a larger scale to unify the missionary, benevolent, educational, and state agencies.

The organization of the United Christian Missionary Society was very strongly opposed from the very first. It was felt by some that the centralization of the agencies was the beginning of ecclesiastical power and control. While the agency was supposed to be a servant of the churches, it was feared that the churches might soon become servants of the agency. Others were certain that the time would come when support of the agency would become the real test of attachment to the movement. Still others maintained that the formation of such agencies and societies was contrary to the Restoration Plea. The church of Christ, they said, is the only missionary society known to the New Testament. Furthermore, it was thought that the tendencies toward abandonment of the Plea, as evidenced in the practice of "open-membership," might crystalize around the organization and give appearance to the world that the movement as a whole was guilty of that practice. However, in the face of the cries of the opposition, the society was formed.

The movement today is bent over this issue. As was mentioned earlier, many would maintain today that non-support of the agency places one outside of the "brotherhood"; others would maintain that support of the agency is a certain sign that one does not belong to the "brotherhood". The attitude of one toward the Christ is being overshadowed by this other consideration. Both attitudes are digressions from the Plea, which through its history has maintained that one's attitude toward Christ and his obedience to Him in all things according to the Scripture is the only test of fellowship, union, and communion among Christians. Some are fearful that division may yet come from this contention within the movement. Only the strict application of the Restoration principle, it seems, will be able to prevent the thing foreshadowed. Meanwhile a strong independent, directly supported, missionary effort has grown up and is doing an exemplary work in many quarters of the globe at home and abroad.

With this much of an analysis of problems confronting the movement in the year 1919 and following, the review of the statements is continued with the presentation of one by Ira M. Boswell. Says Mr. Boswell:

An Analysis of the Restoration movement shows it can be summed up in three main propositions:

1. Purpose: The Restoration of the original unity of the church.
2. Plan: A return of the faith and practice of the apostolic church.
3. Principle: "Where the Scriptures speak, we speak; and where the Scriptures are silent, we are silent."

It seems clear, then, that those of us who believe in the Restoration movement can accept no union which does not plumb with these three propositions. And I am satisfied that it needs no word from me to prove that to accept any union based upon a denial of the deity of Christ, and the authoritative inspiration of the Scriptures, would sever the aorta of our plea, and leave its heart a bloodless piece of flesh. The very life of the Restoration movement is inseparably connected with the two great and essential truths: Jesus, the divine Son, the only begotten of the Father; and the Bible, and the Bible alone, the one authoritative bond of union and the one infallible rule of faith and order.[1]

So writes Mr. Boswell, and so has maintained the Restoration movement. The appeal is to the New Testament and to the New Testament Christ, and represents his answer to the appeals for union and federation.

W. N. Briney states the issue as below set forth:

> This, then, is the historic mission of the Restoration movement: To summon all the disciples of Christ back to the simple original Christianity of apostolic times; to restore, in theory and in practice, the New Testament church—restore it in its name, creed, ordinance, organization and life—in order to Christian unity and world evangelism. The movement was launched and has existed primarily for this great purpose. The Disciples of Christ should never lose sight of this fact.[2]

The statement is simple, but the position stated is clear. When one has restored the elements demanded to be restored by Mr. Briney, he has brought again to the face of the world the simple form of Christianity contained in God's word.

J. B. Briney, dealing with the relation of the Plea to the practice of "open-membership," declares:

> . . . . The question of the reception of the pious unimmersed into the fellowship of our churches began to be mooted, and in accommodation to the notion, and as paving the way for it, "associated membership," a thing wholly unknown to the Scriptures, was instituted. This, however, was a merely temporary makeshift to have its little day, and then give place to the real thing, and it was not long until a few preachers and one paper entered upon the open advocacy of the policy of opening the doors of our churches wide enough to receive all applicants of good character, regardless of the matter of Baptism, and a few churches actually adopted this policy. This is a complete surrender of the historic position of the Restoration movement, and a nullification of the great principle embraced in the two famous aphorisms which say, "Where the Bible speaks, we speak; where the Bible is silent, we are silent . . . ." The paper and preachers that are advocating this reactionary policy, and the churches that have adopted it, are no longer entitled to be regarded as identified with the Restoration movement, nor given recognition in our missionary work or other general enterprises.[3]

This statement, made in 1919, hits the issue square. It has already been stated in this paper that "open-membership" represents a digression from the Plea. Mr. Briney supports the conclusion, but in stronger words. In the face of such statements as this, the advocates of "open-membership" are forced to one of two alternatives: 1) they might retreat behind the supposition that, after all, the traditional concept of baptism as received by the movement is a mistake and that the New Testament meaning of the term is something else, 2) they might begin to attempt to show that "open-membership" is really what the Campbells had in mind but that they took a tangent from their original idea. Both of these positions are held by some. Few would deny this accusation of Mr. Briney, when the matter is considered in the light of the history of the Plea.

Also in 1919, G. I. Hoover wrote:

> We sometimes call this plea "Our plea," "the Restoration plea," but

---

[1] *Christian Standard*, Vol. 55, No. 4, p. 88. [2] *Christian Standard*, Vol. 54, No. 43, p. 1048.
[3] *Christian Standard*, Vol. 54, No. 45, pp. 1095, 1096.

the plea for which our fathers were supremely concerned was the New Testament plea—such a presentation of the gospel as the apostles and New Testament evangelists made, the exaltation of the ideals for the church which Jesus and his apostles clearly taught, and the earnest effort for their realization. It was a plea for the authoritative recognition and the wholehearted acceptance of the ideals of Jesus, those which he taught us in His own person and through His chosen and inspired apostles. It was a plea for the restoration of the apostolic program of Christianity, its doctrines, its ordinances, its fruits. It was a plea for the restoration of the lost unity of the followers of Christ in the one true church of which He is the living head . . . .[1]

The objectives of the Plea, according to Mr. Hoover, are:

1. For the individual—his conversion to God, and his transformation into the likeness of Christ under the sanctifying influence of the Holy Spirit. "Until Christ be formed in you" (Gal. 4:19), "the measure of the stature of the fullness of Christ" (Eph. 4:13).

2. For the church—conceived as a local congregation—the restoration of the New Testament Christian Congregation in its name, its confession of faith, its ordinances, its organization and its life.

Viewed as the whole body of Christ's followers, "one body" (I Cor. 12:12; Eph. 4:4), "No schism in the body" (I Cor. 12:25), "a body fitly framed and knit together by that which every joint supplieth" (Eph. 4:16), "a glorious church, not having spot or wrinkle, or any such thing; but that it should be holy and without blemish" (Eph. 5:27).

3. For human society—its regeneration primarily and fundamentally through the conversion of the individuals that compose it, and through a regenerate church. "The kingdoms of the world are to become the kingdom of our Lord and his Christ" (Rev. 11:15). (Read "The Christian System," essay on regeneration, pp. 281-309, by A. Campbell.)

4. The union of Christians—a unity visible and invisible, organic and spiritual, outward as well as inward, "that they all be one; even as thou, Father, art in me and I in thee, that they also may be one in us; that the world may believe that thou didst send me" (John 17:21).

5. The evangelization of the world (Matt. 28:18-20; Mark 16:15, Luke 24:46-49; John 20:21-23; Acts 1:9).[2]

The above is a very clear and complete analysis of the Plea and of the objectives of its proclamation. It is a little different from many that have gone before, but it is felt that close analysis will prove it to be in harmony with the word of our Lord and in accord with the movement as a whole.

C. C. Spencer writes of the movement and its message in the manner and form following:

. . . . We plead for the obliteration of all party lines, the dropping of all party names, and the abrogation of all party creeds. And we plead for the re-enthronement of Christ as the Head and sole authority of the church. We believe that when His followers again catch the divine vision of the Christ and restore Him to His rightful place and power over the church, the unity of His people will be accomplished, and the Christianization of the world will no longer seem to be a hopeless task. It is because the church lost the vision and dethroned Christ that the unity of the body was destroyed, the church became a Babel of warring factions, and the

---

[1] *Christian Standard*, Vol. 54, No. 49, p. 1199.   [2] *Ibid.*

progress of the kingdom of God was turned into a shameful rout before the hosts of sin, idolatry and pagan philospohy . . . .[1]

Mr. Spencer's appeal is to the Christ, to his re-enthronement. This is basic, and necessary to accomplish the ends contemplated by the Restoration movement, as has been pointed out before in this history of the Plea.

According to C. J. Sharp, writing in the year 1919:

In our judgment, the first ideal of the Campbells and all the rest was, and is, that men and women everywhere should be brought to Christ, discipled, made Christians, with all that this process might imply—not nominal Christians, not formal Christians, but humble, faithful, believing, devout, practicing Christians, living the life and carrying out the purposes, plans, program and commands of the Lord and Saviour. As nearly as we have been able to judge from reading of the mental and spiritual struggles of the forefathers, this was the beginning point.

UNION IDEAL CAME SECOND

Their sentiment *against division first*, and then their earnest desire for union grew out of this first desire. It was a logical and necessary outgrowth. It required no long look and no unusual vision to see that indifference to Christ and the gospel was then prevalent, and all but general. It also required no long look to see that the Christian forces were thoroughly entangled in the meshes of great and small ecclesiasticism, formalism, creedism, division and strife. The life-line which should have been saving the lost was hopelessly snarled, and the followers, like children pulling at a tangled rope, were only pulling one against the other. These men of God, with the one desire to see the church doing the work of Christ in seeking to "save that which is lost," saw first that division and parytism were a hindrance to the church, and, second, that they were unscriptural. Their second logical step and ideal was, therefore, a union of God's people based on God's word alone.

A COMPROMISE WHICH WOULD COMPROMISE NO ONE

This appeared to them as a feasible compromise, which would compromise no one. They were surprised, no doubt, to find almost universal opposition and objection to union itself, union of any kind or on any basis. They were soon fully persuaded that no union was at all possible except a union of the Word alone. Hence the declaration, "Where the Scriptures speak, we speak; where the Scriptures are silent, we are silent." God's silences must be as much respected as His thunderings; His liberties as closely guarded as His commands; His precepts held unchanged and unchangeable, and nothing to be bound upon men except by positive precept of the God of all.[2]

The first paragraph of Mr. Sharp's statement reminds one of Benjamin Franklin's Assertion that we are to unite "on being Christians." Certainly, the early leaders of the Restoration movement were interested in uniting men to Christ, which, they felt, would unite them to one another and enable their working together on the conversion of all mankind. Mr. Sharp's analysis of the development of thought is probably accurate.

Russell Errett, in 1920, makes the following comment on the Restoration movement's plea for the union of all Christians:

This plan of unity is not only Scriptural and catholic, but its demon-

---

[1] *Christian Standard*, Vol. 54, No. 36, p. 872.   [2] *Christian Standard*, Vol. 54, No. 47, p. 1151.

stration has been true to Scriptural precept and example throughout. Beginning in obscurity, and without ecclesiastical organization or prestige, it has spread simply as a leaven, a growing force, permeating the life of the Christian world with a nobler sense of the supreme authority of the word of God, and a new sense of the sinfulness of the human rivalries that have usurped that authority. Always and everywhere it has carried the one message—Christ the only creed; His word the only authority; the terms of membership unconditional surrender to that word.

SECTARIANISM RAISES THE WHITE FLAG

Meanwhile, the hosts of sectarianism, entrenched in wealth and prestige and culture, and vast ecclesiastical establishments, or hierarchies, fiercely holding their own against one another, have united in one thing alone—in unrelenting war on this union movement as a common foe. During all these years, a century or more, no sectarian pulpit or platform has ever been opened to the message of unconditional surrender to God's word, nor consent been given in a union meeting to the declaration of the the Scriptural terms of pardon. With one voice they have justified the divisions in the body of Christ as essential.[1]

The above is an excerpt from a paper read before a Restoration Congress at St. Louis, Missouri. His description of the growth of the movement as leaven, penetrating the life of the Christian world is fine. Such is the precise example given by our Lord as to the manner of infiltration of his people, not as giant organizations clamping the authority of the heads of the church upon the lives of men but the willful submission of men to the authority of Christ leavening the life, the church, and the world. The idea was to change the world by changing men; not to change men by changing the world.

The matter of loyalty and liberty is again brought forward in the next statement by Ernest Hunter Wray, dating in 1919:

Our plea for absolute loyalty to the Lord Jesus Christ not only manifests itself in the acceptance of the Word of God as the rule of faith and practice, but also in that liberty and freedom from the yoke of sin and ecclesiastical bondage from which our Lord sets us free. All the attempts of men to improve upon the original plan and organization of the church by the imposition of creeds and ecclesiastical authority not only not helped the progress of the kingdom but have become actual hindrances to its furtherance. The freedom which loyalty to Christ brings is freedom from all man-made and unnecessary paraphernalia and the joy which comes from the consciousness of having all one's powers dedicated to and used of him.

Then, too, we believe that the way of approach to Christian union is not by way of compromise of anything that is fundamental in any church program, but by way of loyalty that refuses any creed of doctrine not required of Christ and that insists on full acceptance of the elements of the simple scheme of salvation as revealed by the Master. To have union on any other basis than this would be a calamity to the Christian church. Whenever the time comes when men everywhere are willing to be loyal to him who is Lord of all and the Head of his church, then we shall enjoy the full freedom of the Spirit and we shall present to the world the beauty and dignity and the power of a united church. And so on this basis of

[1] *Christian Standard*, Vol. 56, No. 4, p. 1403.

loyalty we are willing and ready to unite with all communions and all individuals who desire to do the will of God.[1]

In the above statement, Mr. Wray is in agreement with J. H. Garrison in the latter's conception of loyalty to Christ and liberty in Christ as presented earlier in this history. This is a fine thought, and is a true and to the point statement of the position of the Restoration movement.

W. H. Book, about the year 1920, wrote as follows:

We hear much, in this day, of "efficiency," "Get together at all costs." "We must have union." One of the leading ministers in the Christian Church recently declared that the union must come, but that he did not know just how. We hear much of the "community church." A church composed of all creeds and no creeds, with only one purpose; viz., "to serve." After a hundred years, denominations which at one time ridiculed the thought of union are now anxious for it; and just at the time when the *one* thing for which Christ prayed and the thing for which we have labored is in sight, and almost an accomplished fact, some of our people have been swept off their feet by this word "efficiency," and are willing to compromise and surrender to the claims of sectarianism.

Paul was a believer in Christian unity; he was a member of that peculiar Christian Endeavor society, and he lays down the only divinely inspired program upon which Christian people can unite without a sacrifice of truth (Eph. 4:1-16). It must be a unity of the Spirit in the bond of peace. There are seven planks in the platform, and there can be no perfect unity if a single one is sacrificed.

One body, *one* spirit, *one* hope, *one* Lord, *one* faith, *one* baptism, *one* God and Father.[2]

When you remove baptism, you *divide* rather than *unite* the people of God. A church without conviction is a church without influence. The religious world loses respect for such a church. If these propagandists are really in earnest, and want to make a contribution which shall be the lessening of denominationalism, and are willing to do it at any price, why do they not unite with sectarian churches, who are already teaching the very things that they teach?[3]

Christian unity—not church union—must be on a New Testament basis; otherwise it can not be accomplished. You can no more bring about Christian unity by cutting out a part of the commission, mutilating the constitution of the kingdom, and compromising one or more of the planks in the divine program, than you can change night into day, light into darkness, death into life, or transmute one species into another.[4]

Mr. Book is clear to state one thing: the union sought by the Restoration movement is not to be gained at any cost. Some things are more important than union, and the divine pattern of things is more important than good natured accommodation. Note also, that he pleads for Christian unity not church union, for oneness with each other through oneness with Christ not merely the cooperation of denominations.

The question of the unit in the unity sought by the Restoration movement has always been a problem. To some it has been the church; to others it has

---

[1] *Christian-Evangelist*, Vol. 56, No. 48, p. 1249.
[2] W. H. Book, et al, *The Watchword of the Restoration Vindicated*, (Cincinnati: The Standard Publishing Company, pp. 99, 100.   [3] *Ibid.*, p. 102.   [4] *Ibid.*

been the denomination. W. R. Walker, in 1921, sets forth the position held by the majority of those pleading the cause of Christian unity, as this research has brought out again and again. However, no one has said it more clearly. "What is the unit in unity?" Mr. Walker answers:

The answer to this question is vitally important. All our thinking on the problem of Christian unity must be in terms of some unit—the elemental factor, or part, composing the whole. Just what are we trying to unite, that the prayer of Jesus for unity may be answered.

Current discussion clearly reveals the fact that most people are thinking in terms of organization. The denomination is the unit, as they see it. Leaders in Christian union movements are planning to bring all existing denominations into one new body, or federate them, somewhat after the model of the United State Government, granting much autonomy to each affiliating body, but requiring subordination to a super-ecclesiastical arrangement.[1]

If the denomination is the unit, it is right to federate, compromise terms of fellowship and urge individual and congregational submission to organized authority, that one great Protestant union may result. If this be the ideal, I wish to respectfully recommend to Protestantism the ecclesiastical machinery of Romanism. Here is a plan of centralized authority, guaranteeing uniformity if desired, preventing disunion in any event.[2]

If, however, a great ecclesiasticism was not Jesus' ideal when He prayed for the unity of His disciples, we are following the wrong program. Let Jesus tell us what His unit is.

"Neither pray I for these only, but for them also that believe on me through their words; that they may all be one; even as thou, Father, art in me, and I in thee." "I am the vine, ye are the branches." Quotations might be indefinitely multiplied from the New Testament on this point, but nothing new would be added. It is impossible to mistake Jesus' meaning. His unit is the individual Christian. Not one passage in the New Testament supports the organizational conception.

Our task and duty in the case now become perfectly plain.

We are to do our utmost to unite individual Christians as they were united in Christ in the ideal New Testament church.[3]

The Scriptural basis of Christian unity is identical with the terms of membership in the New Testament church. This, in turn, is identical with the law of induction into Christ.[4]

The history of the Plea has shown that the statements of the Plea in the aggregate agree with Mr. Walker's statement above. However, it has never before been stated as clearly as here. The simplicity of it is staggering, but we have been adequately warned, "Be not beguiled from the simplicity that is in Christ Jesus."

The Plea was outlined by Peter Ainslie in the year 1924 as follows:

The Disciples humbly present to Christendom the results of their research as far as they have gone in their study for a Scriptural and reasonable way to the peace of the Church: (1) A catholic confession that Jesus is the Christ over against any creedal declarations; (2) a catholic name for all believers, such as Christians, Disciples of Christ, etc.; (3) a catholic book of authority, the Holy Scriptures, emphasizing especially the New

[1] *Christian Standard*, Vol. 56, No. 39, p. 2373.   [2]*Ibid.*   [3]*Ibid.*
[4] *Christian Standard*, Vol. 57, No. 13, p. 3023.

Testament; (4) a catholic mode of baptism, immersion of the penitent believer; and (5) a catholic observance of the Lord's Supper to which persons of all communions are invited on an equality of fellowship.[1]

It is to be noted that Mr. Ainslie is appealing to catholic faith and practice or those things upon which all Christians agree. Note the same element in the following:

> Agreeing with the evangelical Christians on the great fundamentals of our common faith, they sought a basis for union by eliminating those things as tests of fellowship upon which we differ and uniting upon those things on which there is universal agreement, so their message had nothing to do with the formation of a new creed, even if the movement did develop, against their wishes, into a separarte communion. They sought to emphasize the great catholic principles upon which Christendom was agreed and they believed that conformity to these catholic principles would lead believers out of the confusion of denominationalism into the peace of a united Christendom.[2]

Reference is made, in answer to the above, to the statements of the Plea from the earlier periods of the movement. It is thought that the interested searcher will find that the appeal in its greater proportion, has not been to the "catholic" or "universal" points of agreement, but to the faith and practice of the New Testament. Perhaps, however, Mr. Ainslie would answer that all are agreed as to the faith and practice of the New Testament, though not actually in conformity to it. This, of course, may be true. The point was made earlier that all could accept the faith and practice of the New Testament church without any surrender of conscience, not that such was already agreed upon by all, but that all recognized the New Testament to be the record of authority upon these matters. It is supposed that Mr. Ainslie is proposing, then, that all conform to that which all agree upon and that the universal principles suggested earlier constitute those points of agreement.

Mr. Ainslie continues, pointing out the sort of union we seek:

> Christian union is not a doctrine; but, like Christ Himself, it is a life, and only a phase of it is the chief interest to us. The Church is divided by schism and consequently love is marred, life is weakened and the conversion of the world is hindered, therefore above all other issues of Christendom is the union of the Church of God. I do not mean a federation of the communions, as helpful as that is. I do not mean a mechanical union of all Christians, although that is far better than division, but I mean nothing less than a union like that for which Jesus prayed and without which the world cannot be won to Him.[3]

The object of the Plea, as Mr. Ainslie presents it here, is supported by the weight of previous statements. The problem all along has been to persuade conformity to the common agreements, and remains the problem today.

Edwin R. Errett, in 1924, brings forth a notion that is worthy of careful weighing and evaluation. Mr. Errett asserts:

> The people who plead for Christian unity are obligated by every law in heaven and earth to demonstrate it. If our plea for unity means anything at all, it means that we are obligated to prove to the Christian world that

[1]Peter Ainslie, *The Message of the Disciples for the Union of the Church,* (New York: Fleming H. Revell Company, 1924), pp. 25, 26.
[2]*Ibid.,* p. 26.   [3]*Ibid.,* pp. 20, 21.

Christians can maintain their essential unity in Christ and be patient with various differences of opinion as to methods of working; we are obligated to demonstrate to the Christian world that Christians can work through various agencies and be at least as fair to each other as are the competitors of the commercial world; we are obligated to demonstrate that we can be one in Christ without impairing liberty of belief on all non-essential matters; we are obigated to demonstrate to Christendom that we can correct evil conditions without breaking into fragments; we are obligated to demonstrate to the religious world an inherent Christian willingness "to live and let live" when it comes to various efforts at Christian work.

Unless we can demonstrate this ability to maintain our essential unity even when a great missionary agency has gone wrong, we are doomed to be the laughing-stock of the Christian world and the Restoration Movement will go down as a nine days wonder.[1]

To Mr. Errett and to many others no question is involved as to whether or not the missionary agency has gone wrong, but that Christians should excommunicate each other simply upon the ground of support or non-support of the agency, without regard to faith and practice, is basically contrary to the Plea. The agency is not the church. If the agency has been unfaithful to the Lord or to the Plea, which is essentially the gospel of Christ, then it should be repudiated, but care should be taken that, at the same time, some who are yet faithful and loyal to Christ are not also repudiated.

B. A. Abbott presents the concept of uniting upon "common, universal ground" as Mr. Ainslie has presented it above, listing the points as does Mr. Ainlsie in the first paragraph quoted. He then says in the same article, which was printed in 1924:

The proposal of the Disciples is their plea for the union of all God's people on the foundation of the apostles and prophets, Jesus Christ himself being the chief corner stone. It is a call to God's people to come out of their separate and isolated existence and become one in Jesus Christ with his doctrine, work, word, hope and worship as guides in the way of life. It is, therefore, a plea of large friendships and all-inclusive fellowships. It is the plea to all God's people to take the Word of God as their only rule of faith and practice.[2]

The above statement would find general agreement, as we have seen, in the total impact of the movement.

In regard to the question of what the relation shall be between those who practice "open-membership" and those who refuse to practice it, P. H. Welshimer says:

To be sure, we are congregational in government, and every congregation of believers has a perfect right to believe what it desires, teach anything and everything that meets its own approval, let down the bars or build them up at its own pleasure, and tell the rest of the world to go bury itself; but, *a congregation has no right to do these things and still call itself a part of a great movement that stands diametrically opposed to any such course of procedure.* We realize that one church has no right to tell another church what to preach or what to do, *but a church does have the*

[1] *Christian Standard*, Vol. 59, No. 18, p. 454.
[2] B. A. Abbott, *The Disciples, An Interpretation*, (St. Louis: The Bethany Press, 1924), p. 38.

right to take the stand that it will not be hooked up with any other church or churches in a brotherhood of churches, when one or more of those churches willfully departs from the doctrine.

Any church has a right to go into the ditch if it wants to, and other churches have a right to object to going into the ditch with it.[1]

The procedure suggested by Mr. Welshimer is about the only conclusion that can be drawn in the case in point. "Open-membership" is a surrender of the gospel in part and also a surrender of the Plea. It has no place among people who are appealing to the Christians of the world to unite upon the basis of clearly stated elements of the gospel of which Christian immersion is one.

The term "brotherhood of churches" as used above by Mr. Welshimer is strange language in a movement suggesting that Bible things should be called by Bible terms. Such a concept is not to be found in the New Testament. It is a brotherhood, a brotherhood of Christians, but certainly not a "brotherhood of churches." This, it seems, is one of the basic problems among the advocates of the Restoration Plea today. More clear thinking on this point would aid the cause of the Restoration movement immensely.

Z. T. Sweeney is the author of the following statement of the Plea:

Our plea naturally divides itself into, first: our creed: second, our practice.

I. What is our creed? The apostle Peter, in the opening sentence of his second Epistle, addresses it, "to them that have obtained like precious faith with us." In his day the faith of one Christian was like the faith of every other Christian. Not so today. That "like precious faith" was Peter's. If we can learn what was Peter's faith, we can know the faith of all. Peter makes a confession of his faith to the Lord at Caesarea Philippi in the following words: "Thou are the Christ, the Son of the living God." Christ blessed Peter and told him, "Upon this rock I will build my church." *This is our creed . . . .*

There is not an article of that creed that is not essential to Christianity. Moreover, it is the universal faith of all evangelical Christians. Our creed, therefore, is universal. "Well," says one, "is that all?" Yes, that is all—absolutely and unqualifiedly all that a man must believe to be a Christian.[2]

II. What is our practice? In the short space allotted me, I have only time to hint at a few of the important details in our practice:

(1) We call Bible things by Bible names. We call the church by its names in the New Testament. We call the members by New Testament names. We especially call ourselves Christians. Is there anything peculiar in that? Is not the name "Christian" worn by all who profess the religion of Christ? "Oh," says one, "we all claim to be Christians, but some of us wear human names." Well, those names are peculiar, but they are your peculiarity and not ours; our name is universal.

(2) We baptize believers in Christ. Is there anything peculiar in that? Don't all churches baptize believers?

"But we baptize infants also." Well, that is peculiar, but it is your peculiarity. Our practice is universal.

(3) We practice immersion for baptism. Is there anything peculiar in that? Don't all churches recognize immersion as valid baptism? "We prac-

---

[1] *Christian Standard*, Vol. 60, No. 3, p. 52.

[2] Z. T. Sweeney, Editor, *New Testament Christianity*, (Columbus: New Testament Christianity Book Fund, Inc., 1926), III, 84, 85.

tice immersion and also pouring and sprinkling." Here, again, you are peculiar while our practice is universal.

(4) We meet on the first day of the week to break bread. Is there any church that will deny that is right? "We think that is too often, and so practice monthly, quarterly or yearly communion." That, again, is peculiar, but it is your peculiarity. All agree that if any church desires to practice weekly communion it is in harmony with the will of God.

(5) We require Christians to form their character according to the ethics of Christ. The great laws of self-sacrifice and self denial and altruism taught by Him are to form the warp and woof of Christian character; Christ must be formed "in us the hope of glory."

(6) We require all members of Christ's body to live a life of holiness and peace, to walk in the footsteps and teachings of the Master, to grow up in the divine life "unto him who is the head in all things," to "do good unto all men, especially unto them that are of the household of faith."

(7) We present to the Christian world a platform of unity found in the fourth chapter of Ephesians in the following words: "There is one body and one Spirit, even as ye are called in one hope of your calling, one Lord, one faith, one baptism, one God and Father of all, who is above all, and through all, and in you all."

(8) We require all who come into the church to co-operate as they are able in carrying out the command of Jesus to "go into all the world and preach the gospel to every creature." Is there anything peculiar in that? Do not all churches require the same?

Now, I have given as briefly as I can our practice, and I defy you to show that there is anything peculiar in it. It is the universal practice of all evangelical Christians, and entirely unsectarian.[1]

Mr. Sweeney is attempting to show in the above statement that the Restoration movement is peculiar only in that it has no peculiarity and that the faith and practice of the movement is in reality, the faith and practice of all Christians everywhere. The added peculiarities of the sects divide. Again it is pointed out that the argument presented here is not absolutely true. The faith and practice of the Restoration movement might be universally acceptable, since it is the faith and practice of the New Testament church. However, it is not the faith and practice of universal Christianity today.

One thing needs to be pointed out in Mr. Sweeney's statement. In the first paragraph he says: "In his day the faith of one Christian was like the faith of every other Christian. Not so today." In the last section of the first paragaph he says: "There is not an article in that creed that is not essential to Christianity. Moreover, it is the universal faith of all evangelical Christians." This, at first, appears as a contradiction. The similarity in the faith of all evangelical Christians may be found in their common agreement that Jesus is the Christ; the difference in their faith may be noted in the additions which have been appended to that common element. The New Testament Christians had no such additions, so the faith of each was like the faith of every other Christian; today, the additions have been made, so the faith of each is not like the faith of every other Christian. Mr. Sweeney would ask that the appendages be abandoned and that all come to the simple faith of the New Testament and to that alone.

---

[1]*Ibid.*, pp. 87, 89.

In a sermon by Alexander Proctor, published in the year 1926, the ultimate goal of the Plea is emphasized as the following statement begins:

One feels tempted to exclaim: How long have these vain systems, born of the pride of reason and of the heart, yet to trifle and to mock the great wants and woes of the world? How long shall the souls of the dying millions of our race cry out against those who, with these obsolete systems, stand in the way of the world's redemption?

The premises before us are now wide enough to indicate the highest duty of the true men of this generation. It is to call men from these dumb idols to serve the living God; to work and pray for the annihilation of every system which stands in the way of the world's conversion to Christ The position which we have taken as a people, involves nothing less than this. Our antagonism is not to men, but to systems as such. With these there can be no compromise. If there is a man among us who thinks of the possibility of such a thing, he understands neither the principles which he represents nor the people with whom he is identified. If God has given us as a people any mission in the world, it is to turn men from systems—which can not convert any large part of mankind, but which only make religious partisans—to Jesus the Christ, who can and will save to the uttermost all who come to God by him. It therefore behooves every truehearted man to gird himself for the work, to put on the whole armor of God, and enter the contest as if the salvation of the world depended upon his personal success.[1]

When one considers the fact that sectarianism and partyism, with their ecclesiasticism and partizan characteristics, are standing between a sinful world and the Saviour, the urgency of a return to New Testament Christianity and the elimination of every sectarian peculiarity are brought solidly home. Mr. Proctor realizes this and has presented a fine statement of our responsibility in the matter.

In a sermon by H. W. Everest, published in 1926, entitled "The Church of the First Century," the characteristics and marks of that institution are set forth in very clear and accurate terms. Then the following remarks are made:

Every institution of the church has been changed and marred by unholy hands; we must go back to the first sources. All the streams of religious teaching have been polluted by theological speculations and priestly abuses; we must go up and drink at the fountain head. All the offices and organizations of the church have been prostituted to worldly ambition and worldly gain; we must again stand in the presence of the Apostles and see how they administered the kingdom of heaven.[2]

Could we but reproduce the church of the first century in its spirit and power, with our millions of money and our millions of men, and with our peaceable access to all tribes and nations of the earth, how soon all the kingdoms of this world would become the kingdom of our Lord and Saviour Jesus Christ.

As a brotherhood, nearly a million strong, this is our position, this is our endeavor. We present no human creed and no human plan of confederation, but we say: "Let us go back to the days of inspiration and infallible teaching, let us sit at the feet of the Apostles, let us rally around the cross."

Here we stand; we can do no otherwise, so help us God. And, if in the good time coming, whose auspicious signs are already apparent in

[1]Z. T. Sweeney, Editor, *New Testament Christianity*, (Columbus: New Testament Christianity Book Fund, Inc., 1926), II, 80, 81.   [2]*Ibid.*, pp. 19, 20.

the ecclesiastical sky, the contending churches of christendom shall drop creeds or revise them out of existence, cease to glory in party names, and return to the church of the first century, to the foundation of Apostles and Prophets, they will find us a people tenting on that ground and lifting the banner of the cross higher and still higher.[1]

Mr. Everest's statement speaks for itself. It is regretted that we cannot include his remarks on the New Testament Church as an illustration of how well he applied these principles in making the institution of God's new covenant live.

W. M. Forrest is the author of the next statement, which is taken from his book, Do Fundamentalists Play Fair? In the book, which was published in 1926, Mr. Forrest makes the following statement:

. . . . The writer belongs to a religious body that began by making a sharp distinction between the Old and New Testaments, the Law and the gospel. It would not subscribe to any of the creeds, not even the simple Apostles' Creed. It chose to call Bible things by Bible terms, and therefore would not mention the Trinity, nor admit to its hymn books praises to God in three persons. Hence it was long set down as Unitarian and scorned and shunned by the orthodox. Yet it recognized the Father, Son and Holy Spirit, believed in the divinity of Christ, and accepted all the established doctrines of the creeds. Without change in any of those respects, it is now recognized in the company of the orthodox, and the vast majority of its preachers and members are no doubt soundly fundamentalist. If the gentleman who writes about Christianity and Liberalism as two distinct and diametrically opposed religions had been alive a century ago, he would unquestionably have had his church Christian and mine unchristian, by many infallible proofs. If he could be alive a century hence he would undoubtedly regard present day liberalism as Christian, and be proving something else, then new, as non-christian. Why not be of the spirit which can anticipate the verdict of time? Why not admit the other man may be telling the truth when he says that his conception of Christianity is, in other terms, what every man's Christianity has always essentially been.[2]

In short, Mr. Forrest believes that the differences between men who appear to write diametrically opposed views of the church and of the gospel are really non existent. The apparent difference is in terminology and not in the ideas which the terms represent. Thus, according to Mr. Forrest, there is no real difference between Calvinism and Arminianism, no real feud between Arius and Athanasius, no real difference between a man who says that Jesus is the Son of God and one who says that Jesus is a Son of God, nor between the man who says that the Bible is God's word and the man who says that the Bible represents the record of man's quest for God through the ages. This, certainly is not the position that the Restoration movement has historically occupied.

Moreover, Mr. Forrest reveals further his departure from the Plea as he says:

The dead hand of the past has no right to dominate a living church. . . . . Loyalty to founders, constitutions, creeds, and leaders means trying to keep as true to great principles in our day as the fathers did in theirs. That means constant change, and adaption, and reinterpretation.[3]

[1]Ibid., pp. 28, 29.
[2]W. M. Forrest, Do Fundamentalists Play Fair? (New York: The MacMillan Company, 1926), pp. 101, 102.   [3]Ibid., pp. 115, 116.

To restore the New Testament church, then, according to Mr. Forrest, would solve no problems and would not at all represent loyalty to Christ. Christian unity would not necessarily require a connection in faith and practice with the apostles. Yet, this is precisely what the Restoration movement has maintained. To found present day Christianity upon any other foundation than that laid by Christ and his apostles in the New Testament disrupts the historical unity of the church, cuts Christians today off from the Christians of the New Testament day. To have true Christian unity, we must be one with Paul, as well as one with each other today.

William Robinson, in an article published in 1926, presents the following statement on "What the Churches of Christ Stand For":

> What, then, are the positive contributions of this movement, whose growth numerically has been so rapid and shows no signs of abating?
>
> (1) In the first place, it has borne unflinching testimony to the value of the New Testament as the sacred record by which all Christianity must be judged, and it has insisted on the historic method of interpretation. (2) But at the same time it has insisted on the divine character of the church, visible on earth; and the central position within its life of the two great sacraments of baptism and the Lord's Supper. Moreover as to these sacraments, it has maintained that they must be interpreted not only spiritually, but ethically; that is, that they must result in a new life devoted to the will of God. And so it has stood throughout its history for purity and righteousness of Christian life, and has fostered self-sacrifice, zeal and devotion. (3) It has witnessed to the centrality of Christ in Christian discipleship, and so has stressed the conscious yielding of the whole man—intellect, emotions and will—to Him in loyalty and trust, as the test of discipleship. It has therefore rejected that early departure from this vital principle of Christianity which sanctions the administration of baptism—the badge of discipleship—to unconscious infants, who can not exercise choice, being incapable of either belief or repentance. (4) It has witnessed to the spiritual satisfaction which comes from weekly corporate worship centering around the Lord's Supper. (5) By its aversion to creeds and confessions, it has shown how to combine a maxim of liberty with a sane order and orthodoxy, and how to show a united front with a minimum of ecclesiastical organization. (6) And, finally, it has witnessed, with an undying passion, to the need for a real organic unity of Christ's church. This is the historic task of the churches of Christ. They have never ceased in their "earnest efforts to promote both by testimony and practical labors the unity of the people of God." Nor will they cease until "we all attain unto the unity of the faith, and of the knowledge of the Son of God, unto a fullgrown man, unto the measure of the stature of the fullness of Christ.[1]

The testimony of Mr. Robinson concerning the positive contributions of the movement is well stated and truly composed. It has been clear, in this study, that the movement has proclaimed the principles he reviews above. While the above could not be said to be a statement of the Plea, it represents the effect of the plea in operation.

The following statement is by George P. Taubman, who asserts:

> The restoration of the New Testament church in name, creed, doctrine, ordinance and life is the only practical plan offered as a basis for the unity of all believers in Christ. This was in the minds of the fathers; it is

[1] *Christian Standard*, Vol. 61, No. 44, p. 535.

found in the history of every inch of the way we have traveled. It is the plan for Christian unity proposed by the churches of Christ to a world sadly torn with division.[1]

We should note, also, that there is demanded a *complete* restoration of the New Testament church, not only in name and in creed, for that is about as far as some of our people go, but a restoration, also, of ordinance, of doctrine and of life. We have been compromising on some of these items. Each of them occupied an important place in the program of the New Testament church, and seemed to be an important factor in her success. We can not reason otherwise than to insist upon a complete restoration of the New Testament church if we desire New Testament results.[2]

It is worthy of note that in many of the statements since the turn of the century a review of the intent of the original reformers and of the movement in its emphasis through the years is set forth. This is true of the above remarks by Mr. Taubman when he says of the restoration of the New Testament church: "This was in the mind of the fathers; it is found in the history of every inch of the way we have traveled." This is stressed, no doubt, to offset the contention of some, whom we have seen to be on a tangent from the Plea, that the original reformers and the movement has really stood for the position they hold and that the idea of restoration is of late origin in the movement. However, to Mr. Taubman, the movement has always been advocating a "complete restoration of the New Testament church."

That the Restoration movement had found the true ground of Christian unity was not a matter of doubt to the mind of Jesse R. Kellems, who composed the statement below in the year 1927. Mr. Kellems affirms:

There can be no doubt but that the Restoration movement has discovered for the Christian world the method of unity as well as its theory. I am quite sure that our great plea—the large pretension which we have made—commits us to a vital interest in every attempt to solve the unity problem, even though we may not believe at all in the solutions advanced. We must welcome every chance to associate with our Christian brethren of other communions in conference and prayer, in discussion public and private. On every occasion we must let our voice be heard, and in no uncertain advocacy of what we honestly believe the divine plan for reunion to be. But Christian unity is not going to come by committee pronouncement nor by act of parliament. It is never going to come by an acknowledgement of the historic creeds. The only basis of Christian unity is that which unites one Christian to another in the bonds of Christian love and fellowship. The same thing which makes a man a Christian, that which alone is necessary to the salvation of his soul, is the only foundation upon which any enduring unity can be consummated. When men are committed to Christ according to His own great commission and are organized into churches of Christ, they stand upon the only possible ground upon which God's divided people may be one. Our greatest contribution to this noble cause can be made by an unremitting proclamation of the divine way of salvation and an organization of those who accept it into churches of Christ upon the New Testament pattern, and a demonstration by our own unity and liberality that our program is all we claim for it.[8]

Mr. Kellems has grasped well the plan as proposed by the Restoration movement. His suggestion, proposed at the beginning of the statement, to accept

[1] *Christian Standard*, Vol. 62, No. 37, p. 867.
[2] *Ibid.*   [8] *Christian Standard*, Vol. 62, No. 44, p. 840.

every opportunity to present the plan and to discuss the matter of unity with "other communions" is well taken. There is no question that many times the advocates of the Plea have held themselves aloof, refusing all fellowship and co-operation with those at odds with the Plea, and, consequently, the message has gone unheard among those people for whom it is proposed. Denominationalism is not going to come to the Plea to be destroyed; we must take the Plea to those to whom it it addressed.

J. S. Raum, who left the Reformed people to enlist in the movement to restore the church of the New Testament, says:

> You ask me: "What in the Restoration plea especially appealed to me?" I answer: "The conception of the supreme and final authority of Jesus Christ." Were that authority universally recognized today, all human passions would subside, all human traditions and creeds would lose their power, and the will of the many would be lost in the will of the One.[1]

The remarks are from a published sermon, which was preached in 1927 before a North American Christian Convention. The idea of "the will of the many" being lost "in the will of the One" is descriptive of the very goal sought by those who plead for the restoration of the New Testament church. This, indeed, would be the unity of Christians.

That the Plea is a plea for Christ is the position taken by C. C. Crawford, in 1927, as he says:

> The point I make is this: This particular thing that has been called "our plea" is not ours; in reality, it is a plea for Christ, and it is as old as the apostolic message. It is Christo-centric; Jesus Christ is in all, through all, over all; in fact He is *the all* of the plea . . . .
>
> As the Restoration movement stands for the reproduction of New Testament Christianity, it follows that the central thought and theme of its preaching is likewise *the personal Christ*. The Restoration movement differs from Catholicism in that it repudiates all ecclesiastical machines; it differs from Protestantism in that it rejects all human names, creeds and ceremonials. It is a protest, not only against Catholicism, but also against those things which Protestantism has borrowed from Catholicism that are not to be found in the New Testament church. The fundamental message of the movement is the preeminence of Christ. The Restoration plea may be defined in a single sentence as a plea for Christ . . . .[2]

Mr. Crawford then proceeds to point out that the Plea is a plea for: "The Name of Christ," "The Person of Christ," "The Word of Christ," "The Authority of Christ," "The Church of Christ," "The Ordinances of Christ," "Unity in Christ," and "Consecration to Christ," filling in, however, with a more complete description of each point. Certainly Christ is the center of the message of the Plea, since He is the center of the gospel and the faith.

In the year 1927, J. H. O. Smith analyzes the difficulties facing the church and the solution to them, as conceived by the Restoration movement, as he says:

> The supreme authority of Christ and apostles is acknowledged by both Catholics and Protestants, and is therefore non-sectarian. Apostolic succession has been subject to endless discussion. We are united about the

---

[1] *Christian Standard,* Vol. 62, No. 48, p. 934.
[2] C. C. Crawford, *Sermon Outlines, The Restoration Plea,* (St. Louis: Restoration Publishing Company, 1927), I, 44-59.

original apostles, but divided with regard to professed successors, who claim to be the Lord's special representatives, and to hold commission under the head of the church, equal to the apostles. Not Christ and the twelve apostles as interpreted by the head of the Church of Rome, the heads of the Church of England, or any other, but these chieftains measured by the word of Christ and His apostles.

Christ being the Head of the church, the apostles being recognized as His representatives on earth, and the Bible containing their word, we must go back "through the tangled thicket of the years" to find in the Scriptures the plans and specifications for building the church and the only basis of Christian union.

The identity of the church lies not in broken fragments of succession or even in a chain, which can be shaken in Chicago, London or Rome, and clank clear back to the city of Jerusalem. The identity of the church is to be determined by comparing its constitution with the unquestioned, original, divine pattern given by Christ and His apostles.[1]

That the identity of the church is to be determined by reference to the word and not by reference to so called "succession of bishops" is precisely the position of the movement to restore the church of Christ. The clanking chain illustration picturesquely portrays one of the greatest problems involved in the divisions of Christians today.

To suppose that unity could be accomplished without cleansing the churches of error and anti-scriptural traditions was not a part of the thinking of B. J. Radford, and in 1927, to illustrate the point he points out that:

To close and bandage the wounds of a mangled body while leaving them full of septic germs is only making matters worse, yet there are many earnest and sympathetic souls who seem bent on practicing such futile surgery upon the wounded body of Christ. However skillfully closed and stitched with threads of sophistry, and however piously anointed with prayer, the wounds will never heal unless the germs of error are destroyed. Doctors of divinity are astonishingly slow to see the need of sterlization . . . .[2]

The truth presented in Mr. Radford's statement no doctor of medicine would deny today. However, years were needed before the people were able to be convinced of the necessity of sterilization. Years more may be necessary to enable people to see that the same thing is needed in the church.

Wm. E. Sweeney has the following to say about the Plea:

If I understand our aim as a people, and I believe that I do, it is the restoration of all that is essential to the Christianity of the New Testament. This is our *immediate* aim. More *remotely*, we aim at the unity of all believers in Christ. And still more remotely, we aim at the conversion of the world. We have long drawn inspiration for this plea from that tender farewell prayer of the Master's: "For them also that believe on me through their word; that they may all be one . . . . that the world may believe." Here we have apostolic preaching, faith in Christ, unity and world conquest in their logical and chronological order. Surely this is "the wisdom that is from above."

Our first aim is to restore the Christianity of the New Testament, or, which is the same in substance, the *church* of the New Testament. When this is done, it will be a united church. Unity was not an incident of the first church, it was inherent in that body. I see no profit in discussing the

---

[1] *Christian Standard*, Vol. 62, No. 36, p. 843.   [2] *Christian Standard*, Vol. 62, No. 46, p. 883.

question as to whether we aim at restoration or at unity. They are one. I can no more conceive the thought of a New Testament church that is not a unit than I can see the possibility of achieving unity without restoring the New Testament church. Our duty is to restore the church, and unity will come with it. Our pattern is the New Testament. That pattern is clear. It is from the Lord. And if we have not been faithful to that pattern in our efforts at restoration, we will listen cheerfully to any who would show us wherein we have erred.

And, even as unity follows restoration, so the conquest of the world for Christ will follow unity. The Master prayed "that they all may be one . . . . that the world may believe."

We do not claim to be wiser than others. Our plea is not the product of human wisdom. It is essentially an appeal to faith, and a renunciation of worldly wisdom. We do not claim to have builded better than others, but we believe *the Lord* has. Our plea is to men to "trust in the Lord with all thy heart, and lean not upon thine own understanding."

Our position demands the restoration of the church to its *supremacy* as well as its purity. There is no other that can take rank with it. I sometimes hear it said that "one church is as good as another." Those who make this admission should be prepared to accept the conclusions which flow logically from it.

If one church *is* as good as another, our whole history as a people is an effort to build something which is no better than what was already in existence when we began. If this is true, we have no distinctive worthy purpose, and hence no justification.[1]

Mr. Sweeney joins with others quoted in this thesis who see the close association of the Plea, accurately understood, to the prayer of Jesus in the seventeenth chapter of John's gospel. His statement considers the aspects of the unity problem in the same order as set forth by our Lord, apostolic doctrine, faith, unity, and world conversion. 1928 is the date of the statement.

Borrowing a phrase or two from Lincoln's Gettysburg address, Claude Hill stated the plea as follows in 1930:

SIXSCORE years and more ago our fathers in the gospel brought forth upon this continent a movement conceived in liberty in Christ and loyalty to Christ, and dedicated to the mighty task of uniting the church and evangelizing the world. This movement struck its roots deep down in five great and unshakable convictions. By these convictions it began! By them it has lived and spread over the earth! And by them it is today . . . . Believing, as I do that these convictions are sound, I think it is a good day and hour to go back. In order they were, and are, as follows:

First. That Jesus Christ is the only begotten Son of the living God and the only Saviour of the world; that only by Him do men know God, and only through Him can men come to God. The inevitable corollary of this belief is that the gospel of the Lord Jesus is indispensable to the life, the salvation and hope of the world.

Second. That the New Testament Scriptures are a credible and dependable revelation of the mind, and the will, of Jesus Christ as the mind and will of God are made known to the world by Him.

Third. That the church is of divine origin, instituted and ordained of God as the instrument and agency by which the gospel is to be preached to the whole world.

[1] *Christian Standard*, Vol. 63, No. 47, p. 1195.

Fourth. That the church can never function adequately, that it never can be equal to this task, while disunion and division prevail. Our fathers in the beginning believed, and we now believe, that division means waste, and waste means want. They believed more about disunion and division than its inexpediency. We believe more about it than that. We believe the whole thing to be in opposition to the mind of Christ. We believe it to be twofold sin—a sin against God and against humanity.

Fifth. That in the New Testament Scriptures, and among the surely and unmistakably recorded words of the Lord Jesus, there is sufficient non-debatable and uncontested ground to provide an adequate basis for a lasting union of the divided and dismembered church. It will at once be seen, therefore, that we came on the field and into being with both a *passion* and a *program* for union. It was the passion for a united church that led to the search for a program for a united church. And in that search we turned to the only source that ever has, that ever can, or will offer any hope for such a program. We turned to the authority of Jesus Christ, believing that He alone speaks with authority, and that the New Testament records His will. That is to say, we turned to the New Testament itself for a program for union. It was there we found our passion, and it is there we found our program.[1]

No comment is needed on this statement; its proximity to the Plea as it is stated again and again through its history is apparent. Mr. Hill's use of the word union may, in his own mind, refer more to church union than to the union of Christians, though the establishment of the "five convictions" would result in a union of Christians.

L. A. Chapman lists the elements upon which Christians must unite in the form following:

Christian people must and will come together and forsake their divisions and human creeds. Unity can be had only by accepting the common denominator of religious belief—by accepting the common ground. Churches of Christ must be founded upon Christ and the doctrines of the New Testament Church, and these are not difficult to discover. There must be the

1. Common name, Christian or Disciples. "The Disciples were called Christians first in Antioch." (Acts 11:26.)

2. Common creed. "Thou art the Christ the Son of the Living God." (Matt. 16:16.)

3. Common Book—the Holy Scriptures.

4. Common Baptism—that practiced by the New Testament Church. No other is universally accepted. Here is common ground. Roman Catholic, Greek Catholic, Protestant—all agree that the New Testament baptism was an immersion into the name of the father and the Son and the Holy Spirit.

5. Common Fellowship—fraternal relations among all Christians. "By this shall all men know that ye are my disciples if ye have love one to another."[2]

It is, again, a question of all holding to these elements in common, not that they are already the common possession of all. They are available to all, and cause no more sacrifice of ground to one than to another. Mr. Chapman's statement dates in the year 1931.

---

[1] *Christian Standard*, Vol. 65, No. 44, p. 1047. [2] *Christian-Evangelist*, Vol. 68, No. 16 p. 524.

Also from 1931, and similar in outline to that of Mr. Chapman, is the following review of the principles of the church of Christ by Glenn W. Hutton:

In closing, I will give a brief outline of our position as a church.

First, we stand for the unity of all God's people upon the New Testament. We believe that divisions and doctrinal differences are wrong.

Second, we have no creedal statement or interpretation of Christ but ask, as taught in the New Testament, that men simply believe in Him as the Son of God.

Third, we have no authority except the Word of Christ which is the New Testament. This is the final authority in Christianity.

Fourth, we believe that we should glorify Christ by wearing only his name, the name Christian.

Fifth, we believe that if it took a belief in Christ as the Son of God, a repentance from sin and a burial by Christian baptism into Christ to make a Christian in the first church, it will take the same thing to make one today.

Then we believe that holy living in accordance with the teaching of Christ is necessary to complete our policy and make possible our eternal life.

The rules committee of heaven met and gave us these principles in the New Testament and there has never been a meeting of that committee since. Men have met and decided on many changes but until there is a change from God we feel that the New Testament is final.

You have heard of the plea of the Christians. For a hundred years we have stood for the unity of God's people. We believe division is wrong.[1]

The two above statements are not at all outstanding, but are included to illustrate what could be multiplied manifold from the written record of the Restoration movement. Neither of the statements represents a digression from the Plea. The objections of an appeal to "common ground" have previously been dealt with in this thesis.

Edgar DeWitt Jones calls the following statement a "personal confession of faith." Written in 1933, it reveals Mr. Jones' attitude toward and conception of the church and the Restoration movement:

I believe in the movement within the church for the unity of the church, the body known as Disciples of Christ, Churches of Christ, or Christian Churches! There are at least two interpretations of every movement, party, institution. Thus there are two interpretations of the Constitution of the United States, one of the letter, the other the spirit; two interpretations of the Republican party, one narrow, the other broad; two interpretations of the Democratic party, one reactionary, the other liberal. There are two interpretations of the communion of which I am a member, one narrow, the other generous. Progressively interpreted the Disciples of Christ embody a noble plea and an arresting program. They cherish the dream of a reunited church, and make Christ central in teaching and life. They emphasize unity but not uniformity. It is a roomy fellowship, holding to a universal creed; "I believe in Christ as the Son of God and my personal Saviour." For a century this virile body has had its life and witness mostly in the south and middle west where it is strongest. It has produced an able company of preachers, missionaries, prophets of the newer

---

[1] *Christian-Evangelist*, Vol. 68, No. 8, pp. 262, 263.

day. I am of the third generation of Disciples, my brethren have honored me, and I have my reasons to rejoice in the comradeship of such a people. I respect and highly esteem my brethren, conservative and liberal, and of every school of thought. But we cannot stand still else we go back. We do not honor the fathers of our movement by slavishly following in every particular the positions they took, the interpretations they proclaimed. That would be to dishonor them and their ideals. They were human, so are we. They made mistakes, likewise do we. They flung a torch of freedom to us which we must hold aloft and carry bravely forward. With the passing years I am less a denominationalist. I think I could preach from any pulpit of any communion that would give me the liberty of prophesying, but I doubt whether any other body could give me more liberty than I enjoy in this pulpit. I have about as much liberty as I can take care of. I find an increasing joy in the realization of that noble motto: "In faith unity; in opinions and methods liberty; in all things charity."[1]

The logic of the statement that "we do not honor the fathers of our movement by slavishly following in every particular the positions they took, the interpretations they proclaimed" is difficult to understand. In the Restoration movement this would mean that we can not honor Jesus by doing as he requested or the apostles by teaching what they taught, for the appeal of the Restoration movement has always been to that Christ and that teaching. The advocates of the Restoration idea had no doctrine of their own; thus, the statement of Mr. Jones is an open avowal to surrender the Plea and the gospel to which it appealed. The fathers, so called, flung us a "torch of freedom," freedom from all human authorities and doctrines, but not freedom from the gospel of Christ nor the Christianity of the New Testament.

The New Testament is the center of the Plea, as proposed by James A. Burns:

WHAT IS THE RESTORATION PLEA?

1. It comprehends the New Testament. It maintains that where the Scriptures speak, we speak; and where they are silent, we are silent. But the Book needs rightly to be divided in order to an intelligent understanding of it. In a general way the Old Testament may be said to be Israel's book; but God has spoken His final Word to all men through Christ (Heb. 1:1, 2), and this Word is found in the New Testament.

2. It comprehends the New Testament Christ. The modernist talks about the "Master," but the plea presents no milk-and-water Jesus for a dying world. It points to Him of the New Testament, God's only begotten Son, His name above every other name, the Lord of all, the Head of the church with supreme authority in it; and faith in Him is our creed.

3. It comprehends the New Testament church. Its ordinances are simple, easily understood, and their observance would do much to unify a distracted church. Its doctrine concerns Christ, not so much something about him as maintained in speculative theology, but the Christ Himself. "I know Him whom I have believed" is not the word of theology but a gripping experience.

4. It comprehends the New Testament gospel. So vast is the chasm dug by speculation that divides between that "gospel which is the power of God unto salvation" and the "gospel" in many quarters of denominational speculation, that one need not marvel that so few turn to God in our day.

[1] *Central Woodward Pulpit*, Vol. 4, No. 22, n. p.

Verily there must be an inherent religious tendency in the human breast. The New Testament gospel would work its purpose today were men not bewildered by denominational confusion. This ancient gospel consists of facts (about Jesus) to be believed, commands (of Jesus) to be obeyed, and promises (of Jesus) to be enjoyed.

5. It comprehends the New Testament life. Three great ideals mark that life: Loyalty to Christ, His word and His commands; likeness unto Christ as the aim of the Christian; and service for Christ as it may manifest a real helpfulness in His name.[1]

The date of Mr. Burns' statements is 1934. It is clear that the Plea, to him, is a plea to restore the Christianity of the New Testament just as it is recorded in that volume.

Dean E. Walker, in the year 1935, composed the following statement revealing the position and power of the movement to restore New Testament Christianity:

Broadly, the Disciples have stood for five great truths, the impact of which is daily growing in American churches.

(1) They have insisted that the Bible is a book of revelation which is intended to be understood, and therefore possible of being understood, by ordinary scholarship and sanctified common sense. They have made it, and not catechisms, the religious book of the people. This does not mean that they have opposed Biblical criticism—quite the contrary. If the New Testament is not true they want to know it. They have therefore welcomed all light that has come upon the text and its interpretation. But they have consistently drawn the line between discovered facts and theories constructed upon those facts. The significance of these facts has confirmed their confidence in the New Testament as the embodiment of the only norm of Christian faith and practice.

(2) They have insisted that every Christian must believe the Creed of the New Testament—that Jesus is the Christ. They have centered everything in the Lordship of Christ. Theories about his Person have not interested them so much as obedience to His will. The wisdom of this position is being vindicated by both Biblical scholarship and modern philosophy. It is a recognition of Personality as the highest thing we know.

(3) They have insisted that evangelism must be simple and rational, appealing to the whole nature of man, enlisting above everything else his will: that it is in doing that emotion and reason find religious synthesis: that to be a Christian is far more than to have an "experience"; and, on the other hand, that it is far more than ethical perfectionism: that Christ's Lordship is intended to be exercised over every department of life, in the spirit of humility, as His disciples; and that this submission includes the formal or institutional side of Christanity, as well as its intellectual and volitional side.

(4) They have insisted that schism is not only unfortunate—that it is sin. Charged with uncharitableness, they have not been able to tear out I Corinthians from their Bibles. They had laid the responsibility for divisions on the consciences, not on the pocket-books, or on the political expediences or historic witnesses of the Church universal. The sin of the Church has brought it into its present paralytic condition. They have called it to repentance and to first works. They claim, after over a hundred years of experience, that they have demonstrated the practicability of their plat-

[1] *Christian Standard*, Vol. 69, No. 23, p. 397.

form for Christian union. They challenge Christendom to its adoption or to the production of a better plan.

(5) They have insisted that at the bottom the whole disorder in the Church, and failure of its people, is lack of spiritual discernment and life; and that the essence of spirituality lies not in ecstasy, nor in esoteric formulae, nor in ineffable self-assurance; but rather in unification of the whole human personality through devotion to the spiritual realities revealed by the one Person through the ages who has come from the realm of spirit and returned thither to prepare a place for his people. When they have spoken of the inspiration of the New Testament, they have meant that it is the authority of that collection of documents which reveals to man the heavenly things, and how he may attain them. To live by this Sword of the Spirit is to be spiritual.

Such a position is never partizan. It is always free. It is deeply reverent. It is practical. It stakes all upon the essential unity of all life at its best. It is serious. It is joyous. It is humble. It will transform the kingdoms of this world into the Kingdom of God.[1]

Thus, according to the above, the movement has stood by five great truths: (1) The Bible is a revelation not a concealment, (2) Faith in Jesus as the Christ must be central and held by all who would be Christian, (3) Evangelism is rational and not mystical, (4) Division in the body of Christ is sin, (5) Lack of spiritual life is the cause of the disruption; living by the word is the cure.

In the year 1936, Edward S. Ames made the following statements regarding the movement and the Plea:

They and their followers endeavored to make the teaching of the New Testament the basis of union. They felt the need of emphasizing especially the conditions of entrance into the church and so came to formulate the steps—faith, repentance, and baptism—in what they understood to be the plain words of the scripture. The major premise of all their arguments was that of the sufficiency of the New Testament to provide the doctrines, ordinances, and directions for the Christian life, and this premise they held in common with Protestants generally.[2]

Certain phrases in the above statement, such as "They felt the need," "in what they understood," tend to inform one that Mr. Ames is not at all in agreement with their conclusions. He continues:

Now in the course of a hundred years there has developed a better understanding of the Bible, and a more accurate knowledge of the early church and subsequent church history. As a result, the major premise of Protestant authoritarian views of the Bible has been dissolved. It is now seen that the Bible grew out of the church and not the church out of the Bible. Therefore the attempt of the Disciples to build churches upon the Bible, as if that were always the process of building churches, has provided inadequate to the achievement of union.[3]

This statement represents a clear cut repudiation of the Plea, as well as the gospel of the New Testament. If the New Testament has been discovered to be non-authoritarian, then it is not adequate for guidance in any phase of Christian teaching or conduct. The argument that the New Testament is not authoritative because it grew out of the church and not the church out of it is invalid. The message contained in the New Testament existed before the church. The

---

[1]Walker, "Adventuring for Christian Unity," op cit., pp. 52, 53.
[2]Scroll, Vol. 32, pp. 56, 57.   [3]Ibid.

169

word of the Book is a record of the manner in which the church was formulated, of the message it preached, of the faith it held, of the practices to which it conformed.

Concerning the manner of becoming a Christian, Mr. Ames says:

> The basis of membership in the local church is persuasion of the value and urgency of Christian faith and fellowship. This faith is devotion to the spirit and idealism of Christ and to the fellowship of those banded to-. gether in his name and service. It is not a matter of the letter of scripture.[1]

One of the primary conceptions advanced by the reformers was that "Bible things should be called by Bible terms." Their repudiation of the experimentation and interpretations of men was absolute. The above statement is pure and simple interpretation and opinion. It is the abandonment of scriptural language altogether, "not a matter of the letter of scripture," and the use of words and expression which fit the idea in Mr. Ame's mind. Mr. Campbell would say, "I fear that since the words are not Biblical the idea is not Biblical." In any event, it would be difficult to defend the above as being in harmony with the Plea as revealed through the discoveries of this investigation.

Mr. Ames is also an advocate of the adoption of the practice of "open-membership." Every "Disciple Church" should become a community church, says he, for:

> . . . . the essential principle of a community church is that it shall receive all Christians, and of whatever name or sign, into its fellowship, if they desire to unite. Many Disciple churches already exemplify this practice. They do not consider themselves any the less Disciple churches because they seek to serve the whole community or at least all who desire to be served thus. What more need a Disciple church do to become a community church than to relax its insistence upon immersion? . . . . All other denominations, save one, had abandoned or modified the requirement, but they did not plead for union, while the one body that had a history, a plea, and a conscience, on union, allowed that requirement to thwart its practice of union.[2]

So far as is known, the claim has never been made that it was not the desire of the Restoration movement or the church of Christ to serve the whole community or at least those who desire to unite with it. However, it has sought to inclose within the fellowship those who desired to be united with Christ in terms of His will, and, at this point, Christian immersion enters the picture. In gaining the oneness of Christians, nothing may be surrendered which may endanger the oneness with Christ.

Mr. Ames' reasons for excluding baptism are stated as follows:

> . . . . What was so long a support to their cause is now suspected of being a burden. New Testament textual criticism has undermined the last proof-text by showing that the baptismal formula of the "great commission" bears the marks of being no earlier than the third century since the formula is trinitarian in its wording. Thus the assumption that Jesus explicitly commanded baptism falls, and the last element of formalism is removed from his teaching.[3]

The evidence presented is exceedingly slim. Perhaps Mr. Ames would also

---

[1]*Ibid.*, p. 60   [2]*Scroll*, Vol. 33, pp. 67, 68.   [3]*Scroll*, Vol. 37, pp. 341, 342.

deny that Father, Son, and Holy Spirit are mentioned in the New Testament. Dean E. Walker has already suggested that the disciples have always welcomed Biblical criticism, since they, of all people, would want to know it, if the Bible were not true. However, he adds, that they have always distinguished between facts discovered and theories based upon these facts. This is precisely the difficulty with Mr. Ames' position above stated. It is the old mistake in science of becoming so familiar with a theory as to begin to suppose it to be a fact. There are some scholars who are quite certain that the theory advanced by Mr. Ames grows out of "open-membership" and other perversions of gospel truth and not the latter out of the former. Again, it is a matter of abandoning the Plea and the scriptures to which the Plea appeals.

Harold L. Lunger, in the year 1937, suggests the way to unity in the following terms:

> The only way in which we will ever restore the unity of all Christians will be to recognize the equality of all Christians before God. Let denominational boards unite; combine competing churches wherever they are found in local communities. Let each local church follow its own traditions; let each individual follow the dictates of his own conscience. Not until we are willing to treat all Christian churches as *true churches* and all members of these churches as genuine Christians will we have restored the unity of all Christians.

> Christian unity awaits for its appearance upon more of Christ's spirit in the hearts of his followers. When we share his spirit, we too will be pained by the divisions among his followers enough to do something to heal the wounds in his body. We will not be exclusive in our Christian fellowship, but will love and associate with all his followers no matter to what sect they may belong. We will be broadminded and tolerant, willing that others who do not see eye to eye with us shall be on an equality with us in the church. We will have the courage to break even our most cherished traditions, if we find that they cramp the church and hinder her in the work that has been entrusted to her.[1]

No one in the history of the movement has advocated anything other than the recognition of all Christians as on an equality before God, or all Christian churches as *true* churches. The movement has been opposed, however, from its beginning, to the practice of recognizing as fully Christian any but those who have met the scriptural requirements for bearing that name, or as completely Christian churches any but those which meet the pattern set forth in the New Testament. The advocates of the Plea have been careful, however, not to judge the condition before God of those who have met only a part of those requirements, which are clearly taught in the Word. It is a matter of deciding between two alternatives: 1) the recognition of all sectarians and denominationalists as saved and wholly Christians, or 2) the refusing to recognize them as either saved or condemned. Some have, of course, taken a third alternative, that of judging the whole denominationalism and all of its members as lost. Such action, it has been seen, is not in accord with the thinking of the movement, however.

The suggestion of Mr. Lunger in the first paragraph of his statement concerning the uniting of denominational boards, etc., as being the way to unity reveals that Mr. Lunger is thinking in terms of organizations when he speaks

---

[1] *Christian-Evangelist*, Vol. 75, No. 31, p. 1008.

of Christian unity. Whereas it has been the individual that has been considered the "unit in the unity we seek." Mr. Lunger is suggesting a union by good natured accommodation and mutual forbearance. Such would be union, but not Christian union, much less Christian unity; it is certainly not the unity proposed by the Plea.

Edwin Errett reviewed the movement, in the year 1937, setting it forth in the manner and form following:

The first of these distinctive contributions is our consistent declaration that Jeus Christ is the only creed, and that the use of any other creed as a test of faith and fellowship is not only unnecessary, but divisive. Our people have exalted the Christ. Some have been more loyal to Him than ourselves, perhaps. Heroism in His name is no unique possession of ours. But no people has realized so profoundly and no group has preached so persistently the doctrine that Jesus Christ in His own person is the creed of the church. Even with an increasing appreciation of the point upon the part of other peoples, they seem to be as those who see men as trees walking. Either, out of timidity, they will not let go of human summaries of faith or they become so liberal as to sacrifice the person of Jesus in zeal to gather into one company all who will accept his ethical teachings.

We insist that there can be no church of God unless its members have accepted the Christ of God for all He claimed to be, and that when they have accepted Him they have taken the only creed that is necessary or wise for a basis of fellowship.

As our second contribution there is our emphasis upon the rational asceptance of Christ and His salvation. Of course, most of us recognize the service rendered by our pioneers in combating the emotional revivalism of a century ago, but too few of us are aware that we are still servants in this respect. A great many of those denominations that stand with us in love for the Bible are confused upon this point even this good day . . . . Our whole movement is inherently opposed to that phase of Calvinism . . . .

Our third major and distinctive contribution is our emphasis upon the proper division of the Bible, especially the distinction between the two covenants . . . . We have avoided efforts to enforce Christian ethics by disciplines and to enforce Old Testament Sabbaths and to induct infants into the church. We have seized upon the principle predicted by Jeremiah, set forth in Christ, introduced by the apostles and championed by Paul—the law written in the inward parts. No other people has the contribution to make here that we possess.

As a fourth distinctive contribution, we note our plea for unity upon a definite basis. For a long time we stood practically alone in our preaching of the desirability of unity. On that point we have so far succeeded that, while the sense of the need is not by any means unanimous, it is delightfully general. The most important element in the picture now is the lack of a formula for unity. That we have, and, most happily, it is not of our own devising. We do not have to ask the Christian world to come to us. We have the glorious privilege of urging that they all study the primitive church and find unity in the essentials laid down by the Lord and His apostles.

. . . . Even some of the "open membership" advocates declare that their ultimate objective is this New Testament basis.

FINALLY, it is no slight contribution that we have to bring in our preservation of a brotherhood upon a basis of faith and doctrine rather than of organization. We are not without knowledge of certain unhappy differences and factions within our fellowship. But even now there are def-

172

inite healing influences at work, the most distinct revelations of which are the undying consciousness of our brotherhood. We can not forget that we belong to each other, even our vigorous disputes themselves being witnesses.

. . . . There will come a time for us to step back and disappear into the church at large, but that day will come only when human creeds are discarded because Christians put complete confidence in the one Creed and the churches win converts as the apostles did and hold them together under the law of liberty in the pattern of the New Testament church. Until then we must study to proclaim with grace and firmness this plan of unity and to live graciously with all denominationalists.[1]

So Mr. Errett viewed the movement and its Plea. There is no compromise here, in so far as the New Testament church is concerned. The appeal is to the Book, to the creed of the Book, to rational conversion, to the New Testament as the Book for Christians, to Unity upon the basis of winning Christians according to apostolic pattern and to keeping them so through the form of Christianity set forth in the New Testament known as the church of Christ. This is the historic appeal of the restoration movement.

In the same year that the above statement was composed, Willard E. Shelton, then editor of the *Christian-Evangelist*, wrote the following:

We have been, of course, not only a people with a plea—a plea for Christian union—but also a people with a program which we have called "New Testament Christianity." There are those of our number who put this program first in importance and our plea for Christian unity in a secondary place. Our basic task, they say, is to restore the New Testament order and in doing this Christian unity will take care of itself. Such a view, generally held, would, of course, solve our dilemma, for it would remove our plea for unity from a position of major significance and would enable us to go to the world as the Baptists, Methodists, Presbyterians, and all the rest go, with the declaration, "We have the best program; join us."

There are two objections to such a solution, however. One is that history will not down. We did not come into existence pleading for "New Testament Christianity" and believing that Christian union would be a by-product; we came into existence pleading first of all for Christian union, and advocating secondarily as a basis for that union what we conceived to be New Testament Christianity. The second objection is the very practical one that we as a people are not making such marked progress numerically as to lead us to hope that all Christendom will some of these days "join us."[2]

Mr. Shelton misconceives the Plea and movement when he supposes that we plead for union and restoration of the New Testament church as two distinct sections of our message, and in the conception that we have asked anyone to "join us," except in the New Testament sense. The Restoration movement has called for unity upon the New Testament basis, and has never separated the two. Moreover, the movement has pleaded with denominationalists to meet us at the feet of the Lord and his apostles. The message is for all to join Christ and meet each other in Him.

W. S. Willis responded to the above editorial as below:

. . . . I do not believe we are in any "dilemma" except that brought

[1] *Christian Standard*, Vol. 72, No. 16, pp. 367, 368.
[2] *Christian-Evangelist*, Vol. 75, No. 10, p. 311.

about by preachers who refuse to preach the "Gospel of Christ which is the power of God unto salvation to every one that believes."

What we need is preachers who will preach the gospel that will save individuals and not "a gospel" that will tickle the itching ears of the Sectarians . . . . What we need is not to go into union with sectarianism, but to go back to the "Old Pentecostal" gospel, and to the "Apostolic Faith and preaching." When this is done, there will be no empty pews or closed church buildings.

The hardest task I have . . . . is to follow one of our "half-backed" gospel preachers. I find it takes months to bring such a church back to faith and zeal for the truth. May God speed the day when we as "New Testament Christians, will quit seeking union with the "denominational world." And cease to be "ashamed of the gospel of Christ," and learn again that "it is the power of God unto salvation to every one that believes" (its message). I, too, am sick and tired; yes, in the parlance of "Andy," regusted, with our preachers going over the country telling people there are Christians in all denominations (there may be; it is not for me to say). And saying, "Join the church of your choice." Yes, if we are in a "dilemma" it is the fault, and weakness of the preacher and not with our plan or plea.[1]

The conclusion to which Mr. Willis came is the conclusion to which many of the advocates of the Plea were coming at that time, that many who were claiming to be in the line of thinking originated by the Restoration movement had obviously abandoned the Plea and were calling for the union of denominations upon the basis of compromise and "good natured accommodation."

A. W. Fortune advanced the statement following in the year 1937. Speaking of the ideals of the Restoration movement or "the Disciples" he says:

These ideals can be stated in a few words, for they are common to all Disciples. From the beginning we have insisted on the unity of the church. The Disciples have insisted that unity can come by a return to the simplicity of the apostolic church. They have maintained that the Bible is our guide in religion and that each one is to read it and interpret for himself. They have held that inasmuch as Christ is our Sarviour, our Lord and Master, that allegiance to him is of fundamental importance. The Disciples have urged that religion is a reasonable relationship and that the one who is seeking for light need not be left in the dark. They have contended for freedom and democracy in religion, insisting that the local congregation has the right to manage its own affairs and that the church has no right to legislate concerning the conscience of the individual. The Disciples have urged that we should be designated by names which are suggestive of what we are and should be, and that lead to unity.[2]

The ideals, says Mr. Fortune, must be adhered to, since the future of the movement depends upon that, but we must not insist upon uniformity. Freedom of interpretation of these ideals must be allowed. It would be wise to attach a warning to them, however, pointing out that to interpret them out of existence would not be adhering to them.

The year 1940 finds Charles C. Morrison advocating about the same thing he proclaimed in 1912. However, he has developed the thought considerably, as may be seen from a close reading of his book "What is Christianity?" The following excerpt indicates the conclusions of the book, particularly the chapter entitled "Restoring the Body of Christ":

[1] *Christian-Evangelist*, Vol. 75, No. 14, p. 461.   [2] *Ibid.*, p. 454.

Let us now gather up the results of our analysis of the problem of the unity of the church. We have defined this problem as the search for catholicity. And we have found that the catholic functions of the body of Christ are now exercised by sectarian parts of the body independently of the body and with no reference to the body as a whole. These catholicities of the body of Christ are as follows: a catholic church order or "polity," a catholic baptism, a catholic ordination of its ministers, a catholic missionary enterprise, a catholic Christian education of its membership and training of its future ministers, a catholic liturgy, a catholic celebration of the sacrament of the Lord's Supper, and finally a catholic ideology or creed.

Our denominationalism has stripped off all these catholic functions from the church of Christ, leaving the church of Christ without organs through which it might function as a living body. The ecumenical task is that of restoring these usurped functions to the Christian community as a whole where they may be exercised according to their catholic nature as functions of the unity of the church, rather than as functions of schism in the church. This task we have described as that of implementing the body of Christ with the organs and functions which belong to it alone. Formidable as such an undertaking seems to be, it is not, in my judgment, hopeless or incapable of achievement.[1]

The functions named by Mr. Morrison, he says, are functions which belong to the church universal and not to any part or segment of the church. These functions rightly belong to the ecumenical church, must be restored to their rightful owner, and must no longer be exercised by the segments of the church. Thus, a great, central meeting of the church is necessary to decide upon these functions, and once decided upon they must be accepted by every part of the whole. Thus runs the force of his argument. The difficulty is that the New Testament does not place these functions in the hands of the universal church, so called. The Lord has designed his church, as he intended it to be, and he has decided the nature and meaning of the functions Mr. Morrison has described. It is the business of the churches to see to it that these functions, as the Lord has decided upon them, are put into operation in the local church.

The difficulty seems to be that some find it a problem to conceive of the church in terms other than universals. The church or body of Christ is, to them, the world-wide church or the aggregate of every local congregation in existence. While it is true that the word "church" is used in the New Testament to indicate the whole, the church of Christ, as set forth in the Word, is always defined in terms of the local congregation in so far as its polity is concerned. The New Testament knows nothing of intercongregational organizations or control. The church universal, so called, is not composed of congregations or of denominations; it is composed of individuals who have become Christians according to the Divine plan and who assemble in their local communities according to the Divine pattern. The problem, then, is not one of uniting congregations or denominations, but of uniting individuals to the Lord and bringing them into the brotherhood. The moment that one begins to conceive of the church in terms other than that of the local congregation, that moment he begins to think in terms which, carried to their ultimate, would satisfy even the Pope of Rome.

W. R. Walker, in 1941, analyzes the problems confronting the Restoration movement in a manner comparable to the above, when he says:

---

[1] Charles Clayton Morrison, *What Is Christianity?* (Chicago: Willett, Clark and Company, 1940), pp. 317, 318.

Today, almost all Christian leadership is vocal in urging union of churches. A century ago, none favored it. This change of sentiment is attributable to the influence of churches of Christ. However, as often happens, later converts to the idea have failed to grasp its real purpose. The movement, in the beginning, was *not* one advocating *church union*, but *Christian unity*. In certain aspects, the two ideologies are so widely different as to have little relation to each other. Christian unity deals with individuals. Church union deals with organizations. A union of all Protestant bodies might be effected, and Christian unity not be either its major aim or result.[1]

This is precisely the position advocated by Mr. Walker in a previous statement and represents some of the clearest thinking on the matter. It is hard to see how anyone could mistake the reasoning or avoid the truth.

In an editorial published in 1941, R. H. Miller states his conception of the Plea as follows:

> . . . . No plan for healing the divisions of the church of Christ has been proposed which can stand comparison with the proposal of the Disciples that unity is possible only by yielding obedience in utter loyalty to Jesus Christ in faith, in ordinances, and in life. When a better way is proposed we shall be bound by the passion of our purpose to consider it in all sincerity and hope. Unless the teaching of the New Testament in Gospel and Epistle is without validity for all time and all people, unless the gospel is no longer the "power of God unto salvation," unless the death and resurrection of Christ are no longer potent to change life and to maintain the new way of life, then our "plea" for unity by the restoration of the New Testament "way," is not outdated nor in need of modification. The only need is for its sincere endorsement by ourselves and for its thoroughgoing practice.[2]

It would seem that Mr. Miller has a firm grasp and an accurate conception of the Plea and a zeal for its acceptance. However, in 1944, he says:

> It would be well for those Disciples, who assert that they have the only plan for unity in Christ, to consider that in more than one hundred years of our history we have not participated in a single union nor healed one division in the body of Christ.[3]

> The plea for Christian Unity is no longer "our plea." Others have taken it up, and many have entered before us into unity. Disciples themselves have learned that the proposal that every division in Christendom immediately shall scrap its historic witness and deny its special experience and "return to Christ and the apostolic church" is too simple. Divisions within our own household of faith have taught us the rigidity of literalism.[4]

Regarding the first paragraph immediately above, the Restoration movement has never questioned the rightness of the position it assumed. The restoration of the church of the New Testament has always been regarded as the only acceptable plan of unity. However, as we have pointed out before, it is not a unity or union of churches or denominations sought by the Plea; perhaps this will explain why the "Disciples" have not had part in "a single union nor healed one division in the body of Christ" in the sense suggested. However, every person won to the Lord and to oneness with Him, who previously had

[1] *Christian Standard*, Vol. 76, No. 14, p. 333.
[2] *Christian-Evangelist*, Vol. 79, No. 47, pp. 1303, 1304.
[3] *Christian-Evangelist*, Vol. 83, No. 10, p. 231.   [4] *Christian-Evangelist*, Vol. 82, No. 20, p. 471.

followed a party instead of Christ, represents the healing of a breach in the body. This has occurred many times through the history of the movement. In regard to the statement immediately above, it is admitted that the Plea is simple, as simple as asking a Buddhist, Confucianist, or any sinner to accept Jesus as Lord and obey him in all things according to His word. If such is too simple to unite the church in Him, it is too simple to win the world to Him.

Asked to submit his own interpretation of the "overture for Christian unity which is the precious heritage and mission of the Disciples of Christ," Mr. Miller wrote as follows:

That nothing is essential to the conversion of the world and the establishment of Christ's Kingdom of righteousness, justice and peace but the unity of Christians.

That nothing is essential to the unity of Christians, but the restoration of original Christianity in its ideal phases as received from the teaching and spirit of Jesus Christ.[1]

The above bears a striking resemblance to the statement following by Alexander Campbell:

First. Nothing is essential to the conversion of the world, but the union and co-operation of christians.

Second. Nothing is essential to the union of christians, but the Apostles' teaching or testimony.[2]

For comparison of the attitude held by both men, the above two statements may be studied very closely. They do not say exactly the same thing, and it is wondered if they mean exactly the same thing.

In the year 1944, P. H. Welshimer reviewed the movement as below:

This movement, beginning on American soil, grew rapidly. It came to be designated as "The Restoration," and the plea was for the unity of all believers in Christ; the plan was the restoration of the church of the New Testament; and the purpose the evangelization of the world.

SO long as the preachers, the teachers and the churches held to that plea, plan and purpose, we were united, were strong, and made headway. But gradually, through the years, men arose here and there in our groups who began to apostatize from that New Testament position; not that they found new light from the New Testament on problems arising, but fraternizing with the denominational bodies they lost their vision, and in the desire to be broad-minded and to have closer fellowship with all believers in Christ, they gradually began to slip away from those things for which we first contended and which had contributed to our growth in the early years of our history.

This condition has grown until today there is the marked danger of an ugly schism, which threatens the unity among our own people.[3]

The truth of his statement concerning the drift away from the Plea has been shown through this research. It is obvious that there is no longer the unanimity among the statements of the Plea that was to be found in the periods previous to this.

---

[1] *Christian-Evangelist*, Vol. 82, No. 11, p. 256.

[2] A. Campbell, "Principles and Rules of Christian Unity," *op. cit.*, p. 103.

[3] *Christian-Evangelist*, Vol. 82, No. 10, p. 236.

On the question of Christian union and Christian unity, Burris Butler wrote as follows in 1944:

> ONE of the greatest needs at present is to get people to understand the essential difference between so-called Christian union and Christian unity. The former is a plan by which, through the amalgamation of sects, a mighty super sect may be created. It retains its sectarian nature. It involves the sacrifice of fundamental principles of the faith in favor of efficiency in worldly organization and of centralization of control under human leaders.
>
> Christian unity, on the other hand, involves a sacrifice of all human ambitions as well as a quest for personal prestige, in favor of the exaltation of Christ as sole Lord of the church. It seeks the unity of every individual in the Lord. United in allegiance and obedience to Christ, we shall all be united in one another as Christians. "Christian union" appeals to the sectarian mind. Christian unity appeals to those who are opposed to every form of sectarianism.
>
> The way to get rid of sectarianism is not to concentrate it, but to abandon it completely as sin. It is opposed to the will of Christ, who is Lord of the church. The Master asks: "Why call me Lord, and yet do not that which I have commanded?" By recognizing in faith and practice Christ as absolute Master of the church, the presuming claims of sectarianism will necessarily have to be discarded and His Word accepted as the rule of faith. There can be no Christian unity without this surrender.[1]

This is precisely the position this investigation has shown the Restoration movement to take through its history. However, the above does not consider certain terms in exactly their true light, though punctuation suggests something. Three terms must be made clear today: 1) Christian unity is the oneness of the individual with Christ and with others so united to Him, 2) Christian union is the co-operation of Christians in the work of the church, 3) Union or Sectarian union is the amalgamation of sects or their co-operation in propagating the common ends they may have.

Much discussion as to whether the Plea is for "restoration" or for "union" has been made throughout this period of the history of the Plea. W. A. Fite, in 1944, voices his position on this matter:

> Now if we as a people cannot adhere to the basis for unity which marked our origin it would be folly to offer it to a divided Christendom. Yet have not some of us been departing from that basis? We have become so enamored with our plea for unity that we have forgotten the basis of that plea. It is a great thing to plead for Christian union, and we hear many such voices today; but it is almost a futile thing unless we can offer a basis for unity to a divided church, which we have demonstrated as practical among ourselves. It was the glory of our fathers that they not only plead for Christian union, but showed the way. Some of us would retain the plea and forget the way; and perhaps some would retain the way and forget the plea. We need both. It is not a question of "either or" but "both and." The Disciples have two great objectives in their mission: (1) The plea for a united church in divided Christendom, (2) the restoration of the New Testament church in name, creed, ordinances and life. If we can maintain both our objectives we shall keep on the beam and reach the goal. To fail in either is to lose the way and suffer a crash.[2]

---

[1] *Christian Standard*, Vol. 80, No. 24, p. 370.   [2] *Christian-Evangelist*, Vol. 82, No. 8, p. 189.

To the above statement the history of the Plea gives witness. The advocates of the Plea have always insisted that to accomplish a union without the destruction of party creeds and practices would not be a union worth the name, but that to restore the church of the New Testament would attain the only union or unity worth possessing.

An insight into the simplicity of the Plea is shown in the following statement by Burris Butler which was published in 1945:

The divine method of operation for the apostles was the simple proclamation of the divine message. In simplest terms their method was the direct approach of one individual to another with the story of Christ.

As men believed the story and accepted Christ they were gathered into congregations or churches. These congregations met the first day of the week (on which their Lord arose from the grave) and observed the Lord's Supper, in which they remembered their Lord's suffering and death on their behalf. Their simple worship consisted of the singing of psalms, hymns, and spiritual songs, of praise and prayer, of preaching and teaching, of instruction in Christian living, and of giving an offering for the work of Christ's kingdom. Each congregation had its own officers, consisting of elders and deacons. Each congregation was under the direct authority of Christ and the apostles.

Under this apostolic system the Church reached its highest degree of efficiency in carrying out its purpose. By the end of the first century of operation the gospel was known and churches were established throughout the whole known world. Without seeking legislative influence or political favors, and in spite of its greatest opposition, the church went on from victory to victory. As Dean Charles E. Mills points out, in her subsequent history the time of the farthest departure from the apostolic methods was the time of her dimmest witness in a world of darkness.

Today we are pleading for a return to the simple proclamation of the gospel message as the task of the church. We plead for the restoration of the apostolic methods which bring glory to God and not to men, which preserve the unity of the spirit in the bond of peace, and which if faithfully adhered to will bring about the redemption of the world and the fulfillment of the kingdom of God on earth.[1]

The Plea of the Restoration movement has behind it the impact of authority, the authority of Christ and His apostles as expressed in the New Testament. It also has behind it the impact of simplicity. The problems of the church and of the world are not so complicated that they could not be solved one and all by the impact of authority and simplicity which is inherent in the gospel of Christ. This, precisely, is the position of the Restoration movement.

Charles E. Mills presents the Plea of the Restoration movement in this manner and form:

Essentially, the Restoration plea is an appeal to all of Christendom to restore apostolic order to the church of the present day in its faith, ordinances, polity, life, message, and program.

Essential to investigation in any field are one or more basic assumptions which are necessary to any consideration of data bearing on that field. Such are the axioms of an exact science, like mathematics. Every branch of human investigation has one or more related assumptions upon

---

[1] *Christian Standard*, Vol. 81, No. 45, p. 706.

which all considerations and conclusions in that field must rest. So it is with the historical study of the Restoration plea. There are five of these basic assumptions on which an orderly and conclusive consideration of the plea must proceed. If these can not be granted, then there is no basis for deliberation and conclusion:

1. First is the cornerstone upon which not only the Restoration plea, but the entire structure of Christendom, rests; namely, *that Jesus is the Christ, the Son of the living God, and that He speaks with authority for the church as to its faith and practice.* Here, the plea rests upon solid ground. If this condition can not be granted, then the entire structure to which the plea is related has no validity. The basic condition of the plea is the basic condition of the church and of the realm of Christian faith. Further, every deduction relative to the plea must rest ultimately upon this central basic fact of the deity of Jesus . . . .

2. *The apostles, when they spoke by inspiration, stood on the same plane of infallibility and authority in the church as that on which Jesus stood.* That is to say, they had the mind and understood the will of Christ. The instructions they gave and the commands they left are to be looked upon as of equal authority in the church as the words and commands of Jesus . . . .

3. *The New Testament reveals the will of Christ for the church, and is the supreme and ultimate source of authority for Christian faith and practice.* The New Testament, and the New Testament alone, speaks to us from the first century with anything like an authoritative message. If the New Testament does not reveal the will of Christ for the church, then there is no objective standard of authority . . . .

4. *The New Testament reveals an exact and complete model of the church for every successive age.* Only the blind or the obstinate can fail to discern, and only the dishonest will refuse to admit that there is depicted throughout the New Testament a church, the marks of which are presented on almost every page. There was a church! . . . .

5. *The New Testament is intelligible as far as the essentials of faith and order in the church are concerned.* The New Testament was not designed by its Author, and it was not written by its writers, to be a secret document to be understood only by the initiated. The New Testament is a *revelation*, not a concealment! The gospel is good news . . . .

These are the assumptions upon which the Restoration plea rests. The rejection of any one of them will make invalid the entire appeal for the restoration of apostolic order to the divided, impotent, and failing Christendom of the present hour . . . .[1]

The above was written in the year 1945. The history of the thinking of the Restoration movement has shown that when the Plea has been departed from, one or more of those "basic assumptions" has been abandoned.

Sufficient statements of the Plea have been included in this chapter to establish the purpose intended. In the previous period, the statements of the Plea were pretty much the same as they were spoken and published throughout the Christian world. There is little digression from that which was set down in the first part of the movement as the basic principles upon which all Christians could become one in Christ. True, there were questions raised which were marks of something going on in the thinking of the people.

---

[1] *Christian Standard*, Vol. 81, No. 43, p. 677.

The period just considered, named because of certain divergent elements within the movement, saw the coming into reality of the tendencies only foreshadowed in the previous period by the questions. This period proved itself to be a jumble of opinion about the Plea. Some of the statements call into question the very basis upon which the Plea has always called the Christians of the world to unite. Definite action was taken in one instance to divide the movement into two segments, at least in so far as the census bureau of the United States is concerned. Overtures were made to the sectarian bodies for union and co-operation upon any basis. Really and literally, the Plea, in so far as many yet claiming attachment to the movement are concerned, was abandoned as no longer worthy of serious consideration. Others, remaining faithful to the original purpose of the movement, began appeals to the history of the movement, in an attempt to bring back the advocacy of the Restoration Plea to its original intent.

As one views the movement today, he is at once aware of the fact that it is in the throes of a condition prophesied early in the movement by one of its leading thinkers. Said he:

> Two things may be looked for now, in these "movements" toward union.—We must rest perfectly sure that sectarianism will make a long and mighty struggle for its life and power and dominion; it will not yield easily.—It is wary, skillful and strong. If it must meet and yield to the rising plea for Christian union,—it will do it in such a manner as to lose nothing by it;—that is, it will consent to such a union that will leave it in the full enjoyment of its sinful life and dominion. This is one of the things that we must expect, inevitably to see. The other is this:—in the enthusiasm for union, men will hasten to reach their object by ignoring and throwing aside, as obstacles to the realizing of their wishes, often what is essential and positive in the doctrine of Christ, and what can never be yielded up without offending God, without destroying the integrity, and therefore the divine power, of the religion of Christ.[1]

The period just considered has seen the beginnings of these things, and the forces are still at work.

---

[1] *Millennial Harbinger*, Vol. 40, No. IV, p. 183.

Chapter VI

THE ORIGINAL GROUND OF THE PLEA

THE PLEA TODAY

In an attempt to determine present day thinking in regard to the subject of this thesis, a letter of inquiry was sent to 44 representative persons in various sections of the country and in various positions of service. The following is an exact copy of the letter:

I am in the midst of preparation of my thesis for the B.D. degree, which I hope to obtain from the School of Religion of Butler University in the near future. The subject of the thesis is: "A History of the Statements of the Plea of the churches of Christ for Christian Unity upon the Basis of a Restoration of the church of the New Testament." I have sought to trace the written record of our historic plea from its beginning to the present day.

However, I have noticed that my collection of statements does not include one from you. Somehow I have, no doubt, overlooked the publications in which they may appear. Since my thesis would not be complete without a statement from you, I would appreciate it immensely if you would take time from your busy life to set forth, in simple form, the principles of the brotherhood, as you see them, and mail same to me in the enclosed envelope at your earliest convenience.

The statement, should you choose to make it, will stand in the thesis on its own merit. I intend making only sufficient comment to connect the statements into smooth reading form. It is my hope that a reader will be able to trace the course of the statements from the beginning of the movement to today and will be able to note trends and developments within the thought of the movement, without comment from the author.

I sincerely appreciate any consideration you may give this request, and hope that I may be able to include a statement from you in my thesis.

It was thought that this would be the best manner of determining the mind of present day leaders on this subject. The statements would be up to date, and persons who were not apt to have statements published could be reached in this manner.

The following persons received the above letter: Percy E. Kohl, State Secretary of the Alabama Christian Missionary Association; Wesley P. Ford, State Secretary of the Arizona Christian Missionary Association; Clifford A. Cole, State Secretary of the California Christian Missionary Association; Lawrence S. Ashley, State Secretary of the Florida Christian Missionary Association; Chester P. Hensley, State Secretary of the Illinois Christian Missionary Association; Ephraim D. Lowe, State Secretary of the Indiana Christian Missionary Society; John D. Zimmerman, State Secretary of the Kansas Christian Missionary Association; William J. Lineback, State Secretary of the Maryland, Delaware and District of Columbia Christian Missionary Association; S. V. Mattson, State Secretary of the Michigan Christian Missionary Association; Vernon S. Stagner, State Secretary of the Minnesota Christian Missionary Association; James H. Tilsley, Executive Secretary of the Missouri Christian Missionary Association; Thomas Miller, State Secretary of the New England Christian Missionary Association; Charles C. Ware, State Secretary of the North Carolina Christian Missionary Association; Herald B. Monroe, State Secretary of the Ohio Christian Missionary Association; C. F. Swander, State Secretary of the Oregon Christian Missionary Association; and John A. Tate, State Secretary of the Virginia Christian Missionary Association.

In addition to the above the following also received the letter of inquiry listed above: George W. Buckner, Jr., Editor of the *World Call*, Eugene S. Ogrodowski, recently editor of the *Front Rank*, Guy P. Leavitt, Editor of the *Lookout*, John G. Alber, Editor of *Sound Doctrine*, formerly State Secretary of the Nebraska Christian Missionary Association; William H. Alexander, minister of the First Christian Church, Oklahoma City; Reuben L. Anderson, Minister of the Long Beach Christian Church, Long Beach, California; Homer J. Armstrong, minister of the Judson Memorial Baptist Church of Minneapolis, Minnesota, (though listed in the Year Book for 1946); R. M. Bell, President of Johnson Bible College; Harry Bucalstein, minister of the West Morris Street Christian Church, Indianapolis (now of Havre, Montana); Peyton Canary, President of Southwest Christian Seminary, Phoenix, Arizona; A. E. Cory, Professor of Missions, Butler University School of Religion, Indianapolis; H. B. McCormick, Past President of the United Christian Missionary Society; C. O. Hawley, Executive Director of Unified Promotion; Willard M. Wickizer, Executive Secretary of the Department of Church Development and Evangelism of the United Christian Missionary Society; E. K. Higdon, Executive Secretary of the Department of Oriental Missions of the United Christian Missionary Society; Virgil Sly, Executive Secretary of the Department of Africa Missions of the United Christian Missionary Society; Ross J. Griffeth, President of Northwest Christian College, Eugene, Oregon; Orval M. Morgan, minister of the Broadway Christian Church, Lexington, Kentucky, Ernest Laughlin, minister of the West Side Church of Christ, Springfield, Illinois; Fred Smith minister of the First Christian Church, Elizabethton, Tennessee; Woodrow Perry, President of Cincinnati Bible Seminary; C. W. Lipsey, formerly minister of the West Side Christian Church, Amarillo, Texas; Vernon M. Newland, minister of the Christian Church, Crowell, Texas; Russell E. Boatman, President of the Minnesota Bible College; Wm. N. Blakemore, Acting Dean of the Disciples Divinity House, University of Chicago; Guy B. Dunning, formerly President of Nebraska Christian College; Stephen J. England, Dean of the College of the Bible, Phillips University; and Rupert C. Foster, Professor of New Testament, Cincinnati Bible Seminary.

Some of the above failed even to reply. Others graciously submitted statements to be included in the thesis. Still others referred to writings previously published which contained statements which were considered to be satisfactory. In order to be absolutely impartial, the reply which each submitted will be included later. In all, however, it seems that a cross-section of thought is represented in the statements received for inclusion. The replies to the letters will be taken up in order.

The first in the lists given above to make reply was Lawrence S. Ashley, who wrote as follows:

Thank you for the invitation but I don't think that I have anything to contribute which you do not already have.[1]

Chester P. Hensley is the next in the list who made reply. Says Mr. Hensley:

It was good to get your letter saying you are writing a thesis on "A History of the Statements of the Plea of the Churches of Christ for Christian Unity Upon the Basis of a Restoration of the Church of the New Testament." I shall be quite interested in reading it when it is completed.

It is noted that you are interested in tracing the written record of our historic plea from its beginning to its present day.[2]

The following is the letter received from Ephraim D. Lowe:

Really, I am ashamed in my not being able to get the statement to you for your B.D. thesis.

My counsel would be, Harold, that you not depend upon this, which is a bit hard to explain, since it has to do wholly with the fact that I have not had the opportunity to give it the needed thought. However, I thought today that you should know, so if you haven't done so, would feel free to proceed in the completion of your thesis without it.

You will please know that this is in no sense intentional, and that I am sorry about it.[3]

John D. Zimmerman enclosed a tract entitled "Studies in Evangelism" in his reply. From that tract we quote the following:

The Disciples came into being as a protest against the sectarian spirit, and in an earnest plea for the oneness of all followers of Christ. The motto of our pioneers is a good one: "Where the Scriptures speak, we speak; where the Scriptures are silent, we are silent."

In our preaching and church work we are not hindered by the necessity of explaining or defending human names or creeds, or rituals or customs. We believe, "Bible things should be called by Bible names."

The Plea is for Christian unity, in answer to the prayer of Jesus, "They may all be one." "In faith, unity; in opinions, liberty; in all things, love." There is one: Body, Spirit, Hope, LORD, Faith, Baptism, God. Eph. 4:4-6.

The Plan for unity is the "Restoration of the New Testament church; in its doctrines, its ordinances and its life." Oneness is not in creeds, but in Christ. The path to unity is by giving up the things that divide, and coming together in Christ and upon His word. "No creed but Christ, No name but Christian, No law but the Lord's, No book but the Bible."

The Purpose is to win humanity to God, and fulfill the prayer of Jesus, "That the world may believe." Christian unity is not for the sake of economy, or prestige, but for service. "When Christians are ONE the world can be WON."[4]

This statement is typical of many that have been included previously in the thesis. Mr. Welshimer's statement on page 143 is cited as example.

To the letter of inquiry Vernon S. Stagner replied as follows:

Would like very much to share in your thesis and will be interested in reading your completed work. Terribly sorry that schedule is so jammed for rest of summer and fall that I just can't see how I could prepare even

---

[1]Letter on file.   [2]Letter on file.   [3]Letter on file.

[4]John D. Zimmerman, *Studies in Evangelism*, (Topeka: Privately Printed, n. d.) pp. 43, 44.

a simple statement that would add anything to what you would already have. Please forgive me.[1]

The next statement was received from Thomas Miller. Due to the length of it, it cannot all be included. In the main, the statement is a comparison of the relative merits of the "atomistic" and "organic" conceptions of the church and the means by which union will be achieved. The former is the conception of the freedom of the local congregation, which Mr. Miller seems to favor because "it was divinely given and hence is the best form." The latter is the conception of the church as held by the Presbyterians and Episcopalians. Mr. Miller seeks to demonstrate that the "atomistic" churches have seen more union accomplished and hold better those who are won than the churches of the "organic" conception. He then reviews the various trends within the disciples of Christ, the organ question, the open-membership question, and the missionary question.

In discussing the relationship of persons who are members of denominations to those who are members of the church of Christ, Mr. Miller asserts:

In what matter of Christian fellowship do we not freely join them? From what matter of Christian fellowship are they debarred in any of our churches? In what do we make a distinction between the immersed and the unimmersed? In two things and two things only. These are the right hand of fellowship and the church roll of members—two things about which the scriptures are as silent as the grave. "Where the scriptures speak we speak, and where the scriptures are silent we are silent." Are we? No. In this we are as vocal as the voice of the clouds. The New Testament church had no roll of members as far as we know; nor did they have the right hand of fellowship as we have it now. Whatever may be our theory or intention we freely and fully receive them in all things that pertain to Christian fellowship. Here the heart prevails over the head.[2]

Mr. Miller goes on to say that this practice merely eliminates certain ones from membership in the Disciples, "Our body," "We as a people."

The statement is concluded as follows:

. . . . Since so many Disciples are doing nothing for union we ought to consider what we ought to try to do.

(1) We ought to lay more stress on the importance of union, and the exceeding sinfulness of disunion. Preparatory to this we ought to make a new and more diligent study of the scriptures bearing on the subject.

(2) We ought to discourage the idea of union by absorption with all of its implications of superiority. While we must strive to reproduce the New Testament church as far as practicable we must realize that in some respects it cannot be reproduced, and in some respects it is not desirable to reproduce it. We ought to realize that it is no longer good policy, saying nothing about good Christianity, to so antagonize the denominations as to turn their ears from our message. We ought to try to reach them not to proselyte them but to prepare them for the united church.

(3) For reasons given above we ought not to adopt the policy of "open membership," for the present at least. Possibly the time may come

[1]Letter on file.

[2]Thomas Miller, *The Disciples and Christian Unity*, (An unpublished Manuscript Loaned by him and returned, 1948), p. 11.

when in the interest of union it might be well to do so; but that time, or those conditions, has not yet come.

(4) We should continue to cooperate with all union movements as far as possible.

(5) Especially we ought to cooperate with the Christian Unity League, if they will allow us to do so without espousing "open membership." (The Christian Unity League, Mr. Miller explains, rejects Disciples, because of their refusal to accept all "Christians," and Episcopalians, because of their insistance upon apostolic succession).

(6) We ought to prosecute our endeavor for union with the Baptists. There are as far as I can see but two obstacles in the way. We would be loth to accept the name Baptist . . . . The other obstacle is the frequency of celebrating the Lord's supper . . . . A majority in any local church would decide.

(7) When this has been accomplished and when pedobaptists have united then we should consider uniting with them. But that is too far away to need discussing now.

(8) And still farther away is the consideration of union with Episcopalians and Roman Catholics, not because such a union is not desirable, but because for the present at least it is so utterly impossible.

(9) As far as my reading on the union movement goes the Friends have not been considered. So it might be well for us to examine their position on the ordinances and Christian living. If pure Christ-like living can be brought about as well without the ordinances as with them, why continue them? If this would settle the matter between Baptists and Pedobaptists the continuation of the ordinances would be a sin.[1]

Mr. Miller's position seems perfectly clear from the statements quoted. As to whether it is the position historically taken by the movement, reference to the statements previously stated must be made.

Charles C. Ware cited his book, *North Carolina Disciples*, in response to the request for a statement of the Plea. The statement cited follows:

In the teaching service of the Disciples a change of emphasis was proper and inevitable. Their movement was born of a pure desire to help answer the prayer of Christ for the union of all His people. They conceived that this could be realized only if the Bible alone were recognized as the standard of faith which all Christians might adopt without offense of mind or conscience. They emerged as a separate Communion by reason of intense opposition. Thomas Campbell's ideals of Christian union were an age ahead of his day. By stern necessity succeeding pioneers adapted these to denominational means. Thus grew the Disciple movement.

When the sin of division shall have disappeared, God's people will again appear wholly undenominational. This indeed they must be in spirit if they are truly His at any time. It was a denominational world in which the Disciples lived. They were subjected to all that this implied. Their principles would not bless the world save as in the grace of God they fought, lived and died for them.

This necessitated, at first, a polemical pulpit, press, and forum. As the Disciples served, however, they were impressed with that which was good in their neighbors. This candor and open-mindedness to all truth has saved representative Disciples from becoming a sect. Much that they have

---

[1]*Ibid.*, pp. 12, 13.

fought for has become a reality in surrounding communions. Disciples have appropriated likewise something of the zeal and self-sacrifice of Methodists, the piety of Presbyterians, the loyalty of Baptists, the esthetics in worship of the Episcopalians, and attention to child culture of Roman Catholics. If the emphasis in the Disciple's message has shifted it is because they have lived in a changing world. They are progressive. This largest communion of American origin has had the genius of America in its development.[1]

The above statement is more of a review of the shift in emphasis of the message of the Disciples and of their adoption of what was good in the denominations. However, it helps, at least in part, to understand Mr. Ware's position toward the disciples and their historic plea.

In answer to the letter Herald B. Monroe replied:

I appreciate the honor you have conferred on me in asking for a statement from me concerning the pleas of the Churches of Christ for Christian Unity. I feel that the honor was undeserved.

I regret to say that, due to the heavy press of activities we must carry on in helping our Churches in the State and due to the frequent calls that are made upon this office for help in writing theses, I must regretfully decline the honor. I believe you will understand that the preparation of such a statement would take considerable time and I am sure you will sympathize when you understand that this makes about the sixth request for help that we have recently received.

I might say that my position is the same as that which has been traditional with our Brotherhood.[2]

John A. Tate replied as follows:

Your letter of August 16 is before me. I have so many requests from students preparing their thesis for historical information on our work in Virginia that it just takes more time than I have to give to it. I would not send you anything except what was correct and I must confess it is utterly impossible for me to find time to write out what you would want now. I regret my inability to comply with your request.[3]

George Walker Buckner referred to his booklet *The Winds of God* in answer to the request. In this booklet Mr. Buckner points out the fact that most Christian groups arose as a result of emphasis upon some point of Christian doctrine or thinking which was considered to be not emphasized sufficiently by the other groups. The Disciples of Christ, he indicates, came into being through emphasis upon the problem of disunion and through preaching a new idea or a new emphasis upon an old idea of restoring the church of the New Testament. One is reminded of the statement of W. S. Russell as quoted earlier in this research.

In addition to the above Mr. Buckner says:

A second essential to the understanding of the significance of the movement of Disciples of Christ for the unity of the church is to recognize the principle which they proposed as a basis for unity. This principle was to return to the simple and basic teachings and practices of the Christian religion as constituting the sole test of fellowship and basis for a common Christian life. It was, they insisted, the developed theologies and ec-

[1] Charles Crossfield Ware, *North Carolina Disciples*, (St. Louis: Christian Board of Publication, 1927), p. 230.   [2] Letter on file.   [3] Letter on file.

clesiastical organizations of the post-New Testament years which caused men to divide. The solution they saw as a return to the simple faith of the New Testament church which they held to be that of personal acceptance of and loyalty to Jesus Christ as "the son of the living God" and obedience to Him in all things. Thus they came to stress the idea of the restoration of the New Testament church.

In this emphasis the Disciples of Christ were not unique, for practically every other Protestant communion from the Lutherans to this day has conceived of itself as restoring primitive Christianity. Their idea of what restoration involved was unique, but not the idea of restoration itself . . . .[1]

A third essential to the understanding of the Disciples of Christ is to sense the degree to which they gave expression to a spirit which they believed must accompany every sincere effort for the unity of the church. That spirit was expressed in an unprecedented emphasis upon the principle of Christian liberty of opinion. Their antagonism to written creeds was based upon the belief that these are divisive. The solution to division they held to be that of Christian liberty . . . .[2]

. . . . In a day of general insistence upon conformity, these men permitted none to intimidate or coerce them—neither secretaries, conventions, nor editors. It is not possible to understand them and the movement with which they were identified except in the light of their unprecedented emphasis upon the principle of Christian liberty of opinion.[3]

A recurring danger of the movement of Disciples of Christ is the danger of the institution. It is always a calamity when an ideal once warm and vigorous, becomes a hard and excluding institution. Just such a calamity confronts the Disciples of Christ today if they permit their ideal of the church universal to be dimmed by their devotion to the institution which has grown out of it. It is not enough for Disciples of Christ to prove to all comers the soundness of the position they have developed with respect to the beliefs and practices of the church. If the ideal of their fathers is to live and prevail, it will not be because its adherents seek to debate the world into submissive acceptance of their position. That ideal will not be made to live by those who set forth in cold terms of legalism a position which they call upon others to accept on a take-it-or-leave-it basis. The ideal will have life and power only as those who hold it join hands with others of the followers of Christ in seeking anew the will of God as to the unity of his church. Only those who seek light have the right to offer to shed light upon the problems of others.[4]

It is believed that the essence of the rather lengthy statement of Mr. Buckner has been gleaned and set forth above. Attention is called particularly to the last paragraph for comparison with other statements set forth herein.

Guy P. Leavitt, in reply to the request, contributed the following statement:

I remember praying as a child of 10 years, that I might live to see the day when all Christians are united in their stand for the deity of Christ, the authority of the Scriptures as a divine revelation, and their adherence otherwise to the pattern of primitive Christianity, its doctrine, its ordinances and its fruits. That prayer has not changed. I am still praying for this unity.[5]

The simplicity of this statement and its apparent harmony with the majority of the statements in this thesis is evident. It is clearly one with the main thought of the movement.

---

[1]George Walker Buckner, *The Winds of God, Christian Unity, Cooperation, World Fellowship*, (n. p., n. d.), p. 29.   [2]*Ibid.*, p. 30.   [3]*Ibid.*, pp. 30, 31.   [4]*Ibid.*, p. 31.
[5]Letter on file.

In response to the inquiry John G. Alber submitted several copies of his little paper *Sound Doctrine* from which the following is taken:

For forty and three years I have preached the gospel. My faith in the Bible as God's Book and in Christ as God's Son has never wavered. To me the church has always been a divine institution; the family of God; the Kingdom of God; the House of God and Gateway to Heaven. It is the Pillar and Ground of Truth. It is the Body of Christ, the Candlestick of Light and Beauty, the Tabernacle of Jesus, the Temple of the Most High, in whose Shekina dwelleth the eternal God. It is the appointed place where Jesus meets his people. No man can preach these things uncompromisingly, in an age of doubt, without creating opposition.

If the Bible does not mean what it says it is no divine revelation. I feel that those who explain it away and whittle Jesus down to the size of a man are the enemies of my Lord. Therefore they are my enemies and I shall fight them as long as this old battle wagon in which I ride stays afloat. Until it goes down, all of her guns shall be ablaze . . . .

I am deeply distressed over the doctrinal breakdown in certain quarters of our brotherhood. The ideology of German Rationalism, which so completely wrecked that nation, and brought on a world catastrophy, has found its way into our educational system and reflects itself in Christian Colleges, and pulpits. Its blighting effect is devastating . . . .

We should not let this situation go unchallenged. We should seek to lead the Church back to the crystal waters of the Fountainhead. We should stress again the great fundamentals of our faith, the reality of a personal God; the divine lordship and deity of Jesus; the authority and authenticity of the Bible; the divine origin and constitution of the Church; the logic and scriptural soundness of the historic position of our movement all of which comes to its glorious fruition and climax in the bright hope of immortality.

We should refute the superficial and illogical notion that it makes no difference what we believe so long as we are sincere. How can one believe what is false and being influenced by it live a life that is true? How can one hold views of Christ that are untrue and have true fellowship with God through Christ? . . . .[1]

Certainly Mr. Alber's regard for the Plea and for the church is unquestioned when the above statement is considered carefully.

Homer J. Armstrong wrote as below:

As I see the movement of the Disciples of Christ it would appear to me that in the beginning the main objective of the Disciples of Christ was to restore primitive Christianity. This plea was based on the assumption that in the New Testament we have a clear cut blue print of the Apostolic Church. The matter of Christian union, I believe, was a secondary consideration.

As I see the movement as it is today, Disciples are divided over the first item. The more conservative brethren of the brotherhood still think in terms of a hard and fast pattern in the NT and seek to "restore" the Apostolic Church according to that Pattern. The more liberal group among the Disciples recognize that it is impossible to "restore" in detail a Church which is not uniform in the New Testament itself, and have therefore shifted their emphasis to *Christian unity* rather than "restoration."

The plea of the Disciples as I see it now is one for Christian unity. We should be more concerned in getting Christians together, than in setting up

[1]*Sound Doctrine*, Vol. I, No. 1, p. 1.

some infallible ecclesiastical pattern. Apart from our passion for unity we really have no right to exist in Protestantism, for all other bodies assume primitive Christianity.[1]

Mr. Armstrong has faced the situation honestly and has analyzed the problem accurately, from his own point of view. It is to be noted that he admits a "shift" in emphasis. This is a shift that many have made but few will admit. In addition, it seems only fair to state that those advocating a restoration of the primitive church would be ready at once to admit a variance in practice which would not exceed the variance in practice in the New Testament church, if such could be shown to have existed.

Liberty of opinion has always been one of the watch cries of the Restoration movement, and that there was variance in the opinions of the New Testament Christians would never be denied. However, it is strange that those who cry the loudest for liberty of opinion would cite the differing opinions of the early Christians as examples of the fact that the church "was not uniform in the New Testament itself," and thereby attempt to justify glaring differences in fundamental faith and practice. As has been demonstrated in this history, the Restoration movement, while admitting differences in the opinions of the Christians of the apostolic age, has at the same time held that those Christians were united in the acceptance of a core of fundamental elements and that these constitute the very identity of the church. It is not for unity of opinion that the Plea has called but for unity of basic faith and doctrine. The church does not find its identity in opinions held by its constituents but in its continuance of the faith and teaching of the apostles of Jesus Christ, who themselves held differing opinions.

The weekly bulletin cover of the West Morris Street Christian Church was included in the reply made by Harry Bucalstein. On this cover is printed the following statement of the position of the Restoration movement:

We came into being with the purpose of presenting to divided Christianity a platform of unity, namely, the restoration of the church according to the form, purpose and spirit given by the divine Founder through His Apostles. Our only creed, therefore, is that confession of truth on which Jesus said He would build His church (Matt. 16:17, 18), when Peter first expressed that faith (Matt. 16:16). Our only book of form or discipline is the New Testament, in which the church is described by inspired men.

Our desire to follow the teaching and example of Christ and His Apostles is our reason for granting the privilege of immersion for remission of sins (Acts 2:38) to penitent believers who confess Christ before men. For the same reason we eat the Lord's Supper weekly (Acts 20:7) until He shall return (I Cor. 11:26). Whatever the New Testament enjoins in command or approved example, we strive to follow. In all other matters we allow the widest latitude of opinion and practice.

We offer a religious home and brotherhood to those who are looking for a sane and practical creed, and for democracy under Christ in the government of the church. OUR CREED IS CHRIST ALONE: OUR PATTERN OF LIFE IS THE NEW TESTAMENT ALONE: OUR SERVICE IS FOR ALL MANKIND.[2]

---

[1]Letter on file.   [2]Bulletin on file.

Here is a complete statement of the position of the movement. It is similar to many that have already been considered in this history.

The following is the reply received from Willard M. Wickizer:

Your letter of August 17 reached my desk while I was absent on vacation and this is the first opportunity I have had to make reply. I am sorry to turn down your request for a statement from me, setting forth the basis upon which I think we should seek to establish Christian unity, but I just do not have time to prepare such a statement for you. I would not be content simply to "dash off" a few thoughts, but if I did submit such a statement I would want it to really represent my best thinking in the matter and it is this kind of a statement that I do not have time to prepare. In the midst of a very busy field schedule, I am working on a ten-year program of advance statements covering the work of my department. This will require all of the time I can possibly marshall between now and the first of December.[1]

The following statement by Ross J. Griffeth was contributed in response to the letter of inquiry:

Three vital factors have been present in the thinking of those who have advocated Christian unity upon the basis of a return to New Testament teachings, namely: (1) restoration, (2) unity, (3) liberty. While ardently proclaiming fidelity to one or the other of these factors at one time or another, there has been no adequate clarifying of the meaning of these three terms as they are used or to a bringing of them into balance. Obviously no brief statement will resolve the matter but an outline of views may stimulate further thinking.

When the emphasis is given to *restoration*, the tendency is to restrict the area of liberty because the restorationists not only appeal to the New Testament Scriptures as authoritative but also, although unconsciously, emphasize a dogmatic interpretation of the Scriptures which they hold to be authoritative. Also, the appeal for unity is apt to be minimized in favor of emphasis upon restoration.

When *unity* is viewed as the most significant factor in the total movement toward Christian unity, the tendency is to compromise in the areas where various Christian bodies disagree in belief and practice in order to gain a working basis among various professed disciples of Christ without securing uniformity of belief even in restricted areas.

When liberty is the dominant emphasis, chaos usually follows in the area of practical problems. The result generally is a tendency to move away from unity and to miss much that is taught in the New Testament, such as kindness, meekness, self-control.

In the light of experience, it may well be seen that the achievement of Christian unity, however defined, is not as simple and easy as was once thought. It cannot be achieved simply by agreeing upon the steps by which one becomes a Christian or by inviting to the Lord's table all who care to participate. Even restoration of the New Testament ideal of unity poses the question as to whether that which is not forbidden is permitted. Thus it appears that Christian unity can only be approached by continual effort and, even if once achieved, will not necessarily be self-perpetuating.

From the point of view most commonly held, the areas of possible or desirable unity may be given a fourfold classification: (1) organization,

[1]Letter on file.

(2) ordinance and worship, (3) creed, (4) Christian social service. Approaches to unity must deal with these matters.

Concerning organization, congregational autonomy with voluntary co-operation is generally regarded as desirable and conformable to New Testament teachings. As to ordinances, baptism (immersion) into Christ and the Lord's table spread weekly and open to all, may be accepted as basic and any realization of Christian unity would of necessity include this minimum. The expression which worship takes may be varied according to custom and interest so long as not contrary to New Testament teachings. As to creed, there can be "no creed but Christ," the resurrected Saviour. Statements of belief may be written or spoken *ad infinitum* so long as they are not held to be binding or essential to unity. And on one can make an authoritative interpretation for another of this basic creed.

Actually the most practical immediate approach to Christian unity is through Christian social service. As professed followers of Christ work together they should learn to respect one another and make possible a unity of spirit in the bond of peace even before all differences are resolved.

Attainable and desirable Christian unity will not be uniformity except in minimum areas as indicated above which are basic. It will not be reached easily. Much study, prayer, work, and Christian love must be exercised before a clear realization of what Christian unity in all its phases can or should be. And we pray that we may adequately apprehend the meaning of our Lord when he prayed, "That they all may be one; as thou, Father, art in me, and I in thee, that they also may be one in us: that the world may believe that thou hast sent me."[1]

This statement should certainly take its place along side of others in a history of the Plea. Mr. Griffeth has sought to reduce the problem to basic essentials, and has admirably succeeded, though perhaps there would be question about achieving even Christian social service before unity in the basic essentials is achieved.

Fred W. Smith submitted the brief articles on the inside of the cover page of three issues of the publication which he edits, *The Plea*. They read as below:

The source of authority in Christianity is God who gave both heavenly and earthly authority to his only begotten Son. Jesus, in turn, carefully selected his apostles and empowered them to be his witnesses. After receiving the baptism of the Holy Spirit the Apostles presented to the world the teachings and commandments of Jesus. When we continue steadfastly in the Apostle's Doctrine we are building upon a sure foundation. When we succumb to the pressures of contemporary culture and listen to the denominational doggeral of our times we are building upon uncertainties. Christianity stands or falls with the Lordship of Jesus and the credibility of the Apostles. It is here that believers must be united. To force opinions upon others through subtle innuendo, or ecclesiastical pressure politics, or written ridicule, is to create division. And this is sinful! To restore the doctrine of Christ and his apostles to the place of paramount authority is our PLEA.[2]

The Oracles of God are given by Divine inspiration and designed to MAKE THE MAN OF GOD PERFECT. II TIM. 3:16, 17. THE SPIRITUAL PERSON DISCERNS IN THE SACRED WRITINGS THE DOCTRINE THAT CENTERS IN THE GREAT SCHEME OF REDEMPTION. For instruction in righteousness, reproof, correction, THERE IS NO COM-

---

[1]Ross J. Griffeth, *Christian Unity*, (Unpublished Manuscript, 1948).
[2]*The Plea*, June, 1948.

PARABLE SOURCE OF INFORMATION. HEREIN IS GOD'S REVELATION TO MAN.

This revelation is in language which is understandable. Therefore, we are to study the Scriptures just as we study other writings. We are to consider the setting of the passage under consideration . . . . Who speaks and to whom . . . . What dispensation, etc.

It is a distortion of revelation to spiritualize everything after the manner of Swedenborg. It is a perversion to extract all spiritual implications as the materialist does.

We believe that the more we study the word of God the more we will discern His will. The way of salvation is plainly revealed and the way of Christian living is clearly promoted. To rightly divide the Word of Truth is our PLEA.[1]

The cells in the Body of Christ which is the Church are the individual believers. They are the branches of the True Vine—the sheep of the One Fold—the children in the Family of God.

Super-organizations and denominational groups are not and never were the units of the Body of Christ. There is no Scriptural sanction for them.

High sounding terms like "Ecumenical" which means "universal" may be popular in the mind of the modern theological "big-leader" but to designate a conglomeration of un-Scriptural organizations as the Ecumenical Church is a distortion of the truth.

The universal church of the Lord and Saviour Jesus Christ is composed of all those who are penitent obedient, believers. Only when men return to the simplicity of the New Testament church will they fulfill the prayer of our Lord for unity. This is our PLEA.[2]

The direct and accurate presentation of the Restoration Plea, as given above, is indeed refreshing. The position of Mr. Smith is clear and unequivocally stated. Its harmony with the impact of the movement is unquestioned.

The statement contributed by Vernon M. Newland follows:

I believe that the grandest and noblest position that any child of God can take any time, any where, in this old sect-torn, denominational world is that of being simply a "Christian only." To me, what we have historically called the "restoration" movement is the most challenging, exalted and idealistic "crusade"—for it is still that to me—since the earliest days of Christianity. I believe it is, and, of necessity, must be, the logical next step for the whole Christian world following the Protestant Reformation of Europe.

The Methodists have no hope that all someday will become Methodists, nor do Baptists hope that all someday will become Baptists. But we hope, and if we are ever to have Christian unity it must be, that all someday will drop their divisive, man-made, unscriptural names and become "Christians only." We do not ask that others tear down their buildings and come and "join our church." It is rather for all who have erected them, to remove the humanly-erected barriers to fellowship and unity that have tragically separated us for long centuries, and to rally around Jesus Christ and Him alone,—then we will gradually "drift" back together again, even as we have in the past drifted apart. Practically speaking, however, we ask and challenge those who belong to groups that do not move forthrightly in that direction to come out of denominational-

---

[1] *The Plea*, July, 1948.   [2] *The Plea*, August, 1948.

ism at once and join with others to effect the largest measure of Christian unity in our time, to hasten the day when Christ's prayer for unity may be fully realized.[1]

Further light on Mr. Newland's attitude may be noted in the following:

> But may I observe, in passing, that in all our relationships with our denominational friends there is no place, either in thought or word, for rudeness or unkindness of any kind. He who deals in these things, or fails to manifest anything but great sympathy for the problems and the difficulties faced by those who, in most cases, have known nothing else but age-old and traditional denominationalism, misses the whole point of what we of the "restoration" movement desire to see come to pass in the world . . . . But if some do not see it that way, our attitude and method is still that of winsome, reasoned, persuasive appeal.[2]

The last sentence applies to those to whom we appeal, who find themselves bound in denominationalism, but find it difficult to see the position the Restoration movement takes. This, of course, is the spirit of the Restoration movement through its history, but Mr. Newland has struck a note that many among us need to learn.

Guy Dunning, recovering from a recent automobile accident, submitted the statement below:

> No people could have been honored with a higher ideal than we have enjoyed. The goal of restoring God's pattern of and for the church, and pointing others to their privilege of doing the same and to thus fulfill Christ's prayer, "That they all may be one."[3]

While the above statement is brief, it is to the point. Especially interesting is Mr. Dunning's conception of the privilege of holding the Restoration position.

Stephen J. England cited his book, *We Disciples*, in answer to the request. Says Mr. England:

> I am wondering if you have read my small book entitled "We Disciples." In this you will see some statements that I have made concerning the plea of our people for Christian unity. Probably these are at much greater length than I would care to try to put into a letter. If these statements are adequate for your purpose it would save a great deal of correspondence. Your thesis should be an interesting one and should make a real contribution to the life of our people.[4]

Attempts to locate a copy of Mr. England's book have been to no avail. The School of Religion Library reports that it is not available at this time.

The last of the responses to the inquiry was by Rupert C. Foster, who called attention to his book, *The Everlasting Gospel*. Reference to this volume and to the section cited brought to light the following statement:

> What is the hope of the church in this critical age? It is to preach the gospel. By forgetting the gospel, the church has fallen into devious ways, and only by the persistent proclamation of the gospel can the church be called back to the straight path that leads to the redemption of the world. The whole gospel must be preached, and with the New Testament emphasis.

---

[1]Letter on file.   [2]*The Midwest Christian*, April, 1946. p. 7.
[3]Letter on file.   [4]Letter on file.

The Protestant world speaks with one voice concerning the gospel, except in respect to certain phases of the message and certain institutions of the church. Common honesty demands that, instead of hiding our doctrinal differences under a bushel, we bring them forth into the white light of the gospel, and allow only that which is able to stand this searching test to remain.[1]

The last paragraph of Mr. Foster's statement is especially interesting. The appeal to bring differences into the open would certainly be more effective to the desired end than covering them up. After all is said and done, the differences are the things that divide. If unity is to be achieved, the differences are going to have to be reconciled. If they are reconciled through reference to the word of God, the purpose of the restoration movement shall have been achieved.

At first consideration, it may appear that nothing has been accomplished through the sending forth of the letter of inquiry and through the inclusion of the responses in this thesis. However, several things may be noted which may aid in understanding the impact of these statements. In the first place, only one statement emphatically states that a change in emphasis has been made, a shift from restoration to unity. This same truth may be detected in others, which do not pointedly admit to a shift in the aim of the movement. In addition, the statements are of varying degrees of enthusiasm for the Restoration idea. A few of them scarcely mention it; others mention little else. Some have asserted that we have overemphasized certain elements of the Plea and have called for a readjustment in our thinking in the matter. The meaning of at least one statement is almost entirely lost in beautiful language.

It may be argued that the lack of response destroys the effectiveness of the method used. To this argument, it is proposed that the refusal to make statements speaks volumes unuttered. If the churches of Christ have any message for unity at all for the Christian world, certainly anyone who is acquainted with that message would not or should not hesitate to speak it to one who inquires, provided it is in harmony with the gospel and with the historical record of the message. Too, one well acquainted with the message could set it down on paper in a very short time. The fact that some did not respond at all to the inquiry is less important, but again the lack of response could not have been based in like reasons in all cases. Of those who did respond the majority were those who had some knowledge of the Plea and were, for the most part, in harmony with its history. This, in itself, is most significant for our purposes. Some do not respond. Others refuse to make a statement. Still others more emphatically refuse. Some admit to a change in emphasis. Some advocate a rethinking of our emphasis. Others make a statement of the Plea with reservations. Finally, some make outright statements that bear harmony with the total impact of the history of the Plea.

REDEFINITION OF TERMS

One basic problem seems to lie at the root of the troubles of the Restoration movement today. This is a problem of definitions. A first year student in logic would know the basic law of that science, and particularly the law that follows immediately upon it, that a term must be defined exactly equal to its class

[1] Rupert C. Foster, *The Everlasting Gospel*, (Cincinnati: The Standard Publishing Company, 1927), pp. 95, 96.

196

and that the term must remain exactly the same in meaning throughout any given problem of argumentation. If the meaning of a term is changed within the course of discussion, a valid conclusion will never be reached.

This law of logic may be demonstrated to have been violated in many ways in regard to thinking being done today concerning the church. The New Testament gives us a picture of the church, however brief that picture may be said to be by some. That is, the term "ecclesia" referred to something definite in the New Testament day. Its meaning was established. A close reading of the word of God will bring to light the church as it was established, as it worked, and as it grew. Something else is not the church. The meaning of the term must forever conform to the meaning set forth in the New Testament, if sound thinking is to be done about it, and it must forever remain identified with the doctrine and practice of the apostles.

The church, in its original connotation, cannot be both as it is pictured in the New Testament and as we see it today. The basic laws of logic are violated. What we see parading as the church, and the church of the New Testament, are mutually exclusive. One or the other is not the church. Both cannot be. It will be argued that the church could not be the same today as it was in the day of the apostles; just as the giant oak is not the same as the acorn. No one has proposed that the church ought not to grow. This, of course, is the object of our labors. It is argued, however, that the church ought not to change, and when it does it changes into something not the church.

The Restoration movement has bandied about three other terms which have to do with this problem, but has somehow failed to define those terms adequately and has also failed to use them in the same meaning at all times. The terms are: Christian unity, Christian union, and union. The very thing for which the movement has been pleading has not been clear in the minds of those who were pleading, sometimes those who were pleading the most loudly. Needless to say, these terms, of all that might be defined, need to be defined clearly and concisely and must be used consistently, if we are to accomplish the object for which we plead. They will be considered one at a time.

Christian Unity:—There are at least four conceptions of Christian unity abroad in our thinking today, as has been pointed out previously and may be noted through careful reading of the statements included in this thesis. Is it any wonder that so little clear thinking is being done about it?

Most people, particularly those outside of the Restoration movement, seem to be thinking in terms of denominational co-operation or federation, when Christian unity is discussed. When asked how such a joining together is to be accomplished it appears that the answer is: through good natured accommodation, through giving over to the other man, through forgetting our differences, through admitting something less than Christianity to be Christianity. Denominations are to co-operate with one another, but are to continue in their own way and under their own banner. Sincerity is to be the rule of faith and acquiescence the rule of action in this "brotherhood of man."

The unit is the denomination, and the object is the co-operation of them all. If one thinks long enough and clearly enough about such a position, especially from the point of view of the New Testament and of the Restoration movement as it has been presented in this thesis, he must finally conclude that such would be neither Christian nor unity, let alone both. The church is certainly not a brotherhood of denominations.

Others seem to be thinking in terms of local congregations. Christian unity to them is simply the accommodation of the faith and life of every local congregation to all others in the same community in a free exchange of membership, if not actual merging of congregations, simply upon the basis of membership in "some church." This position would be the application of the "denominational" concept in the local field.

Some, who are preachers of churches of Christ, and who certainly should know better, often speak or write of a "brotherhood of churches" which is equally erroneous with the expression "brotherhood of denominations." The brotherhood of Christ, as is true of any brotherhood, is a brotherhood of individuals and not of denominations nor even of local congregations. The church universal, if such there be, is not composed of denominations nor of churches, but of individual Christians. It is not a church of churches, but a church of individuals.

Still others appear to be thinking in terms of two or more persons. When overtures for Christian unity are made, these persons think in terms of uniting "John Jones" with "Joe Smith," of uniting two or more human being to each other. This conception, from the Restoration point of view, is more nearly right than the first two above mentioned, for it brings the unit down to the individual where it belongs. It makes the individual the branch of the vine and not churches or denominations. Certainly, it must be concluded that it is a step in the right direction. However, it leaves out a very important factor Individuals may be united in a manner and form which could not be concluded to be Christian in any sense. Individuals must be united through their relationship to a third person, if the unity is to be Christian.

This brings the thought to the fourth concept of Christian unity, thinking upon that subject in terms of Christ and the relationship of the individual to Him. Christian unity is the uniting of the individual person to the Lord Jesus Christ through the means prescribed in the New Testament. The Restoration movement pleads for Christian unity—the uniting of every individual in the world to the Lord Jesus Christ, through his acceptance of Him as Lord and Saviour through baptism into Him. Jesus said, "I am the vine, ye are the branches." It is not the uniting of denominations, nor of churches, not even the uniting of branch to branch, but the uniting of the branch to the vine for which we give our lives and to which we dedicate our efforts. This alone is Christian unity, and in that meaning alone the term should be used.

Christian Union:—Here again the notions run wild in the world today. A common meaning for the term is hard to find, even among those who ought to know. Consequently no sound reasoning will ever be possible until the term is adequately defined and agreed upon by those who would discuss the subject.

Again, as in the case of Christian unity, some are thinking in terms of denominations. The two terms are used interchangeably by some, and are used one for the other without distinction. Too, many who seem to know what Christian unity is conclude that denominational co-operation is Christian union. It has often been said that Christian unity is the thing we seek, since Christian union can be had through denominational co-operation. This is certainly unsound reasoning. The co-operation of denominations is not Christian Union, particularly it is not Christian.

Others, as before, think of Christian union in terms of local congregations. The joining of local forces is proposed in the interest of eliminating over-lapping expenses. The object sought is the unifying of the unifiable elements of the local work. Such is termed Christian union by many. One thing needs to be realized. The unit of universal Christian co-operation is not the local congregation from the New Testament point of view. It was not the *churches* of Lystra and Iconium that recommended Timothy to the missionary party of Paul. The word says, "The same (Timothy) was well reported of by the *brethren* that were of Lystra and Iconium."

This brings us to the third notion of Christian union. When thinking upon this subject, one should think of the co-operation of Christian with Christian in the work of winning the world to Christ. Christian union is not denominational co-operation, not the co-operation of churches, local or otherwise, but the co-operation of Christians, as the term itself suggests. Thus, Christian unity has to do with the individual's oneness with Christ, while Christian union has to do with the co-operation of Christians in the work of Christ. The notion that it is possible to have Christian union without having Christian unity should be abandoned. Such is simply a confused and false reasoning. The co-operation of Christians cannot be had until there are Christians to co-operate, and there are no Christians until such are united with Christ. First comes Christian unity, the oneness of the individual with Christ, and second Christian union, the co-operation of Christians.

Union:—The discussion of this term is injected here to clarify a little more the other two. This term may be applied to anything. It is possible to accomplish the union of two blocks of wood by simply nailing them together. In order to have unity in such a case the blocks of wood would have to be fused together in such a manner as to make them one block of wood and not just two blocks nailed together.

It is possible, whether practical or not we do not judge here, to have a union of denominations. There are certain elements of work in which it might be possible for all denominations to co-operate. However, in the name of reason, it should be clearly stated and understood that such is a union of denominations. It should by all means be called what it is, a union of sects, and no more.

Furthermore, it would be possible, whether practical or not we do not judge here, to effect a union of churches. In many cases, it is conceivable that some co-operation might be effective in some elements of church work and life. However, such union should be termed for what it is a union of churches, and no more. Nothing could be more wrong than to term denominational co-operation or church co-operation Christian union. You have Christian union only when two or more persons who have been made one with Christ join efforts in accomplishing the will of Christ. Such and such only is Christian union.

So, in order to keep the record straight and to be accurate in reasoning about these three terms it should be remembered that Christian unity is the oneness of the individual in Christ; Christian union is the co-operation of two or more Christians in the work Christ has given them to do; union is a term that may be applied to any realm of life to indicate the co-operation of two or more things, persons, or groups of persons in any work. Such might even be applied to the co-operation of churches or denominations.

THE PLEA RESTATED

New Testament:—Fundamental to the Restoration Plea is the acceptance of the New Testament as containing God's revelation to man. It is to be thought of as final reference in all matters of faith and practice. The word of the apostles is to be regarded as highly and as authoritative as the word of the Lord Himself. They are His ambassadors and they speak for Him. The Plea will never accomplish its purpose as long as men regard the New Testament in so many different lights. Testimony of the statements of the Plea through the history of the movement is that the movement, as a whole, has always so regarded the New Testament.

However, when the Word is regarded as simply the beginning of the record of the development of the church and that other records of that development in other periods of the church are just as authoritative, the basis for the unity sought is destroyed. The church stands or falls upon the dependability of the testimony of the apostles. Christians today must place full dependence in the Word of God. The Restoration Plea calls them to this.

The New Testament Christ:—The Restoration movement has always maintained that it has no creed but Christ. He is the object of the faith of the man who would be called a Christian. It has always been the object of the Restoration movement to point out the New Testament Christ as the only one worthy of our regard. Some have maintained that we must not force our concept of the Christ upon other persons, but it would seem only right that the New Testament concept of Christ be required of all who would be called by His name.

The New Testament was placed first in this list of Restoration objectives, because all else is limited by it. There is a picture painted in words in the New Testament of a person who took his place in history and walked among men teaching, living, dying, rising again from the dead. The testimony of the Word and of the apostles is that this person is the Christ the Son of God. Those who would be Christian, in the New Testament sense—and there are no Christians in any other sense—must accept all that the Word of God claims of the Christ. The Restoration Plea calls them to this.

The New Testament Plan of Salvation:—Once the Christ has been accepted as the object of faith, one must then conform to the plan set forth in the Word by which he may enter into the salvation provided in the name of that Christ. The steps have been adequately outlined in other statements of the Plea listed in this thesis. They are also clearly outlined in the records of conversion set forth in the New Testament. The Restoration movement is interested in obtaining the same thing in conversion that was obtained in the New Testament day. Thus, the same plan is submitted.

It must be clearly understood that the plan of salvation is effective to a desirable end. It is not merely the passing through of a series of formal social events by which one enters into the social and religious life of the local congregation. The plan of pardon has as its object the redemption of the human soul. Conversion is a matter of obtaining the forgiveness of sins through the acceptance of God's mercy. He outlines the plan, since He is the offended one. Our part is merely the acceptance of the plan He has initiated. The New Testament contains the record of that plan, and the Restoration Plea calls men to this.

The New Testament Church:—Since the gospel of Jesus Christ is universal and is to be proclaimed to the whole world, a form of co-operation has been instituted by our Saviour in order to accomplish this work more efficiently. This form of co-operation has been called the church of Christ. In so far as the church of the New Testament is concerned, it must be defined simply and solely in terms of the local congregation. It has no visible expression outside of the church local. There were no interlocking connecting links between congregations, but each was independent of all others. The local form of Christian co-operation could be attached to nothing outside of itself in order to make it more the church than it already was, and intrusion from without was resented.

The basic difficulty today is to get people to think of the church in simple terms of the association of Christians accomplishing the will of God in any local field. The term church today is so perverted in its meaning that the New Testament meaning is lost completely in the mind of the common man. Most of the problems today arise from the attempts of men to improve upon the plan of God by organizing the intercongregational relationship of churches. The fundamental fallacy here is the notion that the unit of Christian co-operation is the church. Actually, from the New Testament point of view, the unit of local as well as universal Christian co-operation is the individual Christian person. No relation of overlordship should exist between congregations. The only conceivable reason for desiring such a thing would be to obtain control and to regulate the affairs of the local congregation. Certainly the local leadership of the church is more fully acquainted with the local needs and better able to handle them than someone outside.

Whenever men have begun to conceive of the church as needing some form of intercongregational expression in order to work more efficiently, some ambitious person has sought to allow himself to be appointed in control of the whole. Thus, denominationalism arises, including those churches which have welcomed such overlordship. Those churches which refused the outside controls have banded together under various other efforts. This whole concept, however, is foreign to the New Testament.

The word of our Lord contains a record of what His church was like. That some propose the record to be incomplete and maintain that there is no definite picture of the church in the New Testament is known. However, such statements are evolved from a misunderstanding of the New Testament church and from the application of the organizational concept of the church as held today to the New Testament period. The church as a simple association of local Christians, meeting around the Lord's table on the Lord's day, and working toward the evangelization of the community through the week by means of mutual participation in the work and sharing of the load is clearly pictured in God's word. The Restoration Plea would call men to this.

World Evangelism:—The object of accomplishing the restoration of the church of the New Testament is world evangelism, the uniting of every person in the world with Jesus, as Lord and Saviour. Anything less than this would render the movement out of harmony with the word of God. This, certainly, was the object of Christ's coming. It was also the object of the preaching of the apostles. It is, no less, the object of every faithful preacher of the gospel and every advocate of the Restoration Plea, if he understands it correctly.

It has been previously pointed out that the first advocates of the Restoration Plea were primarily concerned about the ineffectiveness of the church and about the fact that so many things were hindering its efforts both locally and abroad that many persons were destitute of its ministrations while living next door to it. Such condition is deplorable, and the world will never be won to Christ as long as such things prevail. What can be done to remedy the situation? The Restoration movement has the answer. Do away with those things that hamper the efforts of Christian evangelism and reduce the tests of fellowship to those basic things which have to do with the uniting of the individual to his Christ and Lord. Less than this we dare not do. Being interested in the conversion of men, we must be certain that we take nothing less to them than those things which will be efficient to accomplish that conversion. The Restoration Plea calls men to this.

CONCLUSION

One of the greatest dangers that have afflicted the advocates of the Restoration Plea is the arrogance that has sometimes arisen over the feeling derived from being right. Some have felt, and correctly so, that the true development would be an attitude of humility and of profound sympathy for those who have for ages been bound in error. However, others have looked upon the Plea as a policy of exclusion rather than of inclusion, and have become so overbearing in their attitude toward those less fortunate than they, that they have hindered rather than aided the cause for which we plead.

No more fitting conclusion could be appended to this document than the following statement by P. H. Canary:

In a certain religious publication I have noticed that the editor and staff writers refer, apparently consistently, to one another and to others identified with their own immediate group as "Brother," but when they have occasion to name someone who is a denominationalist or even to one who is a member of a church of Christ which uses a musical instrument, such a one is referred to as "Mister." At first, I thought the discrepancy was accidental, but the usage continued in issue after issue; then a few days ago I chanced to meet one of these staff writers and asked him if the practice I thought I had detected was merely accidental or deliberate and intended.

"Your observation is correct," he said, "and it is no accident. We won't call anyone *brother*, if he is a member of a denomination, or if he is a member of any but a true church of Christ. We simply call him *Mister.*"

I said, "So far as I can tell, in the light of the New Testament teaching, I am a member of the true church of Christ. But, from your point of view, am I your *brother*? Would you call me *brother*, or am I, too, merely *Mister*?

For several seconds he studied my face in silence; then, I was amazed to hear him say, slowly and with great deliberation, "Yes, Yes, I'd call you my brother, I *think*—an *erring* brother. I classify you as an *erring* brother."

"Surely," I replied, "I am an erring brother. So are we all, all erring brothers. Don't you also err? If you are brother to anybody, aren't you also an *erring brother*?"

His response astounded me. I could hardly believe my own ears, for he said with utter blandness, "Oh, yes, I err but not as much as you do!"

I began to be amused and asked, "How do you know that? Do you keep books for God? Can you prove that my errors and imperfections are greater than your own? Although I freely confess mine while you grudgingly admit yours, would it not require the records of heaven itself to determine which of us is most in error."

"I don't think so," he stubbornly maintained. "Say," he continued, "do you think *any* denominationalist will be saved?"

"Of course," I said. "Don't you?"

"I do not!" he almost shouted. "How could such a one be saved?" he demanded.

I replied, "Just like you or me or anyone else who hopes to be saved: through the love and mercy and grace of God, plus our faith, obedience, and loving service. Of course, I do not believe all denominationalists will be saved, just as I do not think opinionated, sectarian, and palpably unregenerate persons who may have their names on the register of some local *true church of Christ* will be saved. But I hate to think Satan is whipping God to the extent that *only a portion* or fewer than a million souls are being saved, while more than 700 times that many nominal Christians are *all* being lost."

"Do you think the New Testament promises salvation to anyone without Christian Baptism?" my friend demanded.

"No," I said, "not this side of the first Pentecost after the resurrection of Jesus Christ, at least. Neither do I hold any brief for the so-called pious *unimmersed*, who are generally the *stubborn* and *impious* unimmersed. But I am thinking of many who have been scripturally baptized and serve with singular devotion, yet are not members of your particular group; are we all eternally doomed?"

Thoroughly aroused now, this brother, for whom I have only the best will in the world, struck venemously and seemed to enjoy it. "I think *you* will go to hell, Canary, because *you* use instrumental music in public worship," he said.

Only an Irish sense of humor saved me from exasperation! "My friend," I said, "can you give me book, chapter, and verse for that?"   .

"I can!" he asserted, but he did not, and I am confident if he could have done so he would.

Now, all of this should stimulate us to think a little more clearly and to speak and act with more humility and affection.

I take no satisfaction in the fact that this brother mispronounced *err* and *erring* nor in the further fact that he and his close associates occupy a wholly untenable position in their arbitrary and invalid distinction between *brother* and *mister*, in which they are not supported by even colloquial usage. *Brother* merely means equal but *Mister* is the same as *master* and connotes *superiority*, clearly an idea these zealous but ill advised brethren do not mean to assert or even to imply.

But since these brethren are so inaccurate and faulty in such elementary matters as the pronounciation of ordinary household words, and seeing they blunder and stumble over simple and easy problems of high school syntax, can they be trusted or should they be taken too seriously when they essay to deliver themselves pontifically concerning eternal life, the relative weight of errors in human judgment, and other matters definitely beyond their comprehension?

What new kind of absurdity is this, anyway? For nearly a century and a half of honorable history, no competent man among us of any standing in either scholarship or gentility has been so crass as to say that we are the only Christians. If we are the only Christians, then we have no message of unity and peace for other Christians, because according to this cold and banal concept, there are no other Christians to unite!

Although one hesitates to appear offensive by rendering rebuke or offering fuller instruction to an inadequately equipped brother, to refrain from such correction may do violent injury to the cause of Christ in general and to Christian unity in particular. It is only fair and wise, and in the long view really kind, to restrain somewhat our own overzealous boanerges. Let us impress them with the fact that until they learn to employ grownup speech in a responsible manner, they should be seen but not heard from *too much!*

This plea to unite all Christians through restoration of the approved New Testament norm of doctrine and life is a thing of perennial beauty. May it not be marred and disfigured by shallow learning or boorish deportment.[1]

---

[1] *Christian Unity Quarterly*, Vol. 2, No. 4, pp. 7-9.

BIBLIOGRAPHY

BOOKS

Abbott, B. A. *The Disciples, An Interpretation.* St. Louis: Christian Board of Publication, 1924.

Ainslie, Peter. *The Message of the Disciples for the Union of the Church.* New York: Fleming H. Revell Company, 1924.

Ainslie, Peter. *Towards Christian Unity.* Baltimore: Association for the Promotion of Christian Unity, 1918.

Ainslie, Peter. *The Unfinished Task of the Reformation.* Cincinnati: American Christian Missionary Society, n. d.

Allen, F. G. *The Old-Path Pulpit.* Covington: Guide Printing and Publishing Company, 1886.

Bernard, Samuel M. *Our Religious Neighbors.* Louisville: Guide Printing and Publishing Company, 1902.

Book, W. H., et al. *The Watchword of the Restoration Vindicated.* Cincinnati: The Standard Publishing Company, n. d.

Braden, Clark and Hughey, G. W. *Debate On the Action of Baptism.* Cincinnati: Franklin and Rice, 1870.

Buckner, George Walker. *The Winds of God: Christian Unity, Cooperation, World Fellowship,* n. p., n. d.

Burnet, D. S. (ed.). *The Christian Baptist.* Cincinnati: Published by D. S. Burnet, 1835.

Butler, Pardee. *Personal Recollections of Pardee Butler.* Cincinnati: Standard Publishing Company, 1889.

Campbell, Alexander. *Principles and Rules of Christian Unity.* Bethany: M'Vay and Ewing, 1835.

Campbell, Thomas. *Declaration and Address.* Pittsburgh: Western Pennsylvania Christian Missionary Society, 1909.

Cauble, Commodore W. *Disciples of Christ in Indiana.* Indianapolis: Meigs Publishing Company, 1930.

Conversations at the Unity Club. London: Christian Commonwealth Publishing Company, Limited, n. d.

Cowan, J. N., and Sommer, Daniel. *A Debate.* Sullivan, Indiana: Privately Printed, 1926.

Crawford, C. C. *Sermon Outlines.* Vol. I. *The Restoration Plea.* St. Louis: Restoration Publishing Company, 1927.

Elmore, Robert E. *Christian Unity.* Cincinnati: The Standard Publishing Company, 1901.

Everest, Harvey W. *The Divine Demonstration.* St. Louis: Christian Publishing Company, 1884.

Forrest, W. M. *Do Fundamentalists Play Fair?* New York: The MacMillan Company, 1926.

Foster, Rupert Clinton. *The Everlasting Gospel.* Cincinnati: The Standard Publishing Company, 1929.

Franklin, Benjamin. *A Book of Gems.* St. Louis: John Burns, Publisher, 1879.

Franklin, Benjamin. *The Union Movement.* St. Louis: Christian Publishing Company, n. d.

Garrison, J. H. *A Modern Plea for Ancient Truths.* St. Louis: Christian Publishing Company, 1902.

Garrison, J. H. *Christian Union*. St. Louis: Christian Publishing Company, 1906.

Garrison, J. H. (ed.). *The Old Faith Restated*. St. Louis: Christian Publishing Company, 1891.

Garrison, Winfred E. *Alexander Campbell's Theology*. St. Louis: Christian Publishing Company, 1900.

Garrison, Winfred E. *An American Religious Movement*. St. Louis: Christian Board of Publication, 1945.

Hailey, Homer. *Attitudes and Consequences in the Restoration Movement*. Los Angeles: Citizens Print Shop, 1945.

Haley, J. J. *Makers and Moulders of the Reformation Movement*. St. Louis: Christian Board of Publication, 1914.

Hoshour, Samuel K. *Autobiography—Samuel K. Hoshour*. St. Louis: John Burns Publishing Company, 1884.

Kellems, Jesse R. *Alexander Campbell and the Disciples*. New York: Richard R. Smith, Inc., 1930.

Kershner, Frederick D. *How To Promote Christian Union*. Cincinnati: The Standard Publishing Company, 1916.

Kershner, Frederick D. *The Christian Union Overture*. St. Louis: The Bethany Press, 1923.

Kershner, Frederick. D. *The Restoration Handbook*. Cincinnati: The Standard Publishing Company, 1918.

Kershner, Frederick D., et al. *The Watchword of the Restoration Vindicated*. Cincinnati: The Standard Publishing Company, n. d.

Lowber, J. W. *The Who and the What of the Disciples of Christ*. St. Louis: Christian Publishing Company, 1906.

Mathes, James M. *Letters to Thomas A. Morris*, D.D. Cincinnati: George B. Bentley & Company, Printers, 1861.

Mathes, James M. *The Western Preacher*. Vol. I. Bedford: Published for the Author, 1865.

Mathes, James M. *Works of Elder B. W. Stone*. Vol. I. Cincinnati: Moore, Wilstach, Keys and Company, 1859.

McGarvey, J. W. *Evidences of Christianity*. Cincinnati: Guide Printing and Publishing Company, 1886.

McGarvey, J. W. *Sermons*. Louisville: Guide Printing and Publishing Company, 1894.

Milligan, Robert. *An Exposition and Defense of the Scheme of Redemption*. Cincinnati: R. W. Carroll and Company, Publishers, 1869.

The Missouri Christian Lectures. St. Louis: Christian Publishing Co., 1892.

Mitchell, Nathan J. *Reminiscences and Incidents in the Life and Travels of a Pioneer Preacher*. Cincinnati: Chase and Hall, Publishers, 1877.

Moore, W. T. *A Comprehensive History of the Disciples of Christ*. New York: Fleming H. Revell Company, 1909.

Moore, W. T. *The Living Pulpit of the Christian Church*. Cincinnati: R. W. Carroll and Company, Publishers, 1868.

Moore, W. T. *The Plea of the Disciples of Christ*. Chicago: The Christian Century Company, 1906.

Morrison, Charles Clayton. *What is Christianity?* Chicago: Willett and Clark Company, 1940.

Phillips, Thomas W. *The Church of Christ*. Cincinnati: The Standard Publishing Company, 1915.

Power, Frederick D. *Life of William Kimbrough Pendleton*. St. Louis: Christian Publishing Company, 1902.

Radford, B. J. *The Place of the Gospel in the Development of Humanity*. Cincinnati: The Standard Publishing Company, 1923.

Reis, John. *The Union of the Church of God*. Cincinnati: Hygeia Printing Office, 1850.

Richardson, Robert. *The Principles and Objects of the Religious Reformation*. Bethany: Printed and Published by A. Campbell, 1853.

Richardson, Robert. *Memoirs of Alexander Campbell*. Cincinnati: The Standard Publishing Company, 1897.

Rogers, John I. (ed.). *Autobiography of Elder Samuel Rogers*. Cincinnati: The Standard Publishing Company, 1909.

Rogers, John. *The Biography of Elder Barton Warren Stone*. Cincinnati: J. A. and U. P. James, 1847.

Rowe, John F. (ed.). *Biographical Sketch and Writings of Elder Benjamin Franklin*. Vol. I. Cincinnati: Published by G. W. Rice, 1881.

Rowe, John F. *History of Reformatory Movements*. Cincinnati: G. W. Rice, Publisher, 1884.

Scott, Walter. *The Gospel Restored*. Cincinnati: O. H. Donogh, 1836.

Scott, Walter. *The Union of Christians, On Christian Principles*. Cincinnati: C. A. Morgan and Company, 1852.

Shackleford, John Jr., (ed.). *Life, Letters and Addresses of Dr. L. L. Pinkerton*. Cincinnati: Chase and Hall, Publishers, 1876.

Sommer, D. A. *The Church of Christ*. Indianapolis: Apostolic Review, 1913.

Sweeney, John S. *Sweeney's Sermons*. Nashville: Gospel Advocate Publishing Company, 1892.

Sweeney, Z. T. (ed). *New Testament Christianity*, Vol. I Columbus: Privately Printed, 1919.

Sweeney, Z. T. (ed.). *New Testament Christianity*, Vol. II. New Testament Christianity Book Fund, Inc., 1926.

Sweeney, Z. T. (ed.). *New Testament Christianity*, Vol. III. New Testament Christianity Book Fund, Inc., 1930.

Tyler, B. B. *Addresses of Henry Russell Pritchard*. Cincinnati: The Standard Publishing Company, 1898.

Walker, Dean E. *Adventuring for Christian Unity*. Birmingham, Eng.: The Berean Press, 1935.

Ware, Charles Crossfield. *North Carolina Disciples*. St. Louis: Christian Board of Publication, 1927.

Willett, Herbert L. *Our Plea for Union and the Present Crisis*. Chicago: Christian Century Company, 1901.

Williams, John Augustus. *Life of Elder John Smith*. Cincinnati: R. W. Carroll and Company, Publishers, 1870.

Young, Charles Alexander. *Historical Documents Advocating Christian Union*. Chicago: Christian Century Company, 1904.

PERIODICALS

American Christian Review. January, 1856, Vol. 1, No. 1.

American Christian Review. February, 1856, Vol. 1, No. 2.

American Christian Review. December 20, 1859, Vol. 2, No. 51.

American Christian Quarterly Review. 1862, Vol. I, No. 2

American Christian Quarterly Review. 1863, Vol. II, No. 4.

Central Woodward Pulpit. April, 1933, Vol. 4, No. 22.

Christian Baptist. August, 1823, Vol. I, No. 1.

    ,,   ,,   February, 1825, Vol. II, No. VII.

    ,,   ,,   April, 1825, Vol. II, No. IX.

    ,,   ,,   March, 1825, Vol. II, No. VIII.

    ,,   ,,   June, 1825, Vol. II, No. XI.

    ,,   ,,   September, 1825, Vol. III, No. 2.

    ,,   ,,   October, 1825, Vol. III, No. 3.

    ,,   ,,   October, 1827, Vol. V, No. 3.

    ,,   ,,   March, 1829, Vol. VI, No. 8.

    ,,   ,,   August, 1829, Vol. VII, No. 1.

Christian Century. April 18, 1912, Vol. 29, No. 16.

    ,,   ,,   April 25, 1912, Vol. 29, No. 17.

    ,,   ,,   May 2, 1912, Vol. 29, No. 18.

    ,,   ,,   July 4, 1912, Vol. 29, No. 27.

    ,,   ,,   July 18, 1912, Vol. 29, No. 29.

    ,,   ,,   August 15, 1912, Vol. 29, No. 33.

    ,,   ,,   April 17, 1913, Vol. 30, No. 16.

    ,,   ,,   August 28, 1913, Vol. 30, No. 34.

Christian-Evangelist. June 11, 1885, Vol. 22, No. 24.

    ,,   ,,   July 16, 1896, Vol. 33, No. 29.

    ,,   ,,   March 28, 1901, Vol. 38, No. 13.

    ,,   ,,   April 4, 1901, Vol. 38, No. 14.

    ,,   ,,   May 16, 1901, Vol. 38, No. 20.

    ,,   ,,   September 15, 1904, Vol. 41, No. 37.

    ,,   ,,   October 24, 1907, Vol. 45, No. 43.

    ,,   ,,   October 14, 1909, Vol. 46, No. 41.

    ,,   ,,   February 17, 1910, Vol. 47, No. 7.

    ,,   ,,   April 21, 1910, Vol. 47, No. 16.

Christian Evangelist	April 28, 1910, Vol. 47, No. 17.
"	"	August 3, 1911, Vol. 48, No. 31.
"	"	December 21, 1911, Vol. 48, No. 51.
"	"	February 22, 1912, Vol. 49, No. 8.
"	"	November 6, 1913, Vol. 50, No. 45.
"	"	March 18, 1915, Vol. 52, No. 11.
"	"	December 30, 1915, Vol. 52, No. 52.
"	"	September 7, 1916, Vol. 53, No. 36.
"	"	November 27, 1919, Vol. 56, No. 48.
"	"	October 7, 1926, Vol. 63, No. 40.
"	"	September 15, 1927, Vol. 64, No. 37.
"	"	November 24, 1927, Vol. 64, No. 47.
"	"	May 24, 1928, Vol. 65, No. 21.
"	"	February 19, 1931, Vol. 68, No. 8.
"	"	April 16, 1931, Vol. 68, No. 16.
"	"	March 12, 1936, Vol. 74, No. 11.
"	"	March 11, 1937, Vol. 75, No. 10.
"	"	April 8, 1937, Vol. 75, No. 14.
"	"	August 5, 1937, Vol. 75, No. 31.
"	"	August 12, 1937, Vol. 75, No. 32.
"	"	November 20, 1941, Vol. 79, No. 47.
"	"	June 25, 1942, Vol. 80, No. 26.
"	"	October 15, 1942, Vol. 80, No. 42.
"	"	February 23, 1944, Vol. 82, No. 8.
"	"	March 8, 1944, Vol. 82, No. 10.
"	"	March 15, 1944, Vol. 82, No. 11.
"	"	May 17, 1944, Vol. 82, No. 20.

Christian Messenger. June, 1830, Vol. IV, No. 7.

"	"	August, 1830, Vol. IV, No. 9.
"	"	December, 1834, Vol. VIII, No. 12.
"	"	May, 1841, Vol. XI, No. 9.
"	"	June, 1841, Vol. XI, No. 10.
"	"	March, 1842, Vol. XII, No. 5.
"	"	August, 1844, Vol. XIV, No. 4.

Christian Preacher. April, 1836, Vol. I. No. 4.

| " | " | May, 1838, Vol. III, No. 5. |

Christian Preacher. June, 1838, Vol. III, No. 6

       "   "   July, 1838, Vol. III, No. 7.

Christian Quarterly (New Series). January, 1899.

Christian Quarterly Review. July, 1883, Vol 2.

Christian Record. Third Series, February, 1861, Vol. 5, No. 2.

Christian Standard. December 4, 1897, Vol. 33, No. 49.

     "   "   August 20, 1898, Vol. 34, No. 34.

     "   "   December 17, 1898, Vol. 34, No. 51.

     "   "   October 19, 1901, Vol. 37, No. 42.

     "   "   October 26, 1901, Vol. 37, No. 43.

     "   "   December 21, 1901, Vol. 37, No. 51.

     "   "   April 19, 1902, Vol. 38, No. 16.

     "   "   December 12, 1903, Vol. 39, No. 50.

     "   "   January 16, 1904, Vol. 40, No. 3.

     "   "   February 6, 1904, Vol. 40, No. 6.

     "   "   October 8, 1904, Vol. 40, No. 41.

     "   "   August 25, 1906, Vol. 42, No. 34.

     "   "   May 25, 1907, Vol. 43, No. 21.

     "   "   July 16, 1910, Vol. 46, No. 29.

     "   "   August 10, 1912, Vol. 48, No. 32.

     "   "   September 14, 1912, Vol. 48, No. 37.

     "   "   January 24, 1913, Vol. 49, No. 4.

     "   "   May 24, 1913, Vol. 49, No. 21.

     "   "   November 18, 1916, Vol. 52, No. 7.

     "   "   June 7, 1919, Vol. 54, No. 36.

     "   "   July 26, 1919, Vol. 54, No. 43.

     "   "   August 2, 1919, Vol. 54, No. 44.

     "   "   August 9, 1919, Vol. 54, No. 45.

     "   "   August 23, 1919, Vol. 54, No. 47.

     "   "   September 6, 1919, Vol. 54, No. 49.

     "   "   October 25, 1919, Vol. 55, No. 4.

     "   "   December 6, 1919, Vol. 55, No. 10.

     "   "   March 13, 1920, Vol. 55, No. 24.

     "   "   September 17, 1920, Vol. 55, No. 51.

     "   "   October 23, 1920, Vol. 56, No. 4.

     "   "   June 25, 1921, Vol. 56, No. 39.

Christian Standard. December 24, 1921, Vol. 57, No. 13.

    ,,   ,,   May 27, 1922, Vol. 57, No. 35.

    ,,   ,,   January 12, 1924, Vol. 59, No. 15.

    ,,   ,,   February 2, 1924, Vol. 59, No. 18.

    ,,   ,,   October 18, 1924, Vol. 60, No. 3.

    ,,   ,,   August 14, 1926, Vol. 61, No. 33.

    ,,   ,,   October 30, 1926, Vol. 61, No. 44.

    ,,   ,,   September 3, 1927, Vol. 62, No. 36.

    ,,   ,,   September 10, 1927, Vol. 62, No. 37.

    ,,   ,,   October 29, 1927, Vol. 62, No. 44.

    ,,   ,,   November 12, 1927, Vol. 62, No. 46.

    ,,   ,,   November 26, 1927, Vol. 62, No. 48.

    ,,   ,,   August 4, 1928, Vol. 63, No. 31.

    ,,   ,,   November 24, 1928, Vol. 63, No. 47.

    ,,   ,,   November 1, 1930, Vol. 65, No. 44.

    ,,   ,,   June 9, 1934, Vol. 69, No. 23.

    ,,   ,,   August 25, 1934, Vol. 69, No. 34.

    ,,   ,,   July 11, 1936, Vol. 71, No. 28.

    ,,   ,,   May 1, 1937, Vol. 72, No. 16.

    ,,   ,,   April 5, 1941, Vol. 76, No. 14.

    ,,   ,,   June 10, 1944, Vol. 80, No. 24.

    ,,   ,,   October 13, 1945, Vol. 81, No. 41.

    ,,   ,,   October 27, 1945, Vol. 81, No. 43.

    ,,   ,,   November 10, 1945, Vol. 81, No. 45.

Christian Unity Quarterly. April, 1947, Vol. 2, No. 4.

Disciple. July, 1851, Vol. I, No. 1.

Disciple of Christ. March 1, 1884, Vol. I, No. 5.

Disciple of Christ. May 15, 1884, Vol. I, No. 10.

Disciple of Christ. June 1, 1884, Vol. I, No. 11.

Disciple of Christ. July 1, 1884, Vol. I, No. 13.

Evangelist. August 12, 1880, Vol. 14, No. 32.

Evangelist. October 14, 1880, Vol. 14, No. 41.

Evangelist. March 31, 1881, Vol. 16, No. 13.

Gospel Advocate. September 11, 1873, Vol. 15, No. 36.

Gospel Advocate. July 18, 1907, Vol. 49, No. 29.

Gospel Advocate. November 7, 1907, Vol. 49, No. 45.

Gospel Advocate. January 16, 1908, Vol. 50, No. 3.

Herald of Truth. September and October, 1862, Vol. I, No. 5.

Independent Monthly. Vol. II.

Lard's Quarterly. 1864, Vol. I.

Midwest Christian. April, 1946.

Millennial Harbinger. January, 1830, Vol. I, No. 1.

"	"	August, 1830, Vol. I, No. 8.
"	"	April, 1832, Vol. III, No. 4.
"	"	May, 1832, Vol. III, No. 5.
"	"	March, 1833, Vol. IV, No. 3.
"	"	December, 1834, Vol. V, No. 11.
"	"	October, 1835, Extra No. VIII, Vol. VI.
"	"	December, 1837, Vol. I, No. 12, New Series.
"	"	August, 1839, Vol. III, No. 8, New Series.
"	"	February, 1840, Vol. IV, No. 2, New Series.
"	"	January, 1842, Vol. VI, No. 1, New Series.
"	"	August, 1842, Vol. VI, No. 8., New Series.
"	"	November, 1845, Vol. II, No. 11, Third Series.
"	"	January, 1846, Vol. III, No. 1, Third Series.
"	"	September, 1847, Vol. IV, No. 9, Third Series.
"	"	October, 1851, Vol. I, No. 10, Fourth Series.
"	"	April, 1852, Vol. II, No. 4, Fourth Series.
"	"	February, 1853, Vol. III, No. 2, Fourth Series.
"	"	August, 1856, Vol. VI, No. 8, Fourth Series.
"	"	May, 1858, Vol. I, No. 5, Fifth Series.
"	"	December, 1858, Vol. I, No. 12, Fifth Series.
"	"	February, 1859, Vol. II, No. 2, Fifth Series.
"	"	January, 1861, Vol. IV, No. 1, Fifth Series.
"	"	May, 1861, Vol. IV, No. 4, Fifth Series.
"	"	June, 1861, Vol. IV, No. 6, Fifth Series.
"	"	August, 1861, Vol. IV, No. 8, Fifth Series.
"	"	December, 1861, Vol. IV, No. 12, Fifth Series.
"	"	November, 1865, Vol. 36, No. 11.
"	"	January, 1868, Vol. 39, No. 1.
"	"	February, 1868, Vol. 39, No. 2.
"	"	March, 1869, Vol. 40, No. 3.

Millennial Harbinger. April, 1869, Vol. 40, No. 4.

    "   "   July, 1869, Vol. 40, No. 7.

Religious Historian. May, 1872, Vol. I, No. 5.

The Plea. June, 1948

The Plea. July, 1948.

The Plea. August, 1948.

Scroll. October, 1935, Vol. 31, No. 8.

    "   February, 1936, Vol. 32, No. 2.

    "   April, 1936, Vol. 32, No. 4.

    "   November, 1936, Vol. 33, No. 3.

    "   March, 1937, Vol. 33, No. 6.

    "   April, 1937, Vol. 33, No. 7.

    "   June, 1937, Vol. 33, No. 9.

    "   November, 1937, Vol. 35, No. 2.

    "   December, 1937, Vol. 35, No. 3.

    "   September, 1939, Vol. 37, No. 1.

    "   February, 1940, Vol. 37, No. 6.

    "   March, 1940, Vol. 37, No. 7.

    "   April, 1940, Vol. 37, No. 8.

    "   April, 1943, Vol. 40, No. 8.

    "   January, 1944, Vol. 41, No. 5.

    "   May, 1944, Vol. 41, No. 9.

    "   December, 1944, Vol. 42, No. 4.

    "   June, 1945, Vol. 42, No. 10.

Sound Doctrine. January, 1946, Vol. I, No. 1.

South African Christian. September 1, 1928, Vol. I, No. 11

PAMPHLETS AND TRACTS

Allen, F. G. *What Shall We Do About the Organ?* ....: Privately Printed, n. d.

Bucalstein, Harry. *Who We Are.* Bulletin Cover for Summer, 1948, West Morris Street Christian Church, Indianapolis.

Coombs, J. V. *Our Plea.* n. p., n. d. A Tract of a sermon preached by J. V. Coombs, in the Christian Church, Noblesville, Indiana, March 30, 1890. May be found among tracts in School of Religion Library, Butler University, pamphlet box No. 3.

Errett, Isaac. *Our Position.* Cincinnati: The Standard Publishing Company, n. d.

Garrison, J. H. *The World's Need of Our Plea.* Chicago: The Oracle Publishing Company, 1899.

Goode, M. M. *Our Plea.* St. Joseph, Mo.: Combe Printing Company, 1899.

Hayden, W. L. *What Is the Christian Church?* n. p., n. d. A Tract of an address delivered before the Pennsylvania Christian Missionary Convention at Johnstown, Pa., Oct. 6, 1887. May be found in the School of Religion Library, Butler University. (Vol. 9 of bound tract collection of Enos Dowling).

Hayden, W. L. *Centennial Addresses Delivered in* 1909. Indianapolis: By W. L. Hayden, 1909.

Lamar, J. S. *What Is the Christian Church?* Cincinnati: Tract Committee of the General Christian Missionary Convention, 1883.

O'Kelly, James. *Original Truth.* Raleigh: Printed by Joseph Cales, 1807.

Pritchard, Henry Russell. *Innovations, So Called.* Indianapolis: E. B. Schofield, n. d.

Sweeney, Z. T. *Open Membership.* Cincinnati: The Standard Publishing Company, 1942.

Zimmerman, John D. *Studies In Evangelism.* Topeka: Published by John D. Zimmerman, n. d.

UNPUBLISHED MANUSCRIPTS

Griffeth, Ross J. *Christian Unity.* An unpublished manuscript, Eugene, Oregon, 1948.

Miller, Thomas. *The Disciples and Christian Unity.* An unpublished Manuscript, Schenectedy, N. Y., 1948.

Constitution and Minutes of the Silver Creek Association of Baptists. An unpublished record of the formation of the Silver Creek Association, its constitution, and minutes of the meetings from July 24, 1812 to its dissolution in 1837.

INDEX

ADDITIONAL STATEMENTS OF THE PLEA

ADDITIONAL STATEMENTS OF THE PLEA

ADDITIONAL STATEMENTS OF THE PLEA

ADDITIONAL STATEMENTS OF THE PLEA

ADDITIONAL STATEMENTS OF THE PLEA

ADDITIONAL STATEMENTS OF THE PLEA

ADDITIONAL STATEMENTS OF THE PLEA

ADDITIONAL STATEMENTS OF THE PLEA

ADDITIONAL STATEMENTS OF THE PLEA

ADDITIONAL STATEMENTS OF THE PLEA

ADDITIONAL STATEMENTS OF THE PLEA

ADDITIONAL STATEMENTS OF THE PLEA

ADDITIONAL STATEMENTS OF THE PLEA